Global Value Chains and the Missing Links

T0382898

Global value chains (GVCs) are fraught with the phenomenon of fragmentation and dispersion of production across the world. India presents a unique example with its high potential in manufacturing capability but low integration in GVCs. This book examines the reasons why India has failed to integrate within GVCs so far and looks at key examples to understand the impediments in this process. The chapters bring together case studies from across the manufacturing industry – labour-intensive (garment, paper and diamond), capital-intensive (automobile and petrochemical), and knowledge-intensive (semi-conductor microchip, chemical and pharmaceutical) sectors. Together, they present stories of successful integration of some firms in GVCs as well as the difficulties faced by them. The volume also highlights the importance of GVCs in the context of developing countries in terms of benefits such as income and value generation, knowledge and technology collaborations, and advances in systems and processes.

This book will interest scholars and researchers in economics, international trade studies, development economics and business management as well as practitioners, policymakers, government officials, and those in the corporate sector.

Saon Ray is Senior Fellow at the Indian Council for Research on International Economic Relations (ICRIER), New Delhi, India. An economist specializing in industry and international trade issues, her areas of interest include global value chains, technological upgrading of Indian industries, free trade agreements, and trade creation effects. She has published widely on these issues in books and journal articles. Her latest book is *Impact of American Investment in India: A Socioeconomic Assessment* (2014).

Smita Miglani is Research Associate at the Indian Council for Research on International Economic Relations, New Delhi, India. She has an MPhil in Economics from Jawaharlal Nehru University, New Delhi and her areas of research interest include international trade and investment, WTO (GATS) and energy economics. Her work has been published in various reports, working papers, books and journals. Her research has contributed to India's negotiating strategies in signing bilateral trade and investment agreements and other policy reform issues at the domestic level.

Effective participation in the Global Value Chains is indeed one of the most missing elements of India's international trade. We started at independence as an inward-looking country with emphasis on "import substitution" as the primary goal conserving foreign exchange to import the only most essential goods. This licence permit raj of management had reached its limits and we ended up promoting inefficiencies, poor quality and high costs through this protectionism. We moved to the next phase in 1991 effectively opening up trade with "export promotion" replacing our earlier policy of "import substitution."

But so far as being part of an international chain of value addition, thus, importing raw materials or intermediate goods and re-exporting them after processing is concerned, we have miles to go. Schemes such as SEZs, EOUs, EPCG, Advance Authorisation schemes are steps in this direction. However, we have not become a major player in the Global Value Chains. The reasons for this situation are much more than mere EXIM policies or Customs procedures. The entire range of issues which the participating organisations have to deal with including infrastructure, finance, time taken to clear the goods, transport them to the factories and to re-export them need to be looked at. This book precisely and wonderfully does that. It is absolutely opportune that such a study is made at this time in the country.

In addition to identifying the problems in general, it is important to study specific industries and their problems and issues if the studies have to be meaningful and this is the second biggest contribution of the book. I am confident that the book will be extremely useful for policymakers, practitioners, researchers and trade alike and it will encourage others to conduct more studies covering a larger number of industries.

P. V. Subba Rao, IRS (C&CE),
Joint Secretary (COFEPOSA), Department of Revenue,
Ministry of Finance, Government of India

This book is an empirically rich analysis of the reasons for India's poor integration in global value chains (GVCs). The book also looks at what can be done to increase India's benefits from participation and upgrading in GVCs. Its analysis and conclusions should be of interest to both researchers and policymakers.

Dev Nathan, Visiting Professor, Institute for Human
Development, New Delhi; Coordinator,
GPN Studies, New Delhi; and Visiting
Research Fellow, Center on Globalization,
Governance and Competitiveness,
Duke University, US

Global Value Chains and the Missing Links
Cases from Indian Industry

Saon Ray and Smita Miglani

Routledge
Taylor & Francis Group

LONDON AND NEW YORK

First published 2018 by Routledge

2 Park Square, Milton Park, Abingdon, Oxon, OX14 4RN
605 Third Avenue, New York, NY 10017

Routledge is an imprint of the Taylor & Francis Group, an informa business

First issued in paperback 2020

British Library Cataloguing-in-Publication Data
A catalogue record for this book is available from the British Library

Library of Congress Cataloging-in-Publication Data
A catalog record for this book has been requested

ISBN: 978-1-138-70902-7 (hbk)
ISBN: 978-0-367-73450-3 (pbk)

Typeset in Sabon
by Apex CoVantage, LLC

Contents

Figures

Tables

Acknowledgements

The genesis of this book lies in the project on Enhancing India's Participation in Global Value Chains which ICRIER undertook in 2013–15. The project was funded by the Foreign and Commonwealth Office, British High Commission; their support is gratefully acknowledged. The project was jointly conducted by InterAnalysis, University of Sussex. The objective of the project was, to increase India's participation in global value chains through i) a better understanding of India's positioning in the global production system, ii) a greater capacity for value chain analysis, and iii) using an evidence base created to identify regulatory changes necessary to encourage value chain formation and to increase India's share of value-added.

As part of the project, two workshops were held in New Delhi. The inception workshop, "Global Value Chains and Trade in Value Added in India: Concepts, Measurement, Data and Initial Research Results" was held on 3–4 April 2014. The speakers at the workshop included Michael Gasiorek (InterAnalysis Ltd and University of Sussex), Przemyslaw Kowalski and Javier Lopez Gonzalez (Development Division, OECD Secretariat), and Maximiliano Medez Parra, ITEAS Ltd and CARIS, University of Sussex. There was a panel discussion by Przemyslaw Kowalski, Saon Ray (ICRIER), Michael Gasiorek, Pranav Kumar (CII), and Abhijit Das (WTO Centre, IIFT). The second day of the workshop provided training on the use of the TiVA, WIOD, and Trade Sift databases.

The second workshop on "Enhancing India's Participation in Global Value Chains" was held on 16–17 March 2015 in New Delhi. The speakers at the workshop included Anwarul Hoda (Chair Professor, Trade Policy, and WTO Research Programme, ICRIER), Rajat Kathuria (ICRIER), Michael Gasiorek (InterAnalysis Ltd and University of Sussex), Maximiliano Parra (University of Sussex), Smita Miglani (ICRIER), and Saon Ray (ICRIER). Technical sessions were held on automobiles, in the workshop which was chaired by Nisha Taneja (ICRIER), and presentations were made by Biswajit Nag (IIFT), Subhomoy Bhattacharjee (Indian Express), and Sugato Sen (SIAM). The technical session on semiconductors/IT was chaired by Saon Ray (ICRIER) and the speakers were Dev Nathan (IHD), Anupam Khanna (NASSCOM), and Avinash Ramachandra (Dell). The technical session on pharmaceuticals was chaired by Maximiliano Parra (University of Sussex) and the speakers were Mukta Arora (Eli Lilly) and B N Goldar (IEG). A panel discussion on "How can India enhance its integration with GVCS?" was moderated by M K Venu (Amar Ujala) and the speakers were Abhijit Das (Centre for WTO studies, IIFT), Dev Nathan (IIHD), and Michael Gasiorek (InterAnalysis Ltd and University of Sussex).

Both workshops were very well attended and generated a great deal of interest. Participants at both workshops contributed to the discussion and their comments are gratefully acknowledged.

The project involved stakeholder consultations in Mumbai, Pune, Ankleshwar, Vapi, Ahmedabad, Chennai, Hyderabad, Bengaluru, Kolkata, and New Delhi. The team benefitted from the insights of several people, which is gratefully acknowledged. We would especially like to mention the contribution of Ms. Himadree Kaushik in providing crucial inputs for the chemicals sector.

The guidance of Prof. Dev Nathan and Dr Peter Holmes throughout the project and the subsequent writing of this book has been invaluable. This book would not have reached this stage without their inputs. Finally, the guidance of Dr Rajat Kathuria, Director and CEE of ICRIER, throughout the project is also recognized.

Abbreviations

ABS	Acrylonitrile Butadiene Styrene
AEPC	Apparel Export Promotion Council
AF	Acrylic Fibre
ANDA	Abbreviated New Drug Application
API	Active Pharmaceutical Ingredient
APL	Average propagation length
ASI	Annual Survey of Industries
ATM	Automatic Teller Machine
BEC	Broad Economic Categories
BGA	Ball Grid Array
CAD	Computer-Aided Design
CAGR	Compound Annual Growth Rate
CAN	Acrylonitrile
CBU	Completely Built Units
CDSCO	Central Drugs and Standards Control Organization
CII	Confederation of Indian Industries
CIS	Commonwealth of Independent States
CMT	Cut-Make-Trim
CMVR	Central Motor Vehicles Rules
CPCL	Chennai Petroleum Corporation Limited
CPMA	Chemicals and Petrochemicals Manufacturers' Association
CRAMS	Contract Research and Manufacturing Services
CRDI	Common Rail Direct Injection
CST	Central Sales Tax
DDT	Dichlorodiphenyltrichloroethane
DCGI	Drugs Controller General of India
DDVP	2,2-Dichlorovinyl Di-Methyl Phosphate
DeitY	Department of Electronics and Information Technology
DGFT	Directorate General of Foreign Trade
DME	Directory Manufacturing Establishment

DMT	Di-Methyl Terephthalate
DoT	Department of Telecommunications
DPCO	Drug Price Control Order
DPP	Defense Procurement Procedure
DTAB	Drugs Technical Advisory Board
DVA	Domestic Value-Added
EMS	Electronic Manufacturing Services
EO	Ethylene Oxide
EPS	Expandable Polystyrene
ESDM	Electronics Systems and Design Manufacturing
ETP	Effluent Treatment Plants
EU	European Union
EVA	Ethyl Vinyl Acetate
FDI	Foreign Direct Investment
FICCI	Federation of Indian Chambers of Commerce and Industry
FPGA	Field-Programmable Gate Arrays
FVA	Foreign Value-Added
GCO	Global Chemicals Outlook
GDP	Gross Domestic Product
GE	General Electric
GMP	Good Manufacturing Practices
GPPS	General Purpose Polystyrene
GST	Goods and Services Tax
GTR	Global Technical Regulation
GVC	Global Value Chain
HDPE	High Density Polyethylene
HIPS	High Impact Polystyrene
HMC	Hyundai Motor Company
HMIL	Hyundai Motors India Limited
HOC	Hindustan Organics Limited
HPCL	Hindustan Petroleum Corporation Limited
HS	Harmonized System
IBEF	India Brand Equity Foundation
IC	Integrated Chips
ICIO	Inter-Country Input-Output
ICT	Information and Communication Technology
IDDM	Indigenous Design Development and Manufacturing
IESA	India Electronics and Semiconductor Association
IICT	Indian Institute of Chemical Technology
IIP	Indian Institute of Petroleum
INR	Indian National Rupee
I-O	Input-Output

IOCL	Indian Oil Corporation Limited
IP	Intellectual Property
IPR	Intellectual Property Rights
IS	Innovation Systems
ISIC	International Standard Industrial Classification
IT	Information Technology
ITeS	Information Technology Enabled Services
IV	Intravenous
KT	Kilo Tonnes
LAB	Linear Alkyl Benzene
LCD	Liquid Crystal Display
LDC	Less Developed Country
LDPE	Low Density Polyethylene
LED	Light Emitting Diode
LLDPE	Linear Low Density Polyethylene
LMIC	Low- and Medium-Income Countries
LNG	Liquefied Natural Gas
LPI	Logistics Performance Index
M&A	Mergers and Acquisition
MDI	Methylene Diphenyl Di-isocyanate
MEG	Monoethylene Glycol
MEK	Methyl Ethyl Ketone
MNC	Multinational Companies
MNE	Multinational Enterprise
MoU	Memorandum of Understanding
MPFI	Multi-Point Fuel Injection
MSI	Medium Scale Integration
MSIPS	Modified Special Incentive Package Scheme
MSME	Micro, Small, and Medium Enterprise
MSTQ	Metrology, Standards, Testing, and Quality
MT	Metric Tonnes
MTA	Medium Quality Terephthalic Acid
MTPA	Metric Tonnes Per Annum
MUL	Maruti Udyog Limited
NBR	Nitrile Butadiene Rubber
NCL	National Chemical Laboratory
NCR	National Capital Region
NEIST	North East Institute of Science and Technology
NFY	Nylon Filament Yarn
NIC	National Industrial Classification
NIIST	National Institute for Interdisciplinary Science and Technology

NIY	Nylon Industrial Yarn
NOC	No Objection Certificate
NPE	National Policy on Electronics
NPPA	National Pharmaceutical Pricing Authority
NSSO	National Sample Survey Organization
NTP	National Telecom Policy
OECD	Organization for Economic Co-operation and Development
OEM	Original Equipment Manufacturer
ONCB	Ortho Nitro Chloro Benzene
ONGC	Oil and Natural Gas Corporation
OPAL	ONGC Petro Additions Limited
OPPI	Organisation of Pharmaceutical Producers of India
PBR	Poly Butadiene Rubber
PCs	Personal Computers
PCB	Printed Circuit Boards
PCBA	Printed Circuit Boards Assembly
PCE	Polycarboxylic Ether
PCPIR	Petroleum, Chemicals, and Petrochemicals Investment Region
PET	Polyethylene Terephthalate
PFY	Polyester Filament Yarn
PIY	Polyester Industrial Yarn
PMA	Preferential Market Access
PMMA	Poly Methacrylate
PMP	Phased Manufacturing Programme
PNCB	Para Nitro Chloro Benzene
PP	Polypropylene
PPFY	Polypropylene Filament Yarn
PPSF	Polypropylene Staple Fibre
PS	Polystyrene
PSF	Polyester Staple Fibre
PTA	Purified Terephthalic Acid
PTFE	Polytetrafluoroethylene
PU	Polyurethane
PVC	Polyvinyl Chloride
PX	Paraxylene
QTA	Qualified Terephthalic Acid
R&D	Research and Development
RBI	Reserve Bank of India
RCA	Revealed Comparative Advantage
REACH	Regulation on Registration, Evaluation, Authorisation, and Restriction of Chemicals

RIL	Reliance Industries Limited
RTA	Regional Trade Agreements
SAN	Styrene Acrylonitrile
SBR	Styrene Butadiene Rubber
SEZ	Special Economic Zone
SITC	Standard International Trade Classification
SME	Small and Medium Enterprise
SWC	Structural Waterproofing Company
TDI	Toluene Di-isocyanate
TFA	Trade Facilitation Agreement
TiVA	Trade in Value-Added
TPM	Total Productivity Management
TQM	Total Quality Management
TSC	Technical Standing Committee
TSMC	Taiwan Semiconductor Manufacturing Company
TUF	Technology Upgradation Fund
UAE	United Arab Emirates
UK	United Kingdom
UN	United Nations
UNCTAD	United Nations Conference on Trade and Development
UNIDO	United Nations Industrial Development Organization
US	United States
USA	United States of America
USD	United States Dollar
USFDA	United States Food and Drug Administration
UV	Ultra Violet
VAT	Value-Added Tax
VLSI	Very Large Scale Integration
VVLSI	Very Very Large Scale Integration
WEF	World Economic Forum
WHO	World Health Organization
WTO	World Trade Organization

Part I
Concepts and framework

1 Introduction

One of the most enduring images of globalization is that of the Apple iPhone or iPod, with the tag line, "Designed by Apple in California, assembled in China." This is an example of a global value chain, with part of the process being completed in one or more countries (Gereffi and Lee 2012). The phenomenon of production in global value chains (GVCs) has been called "vertical specialization" (Balassa 1967; Findlay 1978), as well as "slicing up of the value chain" (Krugman 1995). Others have called it "international fragmentation of production" (Arndt and Kierzkowski 2002) and "global production networks" (Ernst and Kim 2002) etc.[1]

In economics, value chains refer to the full range of activities involved in value creation of a product from its conception to the end-use stage and beyond. In a globalized world, global value chains can be understood as the sequence of such activities involving more than one country. These chains operate through inter-firm trade networks and the process typically involves movement of intermediate goods[2] through a series of countries where, in each one, a new value is designed, coordinated, and implemented at a regional or global scale (UNESCAP 2015).[3] More than 60% of global trade consists of trade in intermediate goods and services (UNCTAD 2013).[4]

Between 1995 and 2009, income from GVC-related trade increased sixfold for China and fivefold for India (OECD, WTO, and the World Bank Group 2014). Value-added[5] or GVC trade accounts for the value-added of one country (directly and indirectly) contained in the final consumption of another country.[6] The measurement involves two steps: first, computation of output from each country and sector needed to produce final goods absorbed in a given destination (Johnson and Noguera 2012); and second, from the sector-level production, measurement of the value of final goods purchased from each source country along with inputs is evaluated and the value-added contribution is computed along the production chain.

GVCs have arisen from the growing interconnectedness among economies worldwide, which is a result of technological advancements and liberalization of trade and demand-side factors.[7] Another reason for their development is the reduction in trade costs, which includes the whole range of costs incurred by companies from the site of production to the final consumption. These include land transport and port costs, freight and insurance costs, tariffs and duties, costs associated with non-tariff measures, mark-ups of importers, wholesalers, and retailers. It is the tradeoff between transaction costs and production cost that determines the degree of fragmentation[8] of the production process (Jones and Kierzkowski 2001). GVC formation for products happens while keeping in view the tradeoffs between production and transaction costs. These costs determine the extent to which fragmentation of production process takes place, making the GVC for every product different.

Producer-driven GVCs are more common in high technology industries such as semiconductor electronics, automotive, or the pharmaceuticals since research and development (R&D) plays a major role. GVCs enable a firm to utilize both economies of scale and economies of scope. Imports play an important part in generating exports. A large portion of the commodity being exported originates abroad due to the emergence of regional production hubs, especially in automotive and electronics industry (OECD 2014). In buyer-driven chains, usually found in garments and other labour-intensive products, decentralized production networks operate through independent suppliers in developing countries (Gereffi 1999). The lead firm[9] in industries such as shoe manufacturing usually deals with the marketing and sourcing the product from different independent suppliers.

The GVC approach analyzes the global economy from two angles: top-down and bottom-up (Gereffi and Fernandez-Stark 2016). The concept underlying the top-down view is the "governance"[10] of GVCs, which focuses on lead firms and organizations of international industries; the concept underlying the bottom-up perspective is "upgrading," which focuses on strategies used by countries, regions, and other economic stakeholders to maintain or improve their position in the global economy.[11] A number of factors, both structural and policy related, can influence the degree and type of integration as well as upgrading in GVCs. Structural factors, such as geography, size of the market,[12] and level of development, are found to be key determinants of GVC participation.[13] GVCs are embedded within local economic, social, and institutional dynamics. Economic conditions including availability and quality of inputs (of material and labour), infrastructure and access to other resources (such as finance), and social context (which govern the availability of labour and its skill level) are important (Gereffi and Fernandez-Stark 2016). Institutions including tax and labour regulation, subsidies, and education and innovation policy that promote or hinder industry growth and development all play a role. Also, policy decisions and corporate strategies in these areas play an active role in promoting engagement.

Understanding GVC trade is important since bilateral gross exports (and imports) include double counting as inputs cross borders several times in today's world.[14] The point here is that participating in international value chains does not necessarily mean directly trading goods or services across borders, but rather being linked to such activities through the process of value creation. The framework enables an understanding of the organization of global industries by examining the structure and dynamics of participating firms (Gereffi and Fernandez-Stark 2016). The comprehensive nature of the framework allows policymakers to answer questions regarding development issues not addressed by previous paradigms; and it also helps explain the changed global-local trade dynamics that have emerged within the past 20 years (Gereffi 1999). The GVC approach is also a useful tool to trace the shifting patterns of global production, link geographically dispersed activities and firms of a single industry, and determine the roles they play in developed and developing countries (Gereffi and Fernandez-Stark 2016).

The emergence of value chains has major policy implications for economic growth in developing countries. GVC trade accounts for 30% of the gross domestic product (GDP) of developing countries (UNCTAD 2013). As GVCs link firms, workers, and consumers around the world, they in fact provide a stepping stone for firms and workers in developing countries to integrate into the global economy. Additionally, they are important as they encourage learning[15] and upgrading[16] of production processes. Some argue that GVCs have created new opportunities for developing countries to enter global markets as components or services suppliers, without having to build the entire value chain (Taglioni and Winkler 2016). By providing access to networks, global markets, capital, knowledge, and technology, integration in an existing value chain can provide a first step to economic development – a path that is often easier to follow than building a complete value chain (Elms and Low 2013).

Participation in GVCs can facilitate economic growth, as it is quicker and less expensive to generate exports by joining existing GVCs (it might be difficult for some countries to build vertically integrated industries). The performance of countries such as China, Costa Rica, the Czech Republic, Mexico, and Thailand is proof of the fact that participation in GVCs can lead to fast development, industrialization, and access to investment, knowledge, and technology. GVCs can help the economy as they support the spread of responsible business conduct. They act as a channel for ideas which take the form of new knowledge and innovations; the growth of GVCs is driven by cost efficiency and by improved access to foreign markets and knowledge. Integration into GVCs does not seem to have much effect on the employment figures of a country, but it appears to change the composition of the workforce. For instance, in the US, integration into GVCs decreased the number of medium-skilled jobs and increased low-skilled ones. GVCs did push wages down but improved working conditions in the US (OECD 2013).

Multinational enterprises (MNEs) as well as small and medium enterprises are involved in GVCs. However, the multinational enterprises that facilitate these beneficial changes may move out to other countries as wages and costs in the host country cross a threshold. These MNEs may also capture most of the value. Small firms are flexible and can tap quickly into new opportunities. SMEs also play a major role in supplying intermediates to exporting firms but face challenges as they lack the capital to invest in R&D, train personnel, or meet international standards.

The critical question for the developing countries then is how to facilitate GVC-related trade and hence integrate into GVCs across the world. This has emerged as a basic development challenge pertaining not only to the percentage share of value-added on supply chains, but also to the quality of participation in terms of capacity and opportunity to diversify into other activities (Elms and Low 2013).

Motivation for the book

Various studies have analyzed the conditions under which varied patterns for countries occur for entering or upgrading in GVCs. While there are numerous examples of successful insertion of firms and countries into GVCs, there are fewer studies of the difficulties faced by firms in inserting into GVCs, especially in the Indian context. India is a unique example of manufacturing capability in most sectors, but low integration into GVCs (Baldwin 2011; Athukorala 2013). The evidence is available through its low GVC participation index measure,[17] not only when compared with other developed economies but also with developing ones. This provides the rationale for examining cases from India with the aim of understanding the level and type of engagement, as well as why and how integration may be impeded.

Examples of why India has largely lagged with respect to integration into GVCs are provided in this book. There are two questions that are of relevance here: first, are domestically owned Indian firms well integrated into GVCs? Second, for firms that are integrated, what are the prospects for upgrading? This book attempts to examine these questions through case studies in the manufacturing sector. As far as upgrading is concerned, the tacitness[18] of knowledge determines learning outcomes and transfer of manufacturing practices. The case studies provide a wide variety of experience, throwing light on the process of knowledge dissemination and manufacturing practices in various sectors. The bargaining powers of suppliers also play an important role in the entire process. The case studies also illustrate how the governance structure affects the dissemination of knowledge. In this sense, it looks at the ways in which learning and upgrading are taking place through GVC trade in the country.

The questions that motivate this book are: First, what is the evidence of India's lagging in GVC trade? We present evidence from the literature and data using the Broad Economic Categories (BEC).[19] Second, what are plausible explanations for India's lagging in GVC trade? This question is answered by examining the role of lead firms, governance structures in value chains, and diffusion of technology in each chain. The final question that is asked relates to the impediments to India's engagement in GVCs and how can India overcome these barriers? In each case study, barriers in that sector in the Indian context are discussed. Barriers faced in other countries are discussed in Chapter 3. This also provides an opportunity to examine the regulations in each sector and how they should be modified to overcome the problems faced by firms.

Organization of the book

The book is divided into four parts. Part I contains an introduction that motivates the book. The introductory chapter provides an outline of the book. Chapter 2 is the literature survey while Chapter 3 sets out the conceptual framework for the book. Part II of the book contains quantitative analysis: it analyzes evidence of India's integration into GVCs (Chapter 4) and analyzes the results of field surveys (Chapter 5). Chapter 5 also discusses the barriers faced by Indian firms in integration and upgrading.

Part III contains two subsections: Subsection 1 summarizes the results of the sector case studies covering automobiles (Chapter 6), reactive dyes (Chapter 7), petrochemicals (Chapter 8), pharmaceuticals (Chapter 9), and semiconductor microchips (Chapter 10). These are cases where there is successful integration by Indian firms and, for greater value addition, upgrading is critical. Subsection 2 focuses on the lagging sectors where India has limited integration or has failed to integrate into GVCs. Garments are covered in Chapter 11; Chapter 12 focuses on specialty chemicals. Finally, Part IV concludes with Chapter 13 dealing with some other cases through a discussion of sectors where India can venture in the future. Chapter 14 provides a summary of the main conclusions of the study and implications for policy drawing on the barriers of integration identified in the study.

Notes

1 Other terms used synonymously in the literature are "global production networks," "disintegration of production process," "international production sharing," "international unbundling of production," and "international product fragmentation."
2 Raw materials, parts, components, and semi-finished goods (UNCTAD 2013).
3 The process may involve a number of countries, industries, and services depending on the type of product and geographical location of different activities.
4 UNCTAD (2013) indicate that total global trade is worth more than USD 20 trillion.
5 Value-added in a national accounts sense reflects the compensation of resident labour, capital, nonfinancial assets, and natural resources used in production. It also includes "other taxes and subsidies on production," i.e. those taxes and subsidies that are unrelated to the quantity, price of volume of goods, and services produced (OECD 2012). However, measuring flows of value-added reflects only part of the global trade and is discussed later in the chapter.
6 Baldwin (2011) has referred to this process as the "second unbundling" – which since 1980 has lowered the transmission costs but not trade costs. According to him, "the information and communication technology (ICT) revolution has made it possible to spatially separate some of the stages of production without loss in efficiency or timeliness." The first unbundling, which was from the steam engine to the mid- or late-1980s, led to the lowering of trade costs.
7 On the demand side, the emergence of Asia has led to the increase in purchasing power and adding to global demand (World Economic Forum 2016).
8 Fragmentation refers to "a splitting up of a previously integrated production process into two or more components," or fragments (Jones and Kierzkowski 2001).

9 Lead firm can be understood as firms that plays the lead role of coordination and management within a chain. (Kaplinsky and Morris 2001) the role of the lead firm varies from chain to chain and will be discussed in greater detail throughout the book.

10 Governance can be understood in terms of the nature of the relation between a lead firm and other firms in a value chain (Gereffi 2014). This is discussed further in Chapter 2 of this book.

11 This may be understood in terms of economic and social upgrading. Economic upgrading is defined as "the process by which economic actors – firms and workers – move from low-value to relatively high-value activities in global production networks' in order to increase the benefits (e.g. profits, value-added, capabilities) from participating in global production" (Gereffi 2005; Gereffi and Fernandez-Stark 2016). Social upgrading may be defined as the process of improvement in the rights and entitlements of workers as social actors, and enhancement of the quality of their employment. This in turn might also result from economic upgrading (Barrientos et al. 2010).

12 As explained in OECD (2015), larger countries tend to have lower participation rates, with this often attributed to the larger size of domestic markets from which they draw intermediates.

13 GVC participation is defined in the next chapter. There are various ways to measure economies' participation in GVCs. A simple measure is the share of foreign value-added in total exports. It reflects the extent to which an economy uses foreign inputs in producing for exports. A more rigorous measure is Vertical Specialization (VS), which is the share of foreign value-added and pure double-counted terms in total exports (ADB 2015).

14 Feenstra (1998) argue that the rise of intermediate goods trade was caused, in part, by "the disintegration of production in the global economy" leading to double counting of intermediate goods as they found their way through international production networks.

15 Learning plays a central role in technological capacity building of a firm (Morrison et al. 2008). This will be discussed in detail in Chapter 3 of this book.

16 The concept of upgrading (that is, making better products, making them more efficiently, or moving into more skilled activities) has been used in the literature on competitiveness (Porter 1990; Kaplinsky and Morris 2001). Pietrobelli and Rabellotti (2011) define upgrading as innovating to increase value-added. Enterprises may achieve this in various ways; for example, by entering higher unit value market niches, entering new sectors, or undertaking new productive (or service) functions. In addition, in this context, innovation is clearly not defined only as a breakthrough into a product or a process that is new to the world. It is marginal and involve evolutionary improvements in products and processes that are new to the firm, and that allow it to keep up with an international (moving) standard. This involves a shifting into activities, products, and sectors that have a higher value-added and higher barriers to market entry.

17 Several approaches to measuring trade in value-added have been developed. An example is the GVC participation index measure developed by OECD and the WTO using a database called the TiVA (trade in value-added). Using detailed information on international trade and national

accounts, the database allows calculations on where value is created and consumed. The GVC participation index has two components reflecting the upstream and downstream links in the chain. Basically, individual economies participate in GVCs by importing foreign inputs to produce the goods and services they export (backward GVC participation) and by exporting domestically produced inputs to partners in charge of downstream production stages (forward GVC participation). See Timmer et al. (2015).

18 Polanyi (1966) stated "we can know more than we can tell." Tacitness refers to the fact that scientific knowledge is not fully reducible to articulated set of axioms, rules etc.

19 According to Sturgeon and Memedovic (2010), product information in the UN Comtrade database is organized according to several distinct classification systems. Of these, the Broad Economic Categories classification scheme (BEC, revision 3) collects UN Comtrade data into three end-use categories: 1) capital, 2) intermediate, and 3) consumption goods.

References

ADB. 2015. 'Global Value Chains Indicators for International Production Sharing,' https://sdbs.adb.org/sdbs/jsp/GVC/GVCLanding.jsp (accessed on 14 August 2017).

Arndt, S.W. and H. Kierzkowski. 2002. *Fragmentation: New Production and Trade Patterns in the World Economy*. Oxford: Oxford University Press.

Athukorala, P.C. 2013. 'How India Fits into Global Production Sharing: Experience, Prospects and Policy Options,' Working Paper No. 2013/13. Arndt-Corden Department of Economics, Crawford School of Public Policy, ANU College of Asia and the Pacific.

Balassa, B. 1967. *Trade Liberalization among Industrial Countries*. New York: Mc Graw Hill.

Baldwin, R. 2011. 'Trade and Industrialization after Globalization's 2nd Unbundling: How Building and Joining a Supply Chain are Different and Why it Matters,' NBER Working Paper 17716. Cambridge MA, National Bureau of Economic Research.

Barrientos, S., Gereffi, G. and A. Rossi. 2010. 'Economic and Social Upgrading in Global Production Networks: Developing a Framework for Analysis,' Working Paper 2010/03. Capturing the Gains.

Elms, D. and P. Low. 2013. *Global Value Chains in a Changing World*. WTO, Fung Global Institute, Temasek Foundation.

Ernst, D. and L. Kim. 2002. 'Global Production Networks, Knowledge Diffusion and Local Capability Formation,' *Research Policy*, 31: 1417–1429.

Feenstra, Robert. 1998. 'Integration of Trade and Disintegration of Production in the Global Economy,' *Journal of Economic Perspectives*, 12(4): 31–50.

Findlay, R. 1978. 'An Austrian Model of International Trade and Interest Rate Equalization,' *Journal of Political Economy*, 86: 989–1008.

Gereffi, G. 1999. 'International Trade and Industrial Upgrading in the Apparel Commodity Chain,' *Journal of International Economics*, 48(1): 37–70.

Gereffi, G. 2005. 'The Global Economy: Organization, Governance and Development' in N.J. Smelser and R. Swedberg (eds.), *Handbook of Economic Sociology*, 2nd ed. Princeton, NJ: Princeton University Press and Russell Sage Foundation.

Gereffi, G. 2014. 'A Global Value Chain Perspective on Industrial Policy and Development in Emerging Markets,' *Duke Journal of Comparative & International Law*, 24(3): 433–458.

Gereffi, G. and J. Lee. 2012. 'Why the World Suddenly Cares About Global Supply Chains?,' *Journal of Supply Chain Management*, 48(3): 24–32.

Gereffi, G. and K. Fernandez-Stark. 2016. *Global Value Chain Analysis: A Primer*. Duke CGGC

Johnson, R.C. and G. Noguera. 2012. 'Accounting for Intermediates: Production Sharing and Trade in Intermediates,' *Journal of International Economics*, 86: 224–236.

Jones, R. and H. Kierzkowski. 2001. 'A Framework for Fragmentation' in S. Arndt and H. Kierzkowski (eds.), *Fragmentation: New Production Patterns in the World Economy*, pp. 17–34. New York: Oxford University Press.

Kaplinsky, R., and M. Morris. 2001. *A Handbook for Value Chain Research*. Prepared for the International Development Research Centre.

Krugman, P. 1995. 'Growing World Trade: Causes and Consequences,' *Brookings Paper on Economic Activity*, 26(1): 327–377.

Morrison, A., Pietrobelli, C. and R. Rabellotti. 2008. 'Global Value Chains and Technological Capabilities: A Framework to Study Learning and Innovation in Developing Countries,' *Oxford Development Studies*, 36(1): 39–58.

OECD. 2012. *Trade in Value-Added: Concepts, Methodologies and Challenges*. Joint OECD-WTO note.

OECD. 2013. *Interconnected Economies: Benefiting From Global Value Chains*. Report on global value chains, DSTI/IND (2013) 2 Draft 14 February. Paris: OECD.

OECD. 2014. *Global Value Chains: Challenges, Opportunities, and Implications for Policy*. OECD, WTO and World Bank Group Report prepared for submission to the G20 Trade Ministers Meeting Sydney, Australia.

OECD. 2015. 'The Participation of Developing Countries in Global Value Chains: Implications for Trade and Trade Policy,' Trade Policy Paper No. 179. OECD.

OECD, WTO and the World Bank Group. 2014. *Global Value Chains: Challenges, Opportunities and Implications for Policy*. Report prepared for submission to the G20 Trade Ministers Meeting Sydney, Australia.

Pietrobelli, C. and R. Rabellotti. 2011. 'Global Value Chains meet Innovation Systems: Are there Learning Opportunities for Developing Countries?,' *World Development*, 39(7): 1261–1269.

Polanyi, M. 1966. *The Tacit Dimension*. New York: Doubleday.

Porter, M.E. 1990. *The Competitive Advantage of Nations*. London: Macmillan.

Sturgeon, T. and O. Memedovic. 2010. 'Mapping Global Value Chains: Intermediate Goods Trade and Structural Trade in the World Economy,' UNIDO Working Paper, 05/2010.

Taglioni, D. and D. Winkler. 2016. *Making Global Value Chains Work for Development*. Washington, DC: World Bank Group.

Timmer, M.P., Dietzenbacher, E., Los, B., Stehrer, R. and G.J. de Vries. 2015. 'An Illustrated User Guide to the World Input–Output Database: I Case of Global Automotive Production,' *Review of International Economics*, 23: 575–605.

UNCTAD. 2013. *Global Value Chains: Investment and Trade for Development*. New York and Geneva: United Nations.

UNESCAP. 2015. *Asia-Pacific Trade and Investment Report 2015: Supporting Participation in Value Chains*. New York and Geneva: United Nations.

World Economic Forum. 2016. *World Economic Outlook: Subdued demand-Symptoms and Remedies*. Washington, DC: International Monetary Fund.

Websites

www.wiod.org/new_site/database/wiots.htm (accessed on 16 November 2016).

www.wto.exanelish/res_e/statis_e/miwi_e/Explanatory_Notes_e.pdf (accessed on 09 February 2017).

Part II

Evidence of India's integration

Introduction to Part II

Part II discusses the evidence of India's participation in GVCs. In Chapter 4, we discuss the extent of India's participation in GVCs as recorded in secondary sources. Examining India's trade flow data, it is noted that India has had a negative trade balance in goods for most of the years. For value chain activity, intermediate goods are important. We decompose India's imports using the BEC classification to understand the nature of such imports and corroborate the point that India's participation in GVCs is on account of sourcing of intermediates from abroad.

In Chapter 5, we discuss the framework for evaluating India's integration in GVCs through a discussion of sector level survey analysis covered in greater detail in subsequent chapters. The chapter also focuses on the barriers that have been responsible for developing countries such as India lagging behind in integration into GVCs. It identifies government policy related, firm level and other constraints, which have specifically affected transfer of knowledge and learning capabilities in different sectors.

2   Why is GVC engagement limited for some countries?

The international fragmentation of production (wherein different processes of the value chain are sliced up and different fragments are produced in different countries) has transformed international trade. As a consequence, international trade is dominated by trade in parts and components. More than 60% of global trade consists of trade in intermediate goods and services (UNCTAD 2013). This chapter aims to review the evidence of global value chain (GVC) trade and examines why engagement in GVCs is limited for some countries. The literature review provides a key for building the framework on integration and learning which is used in the book (and elaborated in the next chapter). It also helps identify the gaps existing in literature, especially with regard to India.

The review is divided into the following sections: (i) measurement of GVC-related trade and (ii) barriers to integration.

Overview of the literature

Integration into GVCs can occur through backward and forward linkages.[1] Assessment of GVC participation focuses on three concepts: function in the GVC (from both buyers' and sellers' perspectives), specialization and domestic value-added contribution, and position in GVC network and the type of GVC node (Taglioni and Winkler 2016). As we note from the figures in Taglioni and Winkler 2016, China and Germany are important from the buyer's perspective, while the United States of America (USA) is important from the seller's perspective. From the perspective of the buyer, the first indicator to examine is the share of intermediates by Broad Economic Categories (BEC)[2] classification in gross imports. For the low- and medium-income countries, the share of intermediates in gross imports was 71% in the year 2012.[3]

From a seller's perspective, involvement is indicated by share of intermediates in gross output.[4] This measure focuses on domestic production rather than trade. Several measures like intermediate exports can be obtained from the measure previously mentioned. Over time, the measure for a specific country and sector provides an indication whether the country is an important supplier in GVCs. The share of intermediates in gross exports has increased over the last one-and-a-half decades and the share of low- and medium-income countries (LMICs)[5] is higher than that for high-income countries, indicating that such countries export more final goods.[6]

Measurement of GVC-related trade

More than half of the world's manufactured imports are intermediate goods (primary goods, parts and components, and finished products), and more than 70% of the world's services' imports are intermediate services. Yeats (1998) has shown that trade in intermediates is large and growing. Trade and investment barriers have affected the emergence of GVCs during the last two decades, both in the countries which place barriers and on the global economy. However, their implications are not yet fully understood, as limited empirical evidence is available (OECD 2012).

GVCs call for a change in the conventional approach towards measuring international trade. Calculating trade in gross terms can lead to recording of the intermediate products several times along the value chain[7] and thereby to wrong conclusions in which the country of final producer appears to capture most of the value, overlooking the contribution of countries involved upstream. The construction of an inter-country Input-Output model and the estimation of trade statistics in value-added terms is a significant step further. Overall, the economic literature has evolved along different strands of research, using different concepts, methods, and terminology for value chains. Amador and Cabral (2016) point out that the complexity and different scales of analysis make it virtually impossible to define, measure, and map GVCs in a single way. Three main methodological approaches have been used to measure GVCs at the sectoral level – international trade statistics on parts and components, customs statistics on processing trade, and international trade data combined with Input-Output tables. These are discussed in the following subsections.

Measurement of GVC-related trade

Two parallel approaches have been used in the literature to estimate value-added in trade: the first measures the degree of vertical specialization (VS)[8] and imported foreign content in a country's exports using a single country's Input-Output (IO) table. This is based on the work of Hummels et al. (2001). The second approach traces value-added at stages of production across countries using inter-country Input-Output (ICIO) tables.

Hummels et al. (2001) use Input-Output tables to calculate VS share.[9] Estimation of the VS share requires identification of imported intermediates and can be computed from the IO tables.[10]

The second approach traces value-added at stages of production across countries using inter-country Input-Output (ICIO) tables. This approach is described in Johnson and Noguera (2012).[11] It provides a formal definition of value-added exports or the value-added produced in a country but absorbed in another country.[12] Koopman et al. (2014) (hereafter KWW) developed a framework to measure two sets of coefficients by combining information on processing trade[13] share at the sector level from a country's customs data and the country's IO table. The IO table is split into two parts: one that focuses on domestic production and trade, and the other that focuses on processing trade. The value of gross exports[14] is split into four main elements. These four elements are combinations of the nine terms of the KWW decomposition. FV is the measure of value-added from foreign sources embodied in a country's gross exports, while DVA is the domestic value-added. Domestic value-added can be further decomposed into exported final goods, exported intermediates absorbed by direct importers, exported intermediates that return home, and indirect value-added exports (IV). IV is the value-added embodied as intermediate inputs in third countries' gross exports.[15]

Los et al. (2016) provide a parsimonious approach of the same accounting decomposition as the KWW decomposition and show that DVA in exports, expressed as a share of gross exports, is an inverse measure of the degree of a country's vertical specialization in trade.

PARTICIPATION IN GVCS

The GVC participation index is obtained by adding the FV and IV shares.[16] The higher the foreign value-added embodied in gross exports, the higher the value of inputs exported to third countries and used in their exports, the higher the participation of a given country in the value chain.

The length of the GVCs is assessed through the "average propagation length" (APL).[17]

DISTANCE TO FINAL DEMAND[18]

Fally (2011) suggested that the distance to final demand be calculated[19] using the concept of length of the chain when looking forward.

Evidence

Participation in GVCs is measured using the vertical specialization share which was discussed previously.[20] This indicator measures the value of imported inputs in the overall exports of a country, thereby capturing the importance of backward integration. Alternatively, the forward integration or inputs used in third countries for further exports[21] can be combined with the VS share to capture the comprehensive participation by a country in GVCs. The GVC participation index in Organization for Economic Co-operation and Development (OECD) countries for the year 2008 shows that small economies (such as Luxemburg and Belgium) source more inputs from abroad and produce more inputs used in GVCs compared to their larger counterparts like the US (OECD 2013). However, the size of the country is less correlated to share in inputs than in exports. When participation in GVCs between OECD and non-OECD economies is compared, the participation in GVCs is found to be of a similar magnitude in the two groups of countries. Large economies, such as Brazil, China, and India, have a lower share of exports made of inputs taking part in vertical trade,[22] as opposed to small economies, such as Singapore or Chinese Taipei. Looking into the relative performance and involvement of countries in the context of their participation in GVCs, UNCTAD (2013) observes:

• Small economies (Belgium, Luxemburg) source relatively more inputs from abroad and produce relatively more inputs for use in GVCs than bigger economies among the OECD countries. Even outside OECD, larger economies such as India, Brazil, and China have lower import content of inputs than small economies such as Malaysia.[23]
• The stage at which a country is located in GVC (upstream[24] being involved in R&D and designing, and downstream involving assembly and customer service) also determines how much it benefits from being integrated into it.
• Looking at gross exports and value of domestic value-added in gross exports can help assess the participation of a country in GVCs. Countries highly engaged in GVCs have a relatively lower value of domestic value-added (for instance, China). Another

parameter to look at is the ratio of domestic value-added to the gross exports, as this helps assess the extent of foreign value-added in gross exports, and this ratio is highest for large economies and exporters of raw materials. Small economies or economies heavily integrated into value chains have a low value.

• Bilateral trade balance positions can change significantly when measured in value-added terms. Significant exports of value-added from South Korea and Japan pass through China on their way to final consumers; this results in significantly smaller Chinese trade deficits with these countries but also typically higher Japanese and Korean trade surpluses with other countries. Similarly, Korea's significant trade deficit with Japan falls in value-added terms.

The length of the chain in GVCs indicates how many production stages are involved. The average length of value chains has increased between 1995 and 2005, which can be mostly attributed to an increase in the international part, with the domestic length being the same. Data for 2008–09 suggests that there is evidence of consolidation, as the international length has shrunk to the benefit of domestic APL. Television and communication equipment, motor vehicles, basic metals, electrical machinery, and other transport equipment are the five industries that exhibited the highest levels of fragmentation. Services industries exhibit relatively smaller value chains (with the exception of communication and transport).

The distance to final demand is used to assess where countries are located in the value chain – upstream (research and design) or downstream (assembly and customer services). "Distance to final demand" has been used as an indicator for this. Between 1995 and 2008, the increase in the index is high for economies such as Chile, China, Malaysia, and Singapore. EU countries such as Austria, the Czech Republic, Germany, and Denmark have also significantly increased their upstreamness.[25] Countries where the distance to final demand has decreased include Mexico, New Zealand, Poland, Portugal, Romania, the Slovak Republic, Slovenia, and the US.

IMF (2015), against the backdrop of the rise of GVCs in Asia, documented key developments of GVCs and investigated factors causing economies to reap greater benefits from GVC participation. The key findings included: first, moving towards a more upstream position in production and raising economic complexity. This is associated with the country increasing its share of GVC value-added. Second, fostering GVC participation and expanding the share of the domestic value-added in a value chain require efforts to reduce trade barriers, enhance infrastructure, foster human capital formation, support research and development, and improve institutions.

Sturgeon and Memedovic (2010) address the issue of the data gap in the identification of intermediates. The paper analyzes the trend of trade in intermediates by combining the BEC categories of consumption and capital goods as "final goods," and the BEC classified intermediates are treated as "intermediates." The paper finds that, contrary to what would be expected, the trade in intermediates (as a share of world imports) has actually declined. The authors try to address this problem by further modifying the BEC classification as they find it too aggregative in its approach. Thus, the intermediates are split into two categories: generic and true. The paper looks at the trade in three sectors: electronics, automobiles and motorcycles, and apparel and footwear. The main findings with reference to these sectors are that electronic and motor vehicle industries dominate the world trade in intermediate goods. They also observe a production deepening in the case of motor vehicle and apparel sectors. There is a comparison between trade in final goods and the trade in intermediate goods. In the case of the electronics industry, the trade in intermediates has outdone trade in final goods; in the case of motor vehicles, both have grown at roughly the same pace; and in the case of footwear and apparel, trade in final goods has outpaced trade in intermediates.

Trends in intermediate trade have been analyzed with respect to countries by dividing them into developed industrialized; developing; East Asia newly industrialized; Commonwealth of Independent States (CIS); former Eastern Europe, Western Europe, and Scandinavia; and others in between 1998 and 2006. Developing nations are led by China and Mexico and countries within the group East Asia have been found to be growing faster than those in Latin America. Developing countries' share of world manufactured intermediate goods (MIGs) has been found to be growing at a much faster pace than developed industrialized countries. Another important observation here is that intermediate goods tend to rebound strongly after down cycles. This trade is also more volatile and suffers a magnified effect in recessions.

INTERNATIONAL TRADE STATISTICS ON PARTS AND COMPONENTS

The simplest approach to measuring fragmentation compares international trade statistics of parts and components with trade in final products. This approach was initiated with the work of Yeats (1998) and Ng and Yeats (1999), and has been used extensively; its main advantages are the high coverage and low complexity of the data and its comparability across countries, which allows the identification of the bilateral trading partner relations. Drawbacks of this approach are the low accuracy of the measure and its reliance on product classification of trade statistics (Amador and Cabral 2016). Typically, the parts and components aggregate are obtained from the Standard Trade Classification (SITC), which includes products of SITC 7 (Machinery and transport equipment) and SITC 8 (Miscellaneous manufactured articles). The UN classification by BEC also categorizes trade into large economic classes of goods on the basis of their principal use – this has also been used to measure trade in valued-added goods.

Yeats (2001) shows that in 1995 OECD exports of parts and components in the category "Key machinery and transportation equipment" was USD 440 billion, which was 30% of all shipments in that category. However, as he notes, the extent of production-sharing is higher than this since the SITC Revision 2 system does not allow distinction between components and parts in chemicals and other manufactured goods. The data also indicates that trade in machinery and transport equipment has grown considerably faster than the final-stage products in that group in the past decade. Due to the deficiency in the Standard International Trade Classification (SITC Revision 1) system, it was not possible to differentiate between the international trade in components and parts and the exchange of manufactured goods. However, changes in the SITC classification system (Revision 2) allow the approximation of production-sharing.

Several authors have used this approach to measure trade in parts and components; these include Athukorala (2005) for East Asia and Lall et al. (2004) for the electronics and automotive sectors in East Asia and Latin America.

CUSTOMS STATISTICS ON PROCESSING TRADE

Customs statistics include information on trade associated with customs arrangements in which tariff exemptions are granted in accordance with the domestic content of the imported good. Outward processing data is considered to be a narrow measure of fragmentation (Amador and Cabral 2016). Since this data is administered by customs authorities, trade in goods is recorded accurately at a highly disaggregated level. Processing trade data is available from the US Offshore Assembly Programme for the US and the EU Processing Trade Data for the EU. Studies in which this data have been used include Feenstra et al. (2000), Clark (2006) (for US data); while Gorg (2000), Baldone et al. (2001, 2007), and Egger and Egger (2001, 2005) use data for EU. Lemoine and Unal Kesenci (2004) and Xing (2012) use data for China.

INTERNATIONAL TRADE DATA COMBINED WITH INPUT-OUTPUT TABLES

Mirodout et al. (2009) state that two methodologies can be applied to measure trade in intermediate goods. In the first method, trade in intermediate goods is measured using the UN BEC classification, which relies on the breakdown of disaggregated trade flows at the product level, where they can be distinguished according to their use. The BEC classification groups commodities according to their main end use into capital goods, intermediate goods, and consumption goods. The second method is via the use of Input-Output (I-O) tables that directly provide the value of foreign inputs used in the domestic production of goods and services. I-O tables contain information about the use of intermediate goods and services as inputs in different industries. These tables usually consist of a domestic and imported table indicating the use of domestic and imported inputs, respectively. Hence, they allow for the identification of the industry of origin and industry using the input. However, I-O tables suffer from one drawback: they are not bilateral and do not contain information about trading partners. Also, these tables are usually made available after every five years since they have to account for the underlying changes in the structure of the economy and coefficients are not expected to change over a five-year period. For the intervening years, import coefficients are interpolated. Both methods have strengths and weaknesses; depending on the purpose of the study, either one or a combination of the two methods could be used.

OECD (2012) provides evidence of the position of countries within international production networks. It is based on Input-Output tables of 58 countries that account for 95% of the world output. The OECD inter-country Input-Output (ICIO) model details transactions of 35 industries and for five years: 1995, 2000, 2005, 2008, and 2009. It discusses the extent to which countries are involved in vertically integrated production through their participation, the length of the GVC, and the distance to the final demand.

Barriers to integration

Not all firms are equally connected to GVCs. Even within countries, there is usually a variation in the degree to which firms are integrated into these chains. Some countries participate in many and varied GVCs, either as the host countries to lead firms or as suppliers of very specific tasks, while others have lower penetration. There is extant literature today which confirms and explores issues in this context. This section highlights the barriers to integrating in value chains faced by suppliers in developing countries. In GVCs, value is added at each stage before crossing the border to be passed on to the next stage, making it possible to recognize impediments at a disaggregated level by looking at each stage.

The literature suggests that the varying degree of connectedness or integration in value chains is determined by diverse factors. Some of these are exogenous in nature (such as a country's geographic location, market size, cultural characteristics, and endowment of natural resources), while others are endogenous, so that they can be influenced by government policies and firm-level decisions. OECD, together with the WTO and UNCTAD in recent years (see OECD 2013, 2014, and 2015), have analyzed the development of GVCs – including factors determining countries' participation in GVCs and benefiting from such inclusion.

Several elements of policy determine participation in GVCs: regional trade agreements (RTAs); investment barriers to multinational corporations; infrastructure development; speed and flexibility of movement of physical goods and information; effectiveness of legal and regulatory systems; efficiency of services; developing a skilled workforce; friendliness of the business climate; and capacity of domestic firms (often SMEs) to contribute to the supply chain (OECD 2013). Other factors include border administration, market access barriers, and transport logistics (WEF 2012). These issues have also been frequent targets of aid for trade.

OECD (2014) stresses that GVCs do not respond to piecemeal approaches to policy change. A wholesome approach or "whole-of the-supply-chain" policy approach is needed. Some of the supporting policies are horizontal in nature: good infrastructure and connectivity, a business-friendly environment, flexible labour markets, access to credit, innovation, and macroeconomic stability. Other policies are more targeted, such as tariffs and other trade restrictions, subsidies, local content or export-performance requirements, and restrictions on foreign exchange. Apart from ensuring open markets, appropriate and wide-ranging policy frameworks are needed that allow countries and firms to capitalize on their existing productive capacities and spillover benefits from foreign investment, knowledge, and innovations. These include labour market policies, social policies, and competition policies as well as policies for investment in education, skills, technology, and strategic infrastructure.

Some work has also been published specifically in the context of the developing and underdeveloped economies. For instance, OECD (2015) has assessed the determinants and economic effects of GVC participation across developing countries in five developing regions of Africa, the Middle East, and Asia, offering a starting point for policymakers to assess their country's engagement and consider policy options on how to benefit from the reality of increasingly fragmented production. The results of this analysis show that the key determinants of GVC participation are structural factors, such as geography, size of the market, and level of development. In the short-to-medium term, this suggests that policy can affect GVC participation only to a certain extent. However, trade and FDI policy reforms, along with improvements in logistics and customs, intellectual property protection, and infrastructure and institutions, all play active roles in promoting further engagement (OECD 2015).

Another way to look at barriers to integration in GVCs is costs. Costs (production, labour, transport, investment, and tax incentives) are the major drivers of lead firms' decisions to invest or source production in developing countries. Wage differentials, for instance, are primary drivers of the globalization of production. The notion of costs encompasses all other factors. For example, high costs could result from a lack of infrastructure or competition in basic services. They could also result from excessive administrative burdens (including at the border), strict labour laws (i.e. weak business environment), or a high level of insecurity or corruption.

OECD (2015) highlights the importance of trade costs for participation of developing countries in global and regional value chains. Participation indicators are regressed against a set of structural parameters or non-policy characteristics that are hard to shape in the short-to-medium run (such as economic size, level of development, share of manufacturing in gross domestic product (GDP), and distance to economic centres of activity), as well as policy variables (such as tariffs faced or charged, presence of FTAs, and openness to FDI). They find that the structural characteristics of countries are the main determinants of participation – the size and geographical location of countries as well as their manufacturing share in GDP explain most of the variation in participation rates, but trade and investment policies also matter. Removing tariff barriers to trade is important since fragmented modes of production imply multiple border crossings and hence exponential effects.

IMF (2016) studied the impact of various factors in the context of sub-Saharan Africa. Using the gravity model estimation on an unbalanced panel for 185 countries over the period 2007–11, it was found that deeper integration in GVCs (measured by a higher share of foreign value-added (FVA) in one country's exports) is found to be associated with improved indicators of human capital and availability. FVA is hampered by higher tariff levels and difficult business environments. A reduction in tariff rates across sub-Saharan Africa towards the average prevailing in non-sub-Saharan African countries could increase the share of FVA in exports by about 3 percentage points, an increase in access to credit by 2 percentage points, and an increase in education spending and the rule of law to levels seen elsewhere in the world by another 1 percentage point each. The need to improve infrastructure is another important impediment to trade flows. Better access to credit for the private sector and a more conducive business climate are also found to support more intense trade flows and better insertion into GVCs, as do efforts to improve education outcomes.

The Asian Development Bank (ADB) and Asian Development Bank Institute (ADBI) undertook a study (ADB-ADBI 2015) to examine ways of encouraging small and medium enterprise (SME) participation in GVCs. The study explored policy solutions to promote participation and address the financial and nonfinancial issues that SMEs face. ADB surveyed SMEs, government authorities, and financial institutions in four countries to analyze critical constraints on SME involvement in global value chains and to propose financing models and policy directions. An ADB survey was organized for this publication project and conducted in four select countries – Kazakhstan, Papua New Guinea, the Philippines, and Sri Lanka – during September 2014 and February 2015. Enterprises were asked to indicate the five factors most critical to success in integrating into value chains. The report provides a rich set of ideas for encouraging the further penetration of Asian SMEs into global value chains. Enterprises felt that the quality of their products or services was the most critical success factor. The second factor for success in value chains was skilled labour, a key ingredient for product quality and crucial to achieve high productivity and efficiency. The third factor nominated was strength of customer relations, vital when working within and satisfying buyers further down a value chain. The fourth most critical factor was the ambition of the owner, suggesting that enterprises wanting to globalize must seek out opportunities and have the will to succeed. The fifth factor was the education, experience, and international exposure of the owner. Besides these nonfinancial issues, access to finance is also a key factor in determining the success of SMEs in participating in global value chains. The SMEs surveyed in the four countries had a clear demand for long-term funding from formal financial institutions to survive and grow in global value chains. The enterprises surveyed also recognized a range of impediments that could constrain their efforts to internationalize. Among the five key constraints were access to finance, availability of skilled labour, and labour market rigidity. Weak institutional support indicates that governments can – and are expected to – play a role in facilitating SME integration. The most critical constraint was defined as "disadvantages of the business sector." This suggests that the competitiveness of the sector as a whole may be a factor affecting individual firms.

Table 2.1 presents a summary of key factors that have been identified by ADB-ADBI (2015) in the literature as being important in impacting SME manufacturing firm participation in global production networks. These are elaborated in a separate section on barriers later in the book.

The ability of economies to integrate efficiently into the global economy depends, to a great extent, on the quality of hard and soft infrastructure, ranging from transportation, telecommunications, and financial services to border processes, customs practices, and business and regulatory environments. Inadequate infrastructure is identified by countries and providers of trade-related assistance as the single most important constraint. Access to and reliability of electricity is a major binding constraint to trade performance of developing country firms. Electricity has been important for South East Asian countries in their integration process. The OECD-WTO (2015) analysis shows that, in both developing and developed countries, trade facilitation, whether defined narrowly (World Bank Logistics Performance Indicator for customs) or broadly (infrastructure, intellectual property rights or IPR, broadband and electricity) is important for GVC participation.

Cross-border vertical integration requires ease in mobility of production factors, including capital and labour. Improving connectivity with international markets includes reduction of traditional barriers to trade and promotion of trade facilitation. Recent OECD analysis (OECD 2013, 2015) exploring impacts of specific trade facilitation measures shows that addressing procedural obstacles at the border can boost integration into value chains across all regions. Apart from the direct impact on imports, it takes place on production mechanisms in the domestic market and the increased export competitiveness through access to necessary imported intermediate goods. Transportation costs remain, according to developing country suppliers, the main obstacle to entering, establishing, or moving up GVCs (OECD-WTO 2013a).

Table 2.1 Groups of critical factors affecting GVC participation

Group 1: capability and competitiveness	Group 2: international business	Group 3: access to resources	Group 4: macro conditions
Quality of product and conditions	Political stability in foreign markets	Access to insurance	Geographical location
Skilled labour	Foreign rules and regulation	Access to business development services	Fair competition
Strength of customer relationship	Tariff	Joining business associates	Stable foreign currency exchange
Innovation and design	Language	Access to finance	Cost of inputs
Ambition of owner	Familiarity of foreign business practices	Logistics efficiency	Economic conditions
Education, experience, and international exposure of owner			
Readiness of owner to take risks			
Capability of business			
Flexibility of business			
Specialization of business			
Technology			
Training			
Competitive advantage			
Low-cost production			
Relationship with other firms			
Standards and certification			

Source: ADB-ADBI (2015)

Access to trade finance is also identified as a very important binding constraint, especially in developing countries. Trade finance is the lifeline of international trade, with more than 90% of these transactions involving some form of credit, insurance, or guarantee. In particular, small exporters lack adequate access to trade finance (ITC 2009; OECD-WTO 2013b).

Another major constraint is meeting and certifying the technical, health, and safety standards requirements that are necessary to access mature markets and participate in value chains. This could occur due to the unpreparedness of developing countries. However, at other times, standards could also act as arbitrary and unjustified trade barriers difficult to challenge. According to a business survey in the agri-food sector (OECD-WTO 2013c) in which 250 lead firms and suppliers in developing countries participated, about 60% of the firms pointed at the ability to meet quality and safety standards as the main factor influencing sourcing and investment decisions in GVCs. Table 2.2 suggests evidence for the identified factors for different countries.

Conclusion

The international fragmentation of production, wherein different processes of the value chain are sliced up and different fragments are produced in different countries, has transformed international trade. As a consequence, international trade is dominated by trade in parts and components. GVCs call for a change in the conventional approach towards measuring international trade since intermediate goods cross borders several times, leading to double counting. Measurement of GVC participation follows two approaches: first, using the concept of vertical specialization developed by Hummels et al. (2001) to capture imported foreign content in a country's exports and, second, measuring value addition at stages of production across countries using Input-Output tables.

This chapter also reviewed the evidence of GVC trade and examined why engagement in GVCs is limited for some countries. There are four groups of factors that are likely to affect the participation of countries in GVCs. These are capability and competitiveness, international business, access to resources, and macroeconomic conditions. While certain factors or group of factors are crucial for some industries, they may not be so in other cases. A sectoral analysis is important since the sourcing and the length of chain varies by sector.

Table 2.2 Country-level experiences of factors affecting GVC participation

Factor		Region/country (evidence)	
		Success	Disadvantaged/faced problems
Policy related			
Horizontal	Liberalized FDI policy	China, East Asian economies	Kazakhstan
	Business environment	Angola, Burkina Faso, Ethiopia, Guinea-Bissau, Lesotho, Madagascar, Mozambique, and Senegal. Bangladesh and Cambodia in Asia, and Sao-Tome and Timor-Leste (Bhattacharya and Moazzem 2013) IT (microchips) – Costa Rica (ICTSD-WEF 2013)	Zambia, Angola
	Trade policy factor	Sub-Saharan Africa, the Middle East, and North Africa Logistics – Rwanda, Senegal, Djibouti, Uganda, and Tanzania (Bhattacharya and Moazzem 2013)	Democratic Republic of Congo, Cameroon, Djibouti, Rwanda, and Nigeria Morocco and Tunisia
Targeted	Transport and infrastructure	Sub-Saharan Africa, the Middle East, and North Africa	Sub-Saharan Africa, the Middle East, and North Africa Bulgaria (Taglioni and Winkler 2016)
	Institutional and legal frameworks		Africa
Natural			
	Culture	Entrepreneurship, innovation, and networking among SMEs	

(Continued)

Table 2.2 (Continued)

Factor		Region/country (evidence)	
Policy related		Success	Disadvantaged/faced problems
Firm characteristic			
Common	Capability to meet international product and quality standards	Philippines	Kazakhstan
	Access to finance	Agriculture – Cameroon, West Africa, Rwanda Ethiopia, Tanzania, Guatemala, Honduras, Mozambique, Ghana Textile – Bangladesh Fishery – Grenada Dairy – Peru	India (our survey)
	R&D	PRC Japan South Korea Singapore	Specialty chemicals – India (our survey)
	Creating sustainable industrial clusters	Mittelstand (Germany)	India (our survey)
	Low-cost knowledge base	Philippines	
	Technological advancement	China Apparel – Bangladesh Coffee plantation – Ethiopia (Bhattacharya and Moazzem 2013)	Nepal, Mauritania, Burkina Faso, Mozambique, and Timor-Leste (Bhattacharya and Moazzem 2013)

Source: Compiled by authors

Notes

1 Lopez-Gonzalez and Holmes (2011) introduced the concept of backward and forward specialization, in which backward refers to sourcing and forward refers to sales. This differs from the usual concept of backward links, which refers to sales: forward links refer to sourcing (Ottaviano and Puga 2003).

2 BEC or Broad Economic Categories distinguishes products according to their main end use into capital, intermediate, or consumption goods. This is discussed later in the chapter.

3 Taglioni and Winkler (2016) suggest that high shares of intermediate imports in total imports are common for LMICs, reflecting the importance of primary commodities in the import basket of these countries.

4 This measure suffers from two limitations. Taglioni and Winkler (2016) state that if it is to be useful, it has to be quantified at a very disaggregate level. Second, the measure does not indicate whether the intermediate output is used domestically or exported.

5 Low- and medium-income countries

6 On the sales side, the number of downstream stages between the country's producers and the final consumers are provided by the length of the chain. This has also been called "distance to final demand" by Antras and others.

7 Johnson and Noguera (2016) point out that value-added exports were falling over gross export over 1970–2009, indicating that double counting is more pervasive in gross trade data than in the past.

8 Chen et al. (2005) define vertical specialization as a process by which "countries are linked sequentially to produce goods, with each country specializing in particular stages of a good's production sequence." The "sequential linkage" is the cornerstone of GVC trade as "imported intermediates used by a country to make goods . . . are in turn exported to another country."

9 VS share $= \mathbf{u}\mathbf{A}^{M}\left(\mathbf{I} - \mathbf{A}^{D}\right)^{-1}\mathbf{X}/x_{k}$ .... (1)

where $\mathbf{u}$ is a $1 \times n$ vector of 1's, $\mathbf{A}^{M}$ is an $n \times n$ imported coefficient matrix, $\mathbf{I}$ is the identity matrix, $\mathbf{A}^{D}$ is the $n \times n$ domestic coefficient matrix, $\mathbf{X}$ is the $n \times 1$ export vector, and x_{k} is a scalar that denotes the amount of exports from country k. The numerator of equation (1) measures all imported inputs, iterated over the country's production structure, which are needed to produce the exports of a country from all n sectors. This is divided by the value of the total direct and indirect share of a country's exports attributable to imported inputs (VS share).

10 This assumes the ratio of imported trade intermediate inputs to total imports is the same as the ratio of the total intermediate inputs to total absorption. Absorption ratio is the share of imports in consumption.

11 Using this measure, Johnson and Noguera (2012) observe that exports of manufactures have lower value added exports to total exports (VAX) ratios and trade imbalances measured using this approach can differ substantially from gross trade imbalances. Using thee example of US-China trade, they show that this could be 30–40% smaller when measured in value-added terms.

12 For a country this is $\Delta VAX_{it} = \sum_{s} \Delta VAX_{it}\left(s\right)\left(\dfrac{\omega_{it}\left(s\right) + \omega_{i,t-1}\left(s\right)}{2}\right) + \sum_{s} \Delta\omega_{it}$

$\left(s\right)\left(\dfrac{VAX_{it}\left(s\right) + VAX_{i,t-1}\left(s\right)}{2}\right)$ where $\omega_{it}\left(s\right) = \dfrac{x_{it}\left(s\right)}{x_{it}}$ and $\Delta x_{it} \equiv x_{it} - x_{i,t-1}.$

The first term represents the 'within' effect and the second term represents the 'between' effect.

13 Processing exports are characterized by imports for exports with favourable tariff treatment with tariff exemptions on the imported input and other tax preferences from local or central governments (Koopman et al. 2012).

14 Gross exports has three parts: value-added exports (VT) + domestic content in intermediate exports that finally returns home (VS_1^*) + foreign content (VS). Domestic content = (1) DV in direct final goods exports + (2) DV in intermediates export absorbed by direct importers + (3) DV in intermediates re-exported to third countries IV + (4) intermediates that return home via final imports + (5) DV in intermediates that return via intermediate imports + (6) double-counted intermediate exports produced at home. Similarly, foreign content (VS) = (7) FV in final goods exports + (8) FV in intermediate goods exports + (9) double-counted intermediate exports produced abroad. Value-added exports (VT) = (1) DV in direct final goods exports + (2) DV in intermediates export absorbed by direct importers + (3) DV in intermediates re-exported to third countries IV. (3) + (4) + (5) + (6) is part of VS_1 of Hummels et al. (2001).

15 DVAs = GDPs − GDPs*, where DVA is domestic value-added and where GDPs is simply the sum over industry value-added. $GDP_{s*} = \tilde{v}s(1-A_{ss}) - 1y_{ss}$. The right-hand side of this equation contains data that can be taken from national Input-Output data for the country s, with $\tilde{v}$s a row vector of value-added coefficients for the industries in s, the matrix A_{ss}, with domestic intermediate input coefficients, and y_{ss} domestic final demand for domestic products. As before, DVAs = GDPs − GDPs*. This result aligns with the KWW decomposition and provides a rationale for the VS measure of Hummels et al. (2001).

16 $GVC\ participation = \dfrac{IV_{ik}}{E_{ik}} + \dfrac{FV_{ik}}{E_{ik}}$

17 Dietzenbacher and Romero (2007). APL is one if there is a single production stage in the final industry and increases when inputs from the same industry or other industries are used. The index of the length of GVC is calculated as: $N_{ik} = u.\ (I - A)$-1, where Ni k is the index for industry k in country i, u is the unit vector, I is the identity matrix and A is the Leontief inverse. The index is similar to the calculation of the backward linkage in the input-output literature. Distinction can be made between the domestic and the foreign production stages.

18 Fally (2011) and Antràs et al. (2012) have introduced a measure of "upstreamness" that we can refer to as the "distance to final demand."

19 $D_{ik} = u.\ (I - G)$-1, where D_{ik} is the index for industry k in country i, u is the unit vector, I is the identity matrix, and G is the Gosh inverse.

20 VS share introduced by Hummels et al. (2001) and discussed in the section on measurement.

21 VS_1 or the percentage of exported goods and services used as imported inputs to produce other countries' exports (Hummels et al. 2001).

22 Vertical trade (or vertical specialization trade) as defined by Hummels, Rapoport, and Yi (1998) requires three conditions to occur: (1) A good is produced in two or more sequential stages. (2) Two or more countries

provide value-added during the production of the good. (3) At least one country must use inputs in its stage of the production process, and some of the resulting output must be exported.

23 Low shares of intermediate imports in electrical and electronic equipment are also reported in these countries. Sector analysis is very important for this reason, as indicators for the electrical and electronic intermediates imports indicate. The length of the sourcing chain varies by sector. The length measures the number of upstream stages for a specific sector in a specific country. However, this indicator does not reveal if the imported input is used domestically or for exports. For that, it is necessary to decompose this indicator further into foreign value-added in gross exports and domestic value-added in gross exports. There has been an increase in the foreign value-added in India's gross exports in 2011 compared to 2005 (see Figure 4.8, Chapter 4 of Taglioni and Winkler 2016).

24 The GVC participation index has two components reflecting the upstream and downstream links in the chain. Basically, individual economies participate in global value chains by importing foreign inputs to produce the goods and services they export (backward GVC participation) and by exporting domestically produced inputs to partners in charge of downstream production stages (forward GVC participation). *Source:* Timmer et al. (2015).

25 Average distance to final use (Antras et al. 2012).

References

ADB-ADBI. 2015. *Integrating SMEs into Global Value Chains: Challenges and Policy Actions in Asia*. Philippines: Asian Development Bank.

Amador, J. and S. Cabral. 2016. 'Global Value Chains: A Survey of Drivers and Measures,' *Journal of Economic Surveys*, 30(2): 278–301.

Antràs, P., Chor, D., Fally, T. and R. Hillberry. 2012. 'Measuring the Upstreamness of Production and Trade Flows,' Working Paper No. 17819. Cambridge, MA: National Bureau of Economic Research.

Athukorala, P.C. 2005. 'Product Fragmentation and Trade Patterns in East Asia,' *Asian Economic Papers*, 4: 1–27.

Baldone, S., Sdogati, F. and L. Tajoli. 2001. 'Patterns and Determinants of International Fragmentation of Production: Evidence From Outward Processing Trade Between the EU and Central Eastern European Countries,' *Review of World Economics*, 137: 80–104.

Baldone, S., Sdogati, F. and L. Tajoli. 2007. 'On Some Effects of International Fragmentation of Production on Comparative Advantages, Trade Flows and the Income of Countries,' *The World Economy*, 30: 1726–1769.

Bhattacharya, D. and K.G. Moazzem. 2013. *Participation of the LDCs in the Global Value Chain: Trends, Determinants, and Challenges*. Geneva: ITC Mimeo.

Chen, H., Kondratowicz, M. and K.M. Yi. 2005. 'Vertical Specialization and Three Facts about U.S. International Trade,' *The North American Journal of Economics and Finance*, 16(1): 35–59.

Clark, D. 2006, 'Country and Industry-level Determinants of Vertical Specialization-based Trade,' *International Economic Journal*, 20: 211–225.

Dietzenbacher, E. and I. Romero. 2007. 'Production Chains in an Interregional Framework: Identification by Means of Average Propagations Lengths,' *International Regional Science Review*, 30: 362–383.

Egger, H. and P. Egger. 2001. 'Cross-border Sourcing and Outward Processing in EU Manufacturing,' *The North American Journal of Economics and Finance*, 12: 243–256.

Egger, H. and P. Egger. 2005. 'The Determinants of EU Processing Trade,' *The World Economy*, 28: 147–168.

Fally, T. 2011. *On the Fragmentation of Production in the US*. European Trade Study Group.

Feenstra, R.C., Hanson, G.H. and D.L. Swenson. 2000. 'Offshore Assembly from the United States: Production Characteristics of the 9802 Program' in R.C. Feenstra (ed.), *The Impact of International Trade on Wages*, chapter 3, pp. 85–125. Chicago, IL: University of Chicago Press.

Gorg, H. 2000. 'Fragmentation and Trade: US Inward Processing Trade in the EU,' *Weltwirtschaftliches Archiv*, 127: 403–422.

Hummels, D., Ishii, J. and K.M. Yi. 2001. 'The Nature and Growth of Vertical Specialization in World Trade,' *Journal of International Economics*, 54: 75–96.

Hummels, D., Rapoport, D. and K. M. Yi. 1998. Vertical Specialization and the Changing Nature of World Trade,' *FRBNY Economic Policy Review*, 79–99.

ICTSD-WEF. 2013. *Global Value Chains: Development Challenges and Policy Options Proposals and Analysis*, E15 Expert Group on Global Value Chains: Development Challenges and Policy Options Compilation Report. International Centre for Trade and Sustainable Development.

IMF. 2015. 'Reaping the Benefits from Global Value Chains,' Working Paper WP/15/204, IMF.

IMF. 2016. *Trade Integration and Global Value Chains in Sub-Saharan Africa: In Pursuit of the Missing Link*. Washington, DC: International Monetary Fund.

ITC. 2009. *How to Access Trade Finance: A Guide for Exporting SMEs*. Geneva: International Trade Centre.

Johnson, R.C. and G. Noguera. 2012. 'Accounting for Intermediates: Production Sharing and Trade in Intermediates,' *Journal of International Economics*, 86: 224–236.

Johnson, R.C. and G. Noguera. 2016. 'A Portrait of Trade in Value Added Over Four Decades,' Working Paper 22974. Cambridge, MA: National Bureau of Economic Research.

Koopman, R., Wang, Z. and S.J. Wei. 2012. 'Estimating Domestic Content in Exports When Processing Trade is Pervasive,' *Journal of Development Economics*, 90: 178–189.

Koopman, R., Wang, Z. and S.J Wei. 2014. 'Tracing Value-added and Double Counting in Gross Exports,' *American Economic Review*, 104: 459–494.

Lall, S., Albaladejo, M. and J. Zhang. 2004. 'Mapping Fragmentation: Electronics and Automobiles in East Asia and Latin America,' *Oxford Development Studies*, 32: 407–432.

Lemoine, F. and D. Unal Kesenci. 2004. 'Assembly Trade and Technology TransfIThe Case of China,' *World Development*, 32: 829–850.

Lopez-Gonzalez, J. and P. Holmes. 2011. 'The Nature and Evolution of Vertical Specialisation: What role for Preferential Trade Agreements,' Working Paper 2011/41. National Center of Competence in Research.

Los, B., Timmer, M.P. and G. J. de Vries. 2016. 'Tracing Value-Added and Double Counting in Gross Exports: Comment,' *American Economic Review*, 106(7): 1958–1966.

Mirodout, S., Lanz, R. and A. Ragoussis. 2009. 'Trade in Intermediate Goods and Services', Trade Policy Paper No. 93, OECD.

Ng, F. and A.J Yeats. 1999. 'Production Sharing in East Asia: Who Does What for Whom, and Why?' Policy Research Working Paper Series 2197. The World Bank.

OECD. 2012. *Mapping Global Value Chains*. Paris: Trade and Agriculture Directorate Trade Committee. Paris: OECD.

OECD. 2013. *Interconnected Economies: Benefiting From Global Value Chains*. Report on global value chains, Paris: OECD.

OECD. 2014. *Global Value Chains: Challenges, Opportunities, and Implications for Policy*. OECD, WTO and World Bank Group Report prepared for submission to the G20 Trade Ministers Meeting Sydney, Australia.

OECD. 2015. 'Participation of Developing Countries in Global Value Chains: Implications for Trade and Trade-Related Policies,' Summary Paper, www. oecd.org/countries/kenya/Participation-Developing-Countries-GVCs-Summary-Paper-April-2015.pdf (accessed on January 20, 2017).

OECD-WTO. 2013a. *Aid for Trade and Value Chains in Agrifood*. Paris: OECD

OECD-WTO. 2013b. *Aid for Trade at a Glance 2013: Connecting To Value Chains*. Paris: OECD.

OECD-WTO. 2013c. *OECD-WTO Database on Trade in Value-Added FAQs: Background Note*. Paris: OECD.

OECD-WTO. 2015. *Aid for Trade at a Glance 2015: Reducing Trade Costs for Inclusive, Sustainable Growth*. Paris: OECD.

Ottaviano, G. I. P. and D. Puga. 2003. 'Agglomeration in the Global Economy: A Survey of New Geography,' *World Economy*, 21(6): 707–731.

Sturgeon, T. and O. Memedovic. 2010. 'Mapping Global Value Chains: Intermediate Goods Trade and Structural Trade in the World Economy,' Working Paper, 05/2010. United Nations Industrial Development Organization.

Taglioni, D. and D. Winkler. 2016. *Making Global Value Chains Work for Development*. Washington, DC: World Bank.

Timmer, M. P., Dietzenbacher, E., Los, B., Stehrer, R. and G.J. de Vries. 2015. 'An Illustrated User Guide to the World Input–Output Database: The Case of Global Automotive Production,' *Review of International Economics*, 23: 575–605.

UNCTAD. 2013. *World Investment Report: Global Value Chains and Development.* New York and Geneva: United Nations.

World Economic Forum. 2012. *The Shifting Geography of Global Value Chains: Implications for Developing Countries and Trade Policy.* Geneva: World Economic Forum.

Xing, Y. 2012. 'Processing Trade, Exchange Rates and China's Bilateral Trade Balances', *Journal of Asian Economics*, 23: 540–547.

Yeats, A.J. 1998. 'Just How Big is Global Production Sharing?,' Policy Research Working Paper Series 1871. The World Bank.

Yeats, A.J. 2001. 'Just How Big is Global Production Sharing?' in S. Arndt and H. Kierzkowski (eds.), *Fragmentation: New Production Patterns in the World Economy*, pp. 108–143. New York: Oxford University Press.

3 Conceptual framework for the book

The typology of the governance of the global value chains (GVCs) proposed by Gereffi, Humphrey, and Sturgeon (2005) categorize the relation between governance structures, complexity of transactions, ability to codify transactions, and capabilities in the supply base. We elaborate on this typology to create the framework used in this book.

Gereffi et al. (2005) discuss the conditions under which different patterns emerge: the complexity of the information involved in transactions, the possibility of codifying the information, and the competence of the suppliers along the value chain. Governance[1] type captures the ability to exert control over the chain.[2] The governance of the GVC influences how learning takes place, and hence different mechanisms emerge in different chains (Pietrobelli and Rabellotti 2011). Lead firms put pressure on suppliers to innovate but do not become involved directly in the learning process. For example, lead firms exert an external stimulus for learning[3] and innovation among suppliers in modular chains. On the other hand, in captive chains, the codification and complexity of transactions is high but suppliers have low competence.

The nature of the domestic chain (and its interlinkage with the institutions of innovation) has an important role in the process of learning and upgrading. Navas-Aleman (2011) points out that there are learning opportunities for firms in GVCs from domestic and neighbouring markets. The framework used in this book draws on the role of the governance types in fostering learning (and innovation depending on the institutional setup) in a developing country with a large domestic market.

Key determinants of GVC governance In the introduction, we have briefly examined the link between lead firm, governance structure, and diffusion of technology using the typology created by Gereffi et al. (2005) and Pietrobelli and Rabellotti (2011).

The typology developed by Gereffi et al. (2005) is summarized in Table 3.1. There are eight possible combinations of the three variables (complexity of transactions, ability to codify transactions, competence of suppliers). Five of them generate global value chain types. The combination of low complexity of transactions and low ability to codify is unlikely to occur. This excludes two combinations. Further, if the complexity of the transaction is low and the ability to codify is high, then low supplier capability would lead to exclusion from the value chain. While this is an important outcome, it does not generate a governance type per se.

Gereffi et al. (2005) discuss the conditions under which different patterns emerge: the complexity of the information involved in transactions, the possibility of codifying the information, and the competence of the suppliers along the value chain. In modular value chains, for example, complexity of transactions is high, there are capable potential suppliers, and the codification of transactions is high. Suppliers learn to produce components and modules to fully specified technical standards and the need to adhere to these standards induces learning. Lead firms put pressure on suppliers to innovate but do not become involved directly in the learning process. Hence lead firms exert an external stimulus for learning and innovation among suppliers. On the other hand, in captive chains the codification and complexity of transactions is high but suppliers have low competence (Pietrobelli and Rabellotti 2010b).

Table 3.1 Key determinants of GVC governance

Governance type	Complexity of transactions	Ability to codify transactions	Capabilities in the supply base	Degree of explicit coordination and power asymmetry[*]	Examples[**]
Market	Low	High	High	Low	Bicycle
Modular	High	High	High	↑	Electronics
Relational	High	Low	High		Garment
Captive	High	High	Low	↓	Garment
Hierarchy	High	Low	Low	High	Garment

Source: Adapted from Gereffi et al. (2005)

Notes: [*]The degree of explicit coordination and power symmetry increases from Market to Hierarchy. [**]Examples provided are our own.

Link between lead firms, governance structures, and the transfer of technology through GVCs

The GVC literature stresses the role played by leaders[4] in the chain in terms of transferring knowledge to their suppliers. Participation in value chains is crucial for obtaining information on the type and quality of products and technologies required by global markets in order to gain access to them. However, this information needs to be combined with local technological capabilities and this requires substantial learning efforts (Morrison et al. 2008). Pietrobelli and Rabellotti (2011) discuss how learning mechanisms operate in different types of chains either through a pressure to learn or through explicit support and deliberate knowledge transfer. The dynamics of governance patterns is crucial for opportunities for suppliers to move up the value ladder, moving out of the low road to competitiveness (Pietrobelli and Rabellotti 2007). There are several issues that the literature raises: What institutions (e.g. financial system, corporate governance, education and training system) affect the character and evolution of industries and firms (Berger and Dore 1996)? How do learning mechanisms operate in different types of chains – through pressure to learn or through explicit support and deliberate knowledge transfer?

The literature discusses the relation between GVC and innovation systems (IS) as being non-linear and endogenous, and as affecting both (enterprise learning from GVCs contributes to improving the local IS, which affects the decision of local sourcing of inputs and support for local firms' learning and innovation). However, GVC analysis is limited because of the lack of attention to the institutional context within which local firms interacting in GVC are embedded. An effective IS system increases the capability to cope with complex transactions; when investors engage in make-or-buy decisions, they face a tradeoff between lower production costs and higher transaction costs.

The importance of rules, values, and institutions is stressed in the literature. Lundvall (1992) observes that rules and institutions that interact in the production, diffusion, and use of new and economically useful knowledge are important. Also, the role of technology policies, whether through technology imports via licensing or foreign direct investment (FDI), and incentives for local R&D and training are critical. Technology policy can be mission oriented or diffusion oriented. The technology organizations that carry out basic research and the role of the government-run institutions are also emphasized.

Altenburg (2006) observes that those countries with weak institutions, weak contract enforcement, pervasive corruption, cumbersome bureaucratic procedures, multiple barriers to trade, and poor infrastructure find it difficult to capitalize on inter-firm specialization. Country-specific characteristics are likely to be strong determinants of participation rate differences. These include natural factors such as geographical location and cultural affiliation, as well as the political and institutional environment to support business operations (OECD 2015). Apart from these, there are firm-level factors that determine whether firms are able to integrate in GVCs. Traditionally, this has meant the inclusion of comparative advantage in products/services to be traded, financial resources, and the required labour force. All these factors are considered more important for developing countries such as India. Among the international factors, the structure of value chains that firms hold on to is an important factor. For instance, Gereffi et al. (2005) argue that improved standards, information technology, and the capabilities of suppliers can shift the governance structure from captive and hierarchal towards relational, modular, and market governance, which offers more opportunities for joining and upgrading in a value chain.

Learning in GVCs

Learning in GVCs is influenced by the governance of GVCs, and different mechanisms of learning and innovation are likely to dominate in different types of chains (Gereffi et al. 2005). The governance of the GVC influences how learning takes place, and hence different mechanisms emerge in different chains (Pietrobelli and Rabellotti 2011). Learning mechanisms in GVCs are presented in Table 3.2, based on the analysis of Pietrobelli and Rabellotti (2011). In addition to the five governance types discussed in Gereffi et al. (2005) (market, modular, relational, captive, and hierarchy), two other types are also discussed. These are arm's length and vertical integration, which capture the entire spectrum of relationships in the market. The role of the lead firm in fostering learning within certain governance types is clearly illustrated in Table 3.2.

Innovation systems and their interaction with GVC

Inflows of knowledge and technology from external sources are essential components of learning and innovation in developing countries. In the context of GVCs, integration into GVCs helps firms get access

Table 3.2 Learning mechanisms within GVCs

Governance type	Complexity of transactions	Ability to codify transactions	Capabilities in the supply base	Learning mechanisms within GVC	Examples[*]
Market	Low	High	High		Schmitz (2004) – Brazil footwear industry; Tewari (1999) – Ludhiana knitwear industry
Modular	High	High	High	Lead firms impose pressure on suppliers to innovate and keep abreast of technological advancements, but do not become directly involved in the learning process. Transfer of knowledge embodied in standards, codes, and technical definitions.	Quadros (2004) – Brazil for automobile industry; Albornoz et al. (2002) – Argentina automobile industry
Relational	High	Low	High	Relationships tend to be idiosyncratic, difficult, and time-consuming to re-establish with new value chain partners. Mutual dependence is regulated through reputation, social and spatial proximity, long-term commitment, reputation, and in some cases on family and ethnic ties. Linkages are very tight and learning efforts imply sunk costs and take time, which binds parties into continued interaction.	Gereffi (1999) – Garments industry in East Asia – upgraded from assembly to full package requiring the development of capabilities to interpret designs, produce samples, monitor product quality, and meet buyers' price and time conditions; Kishimoto (2004) – Taiwanese computer industry; Villaschi et al. (2007)

(Continued)

Table 3.2 (Continued)

Governance type	Complexity of transactions	Ability to codify transactions	Capabilities in the supply base	Learning mechanisms within GVC	Examples*
Captive	High	High	Low	Lead firms intervene directly in the learning process – risk of lock-in. Inclusion can lead to process and product upgrading but not functional upgrading, leaving firms dependent on a small number of powerful customers.	Bazan and Navas-Aleman (2004) – footwear industry in Brazil; Rabellotti (1999)
Hierarchy	High	Low	Low	Vertical integration occurs in difficult-to-codify and captive buyer-driven chains where small suppliers are dependent on larger, dominant buyers that exert high level of monitoring and control.	
Arm's length	Low	Low	High	Spillovers and imitation which allow firms to capture knowledge, adaptive change, and innovation needed to stay in the value chain.	
Vertical integration		Low		Similar to FDI	

Source: Adapted from Pietrobelli and Rabellotti (2011) and Gereffi et al. (2005)

Note: *Examples provided are from Pietrobelli and Rabellotti (2011).

to knowledge and, through participation in such chains, learning and innovation is fostered.

Innovation has been defined by Schumpeter as an outcome of new combinations made by an entrepreneur resulting in a new product, a new process, a new source of supply for raw materials and/or other inputs, a new market, or a new way of organizing business (Schumpeter 1934). This process may be breakthrough or incremental. Technological learning takes place in firms and is affected by firm-specific characteristics (Lorentzen and Barnes 2004). National innovation systems, developed mainly in the context of developed countries, speaks to the role played by institutions and organizations that affect the rate of technological change in an economic system (Lundvall 1992; Nelson 1993). Application of the IS concept to developing countries, while more recent (Lundvall et al. 2009; Edquist 2001), is more complicated. This is because incremental innovation and absorption of knowledge and technology new to the firm are more frequent (Pietrobelli and Rabellotti 2011) and are based on firm-level activities that are not included in the formal measures of innovation. A large part of the technological activity in developing countries is in the absorption of knowledge and improvement of existing technologies rather than frontier innovation (Lall and Pietrobelli 2005). The linkages between the main science and technology organizations (such as universities, R&D laboratories, and research institutes) and local firms may be weak or non-existent in developing countries. Altenburg et al. (2008) point out that, in the case of China or India, which have IS similar to those of developed countries, the process of learning may be different, as some sectors are world class in these countries.

How do different IS affect the determinants of GVC governance and what is the opportunity for enterprise learning and upgrading? A well-structured and efficient IS can help reduce the complexity of transactions and enable transactions based on arm's length or on weak hierarchical forms of GVC governance, as well as on the risk of falling into captive relationships.

Lundvall (1992) observes that rules and institutions that interact in the production, diffusion, and use of new and economically useful knowledge are important. The importance of technology policies through technology imports via licensing and FDI, as well as incentive for local R&D and training, are all key to this process. The tacitness of knowledge determines the learning outcomes and transfer of manufacturing practices. The bargaining power of the suppliers plays an important role in the entire process of upgrading. The impediments to integration in GVCs and upgrading within chains are explored further in each of the case studies.

The relationship between GVCs and IS is non-linear and endogenous, with each affecting the other. Policies and institutions affecting international flow of equipment and services, human capital, foreign investments, and GVC matter. In the case of firms, GVCs may contribute to improving the local IS, which in turn will affect decisions about local sourcing of inputs and local firms' learning and innovation (Pietrobelli and Rabellotti 2011). Since the absorption of technology and diffusion[5] occur because of adaptations and modifications to suit local needs, learning capacity is not a sufficient condition of upgrading.[6,7] For this to happen, firms must possess the competencies to incorporate the new technology into their production capacity (Lorentzen and Barnes 2004). The challenge is not always about moving into more advanced functions but is often about deepening specific capabilities required to explore new opportunities in the value chain stage in which the firm is currently engaged (Morrison et al. 2008).

The question for most developing countries is how to move from hierarchical chains to market or modular chains. Taiwan's example is often cited since it strengthened its IS by substantial investment in human capital and innovations in science and technology.[8] The relation between governance types, complexity of transactions, and innovation systems are presented in Table 3.3.

The role of the domestic market

The domestic market (and its size) also plays a significant role in the process of learning and upgrading in GVCs. In most countries, domestic (and regional) value chains coexist with GVCs. However, the impact of the domestic chain (and vice versa) on the other needs to be examined more closely. The nature of the domestic chain (and its interlinkage with the institutions of innovation discussed in the previous section) has an important role in the process of learning and upgrading. Navas-Aleman (2011) points out that there are learning opportunities for firms in GVCs from domestic and neighbouring markets. She says that the literature overlooks the potential of the domestic market in such learning; some learning takes place before firms start exporting. Two examples in Table 3.4 provide an illustration of this difference between learning and upgrading: semiconductor microchips versus automobiles. In the semiconductor microchip case, while there is integration in GVC (and there is no domestic chain), there is no upgrading. Only the design is done in India and the upstream and the

Table 3.3 Complexity of transactions and innovation systems

Governance type	Determinants of	Role of institutions	Innovation systems
Market	Low complexity High codifications	MSTQ organizations matter Education, training organizations matter	Well-structured system makes "market" chain more likely
Modular	Low complexity High codifications	MSTQ organizations matter Education, training organizations matter	Well-structured system makes "modular" chain more likely
Relational	Low complexity High codifications	Education, training organizations matter Local systems are complementary MSTQ organizations are less critical	Well-structured system makes "relational" chain more likely
Captive	Low complexity High codifications	MSTQ organizations matter	Poorer and fragmented systems lead to "captive" chains Upgrading restricted
Hierarchy	Low complexity High codifications	Local R&D organizations may benefit from interaction GVC is expected to improve human technical skills	Poorer and fragmented systems lead to "hierarchical" chains

Source: Adapted from Pietrobelli and Rabellotti (2011)

Note: MSTQ stands for Metrology, Standards, Testing, and Quality.

Table 3.4 Role of the domestic chain in learning and upgrading

	Presence of domestic chain (complete)	Whether integration has occurred	Governance of GVC	Whether learning has occurred	Whether upgrading has occurred
Automobiles	Yes	Yes	Relational	Yes	Yes
Chemicals (specialty)	Yes	No	Relational/ modular	No	Limited
Diamond	No	Yes	Market	Yes	No
Garments	Yes	No	Hierarchy/ captive	No	Limited
Petrochemicals	Yes	Yes	Relational/ hierarchy	Yes	No
Pharmaceuticals (Formulations)	Yes	Limited	Modular/ market	No	Limited
Reactive dye	Yes	Yes	Market	Yes	No
Semiconductor microchip	No	Yes	Modular	No	No
Paper	Yes	No	Market	No	No

Source: Authors' compilation based on survey

downstream activities are done elsewhere. The contrast is provided by the automobile sector, where there is evidence of innovation and upgrading in the Indian case (Ray and Miglani 2016).

The examples of learning that do not necessarily translate to upgrading come from the diamond and garments sectors. In the diamond case, learning and diffusion of the latest technologies have occurred but, due to the absence of the full chain in India, upgrading has not occurred. The lead firms have been involved in ensuring that learning takes place. In contrast, in the case of the garments, no learning has taken place (the reasons are discussed in the garments chapter). However, limited upgrading has taken place in the Indian context (Ray et al. 2016).

Conclusion

The typology of the governance of the GVCs proposed by Gereffi, Humphrey, and Sturgeon (2005) categorize the relation between governance structures, complexity of transactions, ability to codify transactions, and capabilities in the supply base. We use this typology to create the framework used in this book. Governance type captures the ability to exert control over the chain. The framework used in this book draws on the role of the governance types in fostering learning (and innovation depending on the institutional setup) in a developing country with a large domestic market. The governance of the GVC influences how learning takes place, and hence different mechanisms emerge in different chains (Pietrobelli and Rabellotti 2011).

Notes

1 Humphrey and Schmitz (2001) explain governance as "some firms in the chain set and/or enforce the parameters under which the others in the chain operate." According to the US Agency for International Development, "Value chain governance refers to the relationships among the buyers, sellers, service providers and regulatory institutions that operate within or influence the range of activities required to bring a product or service from inception to its end use." www.microlinks.org/good-practice-center/value-chain-wiki/value-chain-governance-overview

2 Modular, relational, hierarchical, captive, and market are the different categories of governance structures in GVCs. Arm's length refers to the pre-GVC production relationship where there is no relation between the lead firms and the supplier and each acts independently. Each category has different levels of complexity of transactions, codification of transactions, and competence of suppliers. Hence the learning mechanism within each GVC chain is also different (Pietrobelli and Rabellotti 2010a).

3 Learning has been defined as the absorptive capacity which includes "an ability to recognize the value of new information, assimilate it, and apply it to commercial ends" (Cohen and Levinthal 1990). In the context of a firm, absorptive capacity can be generated through own R&D, and as a by-product of the firm's manufacturing operations.

4 Leaders or lead firms are firms that control the GVC. In the case of a buyer-driven apparel chain, the lead firms are large global retailers and brand owners (Gereffi and Frederick 2010). In the supplier-driven automotive chain, lead firms are multinational companies (MNCs) and are few in number (Biesebroeck and Sturgeon 2010).

5 Technological diffusion is the process by which innovations (new products or new processes or new management methods) spread within and across economies (Stoneman 1995).

6 Upgrading (or industrial upgrading) involves organizational learning to improve the position of firms or nations in international trade networks. Gereffi (1999) show that upgrading occurs in products that are organizationally related through lead firms in GVCs, through forward and backward linkages from production and through marketing. See also Giuliani et al. 2005 and Cattaneo et al. 2013.

7 Upgrading in modular chains leads to positive externalities for the rest of the economy due to spillovers to other sectors served by the same supplier (Pietrobelli and Rabellotti 2010a).

8 Improvement in MSTQ can lead to movement from hierarchy and captive to modular chains, improvement in local systems can lead from hierarchy and captive to relational chains, and IS supporting evolution of suppliers and GVC competences can lead from hierarchy and captive to relational chains (Pietrobelli and Rabellotti 2011).

References

Albornoz, F., Milesi, D. and G. Yoguel. 2002. 'New Economy in Old Sectors: Some Issues Coming From Two Production Networks in Argentine,' Paper Presented at the DRUID Summer Conference.

Altenburg, T. 2006. 'Governance Patterns in Value Chains and their Development Impact,' *The European Journal of Development Research*, 18(4): 498–521.

Altenburg, T., Schmitz, H. and A. Stamm. 2008. 'Breakthrough? China's and India's Transition from Production to Innovation,' *World Development*, 36(2): 325–344.

Bazan, L. and L. Navas-Aleman. 2004. 'The Underground Revolution in the Sinos Valley: A Comparison of Upgrading in Global and National Value Chain' in H. Schmitz (ed.), *Local Enterprises in the Global Economy: Issues of Governance and Upgrading*, pp. 110–139. Cheltenham: Edward Elgar.

Berger, S. and R. Dore (eds.). 1996. *National Diversity and Global Capitalism*. Ithaca, NY: Cornell University Press.

Biesebroeck, J. V. and T. Sturgeon. 2010. 'Effects of the 2008–09 Crisis on the Automotive Industry in Developing Countries: A Global Value Chain Perspective' in O. Cattaneo, G. Gereffi and C. Startiz (eds.), *Global Value Chain in a Post-Crisis World: A Development Perspective*. Washington, DC: The International Bank for Reconstruction and Development/The World Bank.

Cattaneo, O., Gereffi, G., Miroudot, S. and D. Taglioni. 2013. 'Joining, Upgrading and Being Competitive in Global Value Chains A Strategic Framework,' Working Paper No. 6406. World Bank Policy Research.

Cohen, W. M. and D. A. Levinthal. 1990. 'Absorptive Capacity: A New Perspective on Learning and Innovation,' *Administrative Science Quarterly*, Special Issue: *Technology, Organizations, and Innovation*, 35(1): 128–152.

Edquist, C. 2001. 'Systems of Innovation for Development,' Background Paper for UNIDO World Industrial Development Report 2002/03. Vienna: UNIDO.

Gereffi, G. 1999. 'International Trade and Industrial Upgrading in the Apparel Commodity Chain,' *Journal of International Economics*, 48(1): 37–70.

Gereffi, G., Humphrey, J. and T. Sturgeon. 2005. 'The Governance of Global Value Chains,' *Review of International Political Economy*, 12(1): 78–104.

Gereffi, G. and S. Frederick. 2010. 'The Global Apparel Value Chain, Trade, and the Crisis: Challenges and Opportunities for Developing Countries' in O. Cattaneo, G. Gereffi and C. Startiz (eds.), *Global Value Chain in a Post-Crisis World: A Development Perspective*. Washington, DC: The International Bank for Reconstruction and Development/The World Bank.

Giuliani, E., Pietrobelli, C. and R. Rabellotti. 2005. 'Upgrading in Global Value Chains: Lessons from Latin America Clusters,' *World Development*, 33(4): 549–573.

Humphrey, J. and H. Schmitz. 2001. 'Governance in Global Value Chains,' *Bulletin*, 32(3). Institute of Development Studies.

Kishimoto, C. 2004. 'Clustering and Upgrading in Global Value Chains: The Taiwanese Personal Computer Industry' in H. Schmitz (eds.), *Local Enterprises in the Global Economy: Issues of Governance and Upgrading,* pp. 233–264. Cheltenham: Edward Elgar.

Lall, S. and C. Pietrobelli. 2005. 'National Technology Systems in Sub-Saharan Africa,' *International Journal of Technology and Globalisation,* 1(3/4): 311–342.

Lorentzen, J. and J. Barnes. 2004. 'Learning, Upgrading and Innovation in the South African Automotive Industry,' *European Journal of Development Research,* 16(3): 465–499.

Lundvall, B.A. (eds.) 1992. *National Systems of Innovation: Towards a Theory of Innovation and Interactive Learning.* London: Pinter Publishers.

Lundvall, B.-A., Joseph, K.J., Chaminade, C. and J. Vang. (eds.). 2009. *Handbook of Innovation Systems and Developing Countries: Building Domestic Capabilities in a Global Setting.* Cheltenham: Elgar.

Morrison, A., Pietrobelli, C. and R. Rabellotti. 2008. 'Global Value Chains and Technological Capabilities: A Framework to Study Industrial Innovation in Developing Countries,' *Oxford Development Studies,* 36(1): 39–58.

Navas Aleman, L. 2011. 'The Impact of Operating in Multiple Value Chains for Upgrading: The Case of Brazilian Furniture and Footwear Industries,' *World Development,* 39(8): 1386–1397.

Nelson, R.R. (ed.). 1993. *National Innovation Systems: A Comparative Analysis.* New York: Oxford University Press.

OECD. 2015. 'Participation of Developing Countries in Global Value Chains: Implications for Trade and Trade-Related Policies,' Summary Paper, www.oecd.org/coexanes/kenya/Participation-Developing-Countries-GVCs-Summary-Paper-April-2015.pdf (accessed on January 20, 2017).

Pietrobelli, C. and R. Rabellotti. 2010a. 'Global Value Chains Meet Innovation Systems: Are there Learning Opportunities for Developing Countries?,' IDB Working Paper Series No. IDB-WP-232. Washington: Inter-American Development Bank.

Pietrobelli, C. and R. Rabellotti. 2010b. 'The Global Dimension of Innovation Systems: Linking Innovation Systems and Global Value Chains,' in B.A. Lundvall, J. Vang, K.J. Joseph and C. Chaminade (eds.) *Handbook of Innovation Systems and Developing Countries.* Cheltenham: Edward Elgar.

Pietrobelli, C. and R. Rabellotti (eds.). 2007. *Upgrading to Compete: SMEs, Clusters, and Value Chains in Latin America.* Cambridge, MA: Harvard University Press.

Pietrobelli, C. and R. Rabellotti. 2011. 'Global Value Chains Meet Innovation Systems: Are There Learning Opportunities for Developing Countries?,' *World Development,* 39 (7): 1261–1269.

Quadros, R. 2004. 'Global Quality Standards, and Technological Upgrading in the Brazilian Auto-components Industry' in H. Schmitz (ed.), *Local Enterprises in the Global Economy: Issues of Governance and Upgrading,* pp. 265–296. Cheltenham: Edward Elgar.

Rabellotti, R. 1999. 'Recovery of a Mexican Cluster: Devaluation Bonanza or Collective Efficiency?' *World Development*, 27(9): 1571–1585.

Ray, S. and S. Miglani 2016. 'Innovation (and Upgrading) in the Automobile Industry: The Case of India,' ICRIER Working paper 320.

Ray, S., Mukherjee, P. and M. Mehra. 2016. *Upgrading in the Indian Garment Industry: A Study of Three Clusters*, ADB South Asia Working Paper Series, No. 43. Asian Development Bank.

Schmitz, H. (ed.). 2004. *Local Enterprises in the Global Economy: Issues of Governance and Upgrading*. Cheltenham: Edward Elgar.

Schumpeter, J.A. 1934. *The Theory of Economic Development*. Cambridge, MA: Harvard University Press.

Stoneman, P. (ed.). 1995. *Handbook of the Economics of Innovation and Technological Change*. Oxford: Wiley-Blackwell.

Tewari, M. 1999. 'Successful Adjustment in Indian Industry: The Case of Ludhiana's Woollen Knitwear Cluster,' *World Development*, 27(9): 1651–1672.

Villaschi, A., Cassiolato, J. E. and H. Lastres. 2007. 'Local Production and Innovation Systems in Brazil: The Metalworking Cluster in Espirito Santo' in C. Pietrobelli and R. Rabellotti (eds.), *Upgrading to Compete: SMEs, Clusters and Value Chains in Latin America*, pp. 175–190. Cambridge, MA: Harvard University Press.

4   Evidence of India's integration into GVCs

In Chapter 2, we noted that there are several ways to measure participation in global value chains (GVCs).[1] The empirical literature has examined the determinants of GVC engagement, the gains from participating in GVCs, and the outcomes of deeper integration through regional trade agreements (RTAs).[2] The literature on determinants of GVC trade is developing and, according to Kowalski et al. (2015), there is no gold standard for investigating this issue. We discuss the extent of India's participation in GVCs and the gains from participating in GVCs for India in this chapter.

Examining India's exports and imports, we note that India has had a negative trade balance in goods for most of the years. This could be due to either low exports or high imports. From the point of view of imports, it is important to distinguish between intermediate goods and final goods. While intermediate goods could be used for further processing for goods to be sold in domestic markets or exported, final goods are purely for consumption.[3] For value chain activity, intermediate goods are important. We decompose India's imports using the Broad Economic Categories (BEC) classification[4] to understand the nature of such imports. The tariffs in these sectors are also examined to show that all such imports may not necessarily be undesirable from the point of view of the current balance. If these intermediate products are used in products that India exports (or has comparative advantage in), such sectors could lead to value chain activity.

Background

Very few studies have examined production-sharing by India.[5] OECD (2013) observes that India participates strongly in chemicals, electrical equipment, and other manufacturing (jewellery). India's participation is primarily on account of sourcing of intermediates from abroad.[6] OECD (2013) observes that the majority of the final demand for manufactured goods represents value-added that has been created domestically and that the foreign value-added share was 26% in 2009 for India.

Banga (2013) uses the OECD-WTO trade in value-added (TiVA) database to find the ratio of forward and backward linkages for India and other countries.[7] She observes that this is less than one for India, which indicates that the backward linkages outweigh the forward linkage, corroborating the point made previously by OECD regarding India's participation. The ability to benefit from participating in GVCs depends on how much value a country creates in GVCs.[8] Goldar et al. (2017) analyze the import content of Indian exports at the industry level using the approach of Hummels et al. (2001). They find that the import content of India's exports rose steadily during the period 1995 to 2011.[9]

Athukorala (2013) explores the reasons for India's failure to fit into global production networks, particularly in the electronics sector.[10] The study looks into India's overall export share from the 1950s to 2011 and observes that India's contribution to world exports has been very small; in the same period, other developing countries emerged as the export hubs and participated extensively in production-sharing. The reason for this can be traced back to the import substitution policies adopted by the government until as late as 1991, by which time China's and the Philippines' exports had far surpassed India's. India's overall exports have improved since then, but still do not match up to those of other developing countries, with the pattern of trade quite different from that in the rest of the developing nations or Asian countries. No particular product category stands out in the case of India. The product category, "machinery and transport equipment," which accounts for nearly a third of world merchandise trade, makes up a very small share of India's exports, with export expansion mainly in resource-based products and miscellaneous products (clothing, footwear, and other such labour-intensive products). When network trade[11] is compared, India again stands out in comparison to other East Asian countries. Network trade accounted for 22% for India, between 1990–91 and 2010–11, of the total increment in manufactured exports, compared to 70% for East Asia. For India, the exception was road vehicles, and other transport equipment accounted for 28% of total network exports in 2010–11 (compared to an average of 13.2% for East Asia).[12]

Evidence from India's trade

Items which are imported into a country and then exported back with value addition typically are part of value chain activity for a country.[13] We analyze India's exports and imports for this reason.

Examining India's trade figures to the world for the period between the years 2009 and 2016,[14] we note an overwhelming negative trade balance in goods.[15] This is on account of "Animal or vegetable fats and oils" (HS Chapter 15);[16,17] "Mineral products" (HS 25–27); "Products of the chemicals or allied industries" (HS 28–38); "Wood and articles of wood" (HS 44–46); "Pulp of wood or other fibrous products" (HS 47–49); "Natural or cultured pearls, precious or semi-precious stones" (HS 71); "Machinery and mechanical appliances" and "Electrical equipment" (HS 84–85); "Vehicles: aircraft, vessels and associated transport equipment" (HS 86–89); and "Optical, photographic and cinematographic instruments" (HS 90–92).

Of these items, in the category "Animal or vegetable fats and oils," India is deficient and hence the imports are large.[18] "Wood and articles of wood" is a category where the imports are far greater than the exports. This is also the case with "Pulp of wood or other fibrous products"[19] and "Optical, photographic and cinematographic instruments." These categories do not fit into the value chain activity for India. The largest import category is the "Mineral products" category, which India exports, too. This category is a candidate for value chain activity. The category "Natural or cultured pearls" is interesting since India imports a lot in this category and there are large exports, too. This is another category which fits into the value chain activity and we will discuss these two categories in detail later.

The remaining four categories, "Products of the chemicals or allied industries," "Machinery and mechanical appliances," "Electrical equipment," and "Vehicles: aircraft, vessels and other associated transport equipment" lend themselves easily to value chain activity, as has been discussed in the context of the literature[20] and we discuss these in greater detail later. The trade balance in the category "Vehicles: aircraft, vessels and associated transport equipment" becomes positive in the years 2010 onwards as exports exceed imports.[21]

Revealed comparative advantage

If we use traditional trade concepts such as the revealed comparative advantage,[22,23] it is evident that there are many categories in which India did have comparative advantage in 2006 or 2013. These categories are listed in Table 4.2A in Appendix 4.1. The items in which India has a comparative advantage are highlighted in bold. We note from Table 4.2A that the items that were largely imported and have been discussed in the previous paragraph largely do not figure in Table 4.2A, as expected. The exceptions are "Mineral fuels and oils, and products thereof" (HS 27); "Organic chemicals" (HS 29); "Pharmaceutical products "(HS 30); "Natural or cultured pearls" (HS 71); "Aircraft, spacecraft and articles thereof" (HS 88); and "Ships, boats and floating structures" (HS 89). As discussed earlier, these articles then need to be examined for value chain activity.

From Table 4.2A we can see that some items (these include aircraft, spacecraft and parts, pharmaceutical products) in which India did not have a comparative advantage in 2006 are competitive in 2013. Also, there are items in which India has become uncompetitive in 2013 compared to 2006, for example, "Tools, implements, cutlery spoons and forks" and "Works of art."

Trade in intermediate goods[24]

As discussed in Chapter 2, Miroudout et al. (2009) state that two methodologies can be applied to measure trade in intermediate goods. In the first method, trade in intermediate goods is measured using the UN Broad Economic Categories (BEC) classification, which relies on the breakdown of disaggregated trade flows at the product level, where they can be distinguished according to their use. Using this approach, India's intermediate imports are analyzed and are discussed below. The second method is the use of the Input-Output (I-O) tables that directly provide the value of foreign inputs used in the domestic production of goods and services. As discussed before, Goldar et al. (2017) use the input-output approach for India and find that there was a decline in domestic value-added content which was associated with a simultaneous increase in foreign value-added content in the period 1995–2011.[25]

Using the first approach, parts and components are delineated from reported trade data using a list compiled by mapping parts and components in the BEC. Table 4.1 shows the classification of the goods according to the BEC with the Harmonized System (HS) of trade classification at the six-digit level.[26,27] It also shows the value of the imports by India in the period 2009 to 2015. As indicated in Table 4.1, there are 56 groups of intermediate goods in category 111, 86 in category 121, 300 in category 21, 2306 in category 22, 276 in category 42, and 108 in category 53. The total number of intermediate goods categories is 3132 or 61%.

We note that India's imports have been dominated by intermediate imports. Category 22, processed intermediates, is the largest category with 31% share. It is larger than the imports of fuel and lubricants. Table 4.1 also indicates the importance of intermediate imports in India's trade and the backward integration in GVC activity.

Table 4.1 Classification of products according to BEC

BEC code	Category	Use	Number of products	Value of imports (1000 USD) (2009–15)	(%)
1	**Food and beverages**				
11	*Primary*				
111	Mainly for industry	Intermediate	56	2221166	0.08
112	Mainly for household consumption	Consumption	186	33794598	1.19
12	*Processed*				
121	Mainly for industry	Intermediate	86	66902600	2.36
122	Mainly for household consumption	Consumption	273	5139176	0.18
2	**Industrial supplies not elsewhere specified**				
21	Primary	Intermediate	300	224822959	7.93
22	Processed	Intermediate	2306	885007734	31.20
3	**Fuels and lubricants**				
31	Primary		9	872791667	30.77
32	Processed		2	35473391	1.25
321	Motor spirit	Not classified			
322	Other	Intermediate	16	85371303	3.01
4	**Capital goods (except transport equipment) and parts and accessories thereof**				
41	Capital goods (except transport equipment)	Capital	614	271336938	9.57
42	Parts and accessories	Intermediate	276	177767751	6.27

(*Continued*)

Table 4.1 (Continued)

BEC code	Category	Use	Number of products	Value of imports (1000 USD) (2009–15)	(%)
5	**Transport equipment, and parts and accessories thereof**				
51	Passenger motor cars	Not classified	8	2742440	0.10
52	Other				
521	Industrial		19	25139655	0.89
522	Non-industrial	Consumption		1934067	0.07
53	Parts and accessories	Intermediate	108	65628222	2.31
6	**Consumer goods not elsewhere specified**				
61	Durable	Consumption	159	35611966	1.26
62	Semi-durable	Consumption	384	20495882	0.72
63	Non-durable	Consumption	222	21905337	0.77
7	Goods not elsewhere specified	Not classified	19	2093859	0.07
	n.a.		2		
	Total		5092	2836180710	100.00

Source: Authors' compilation using UN Comtrade database

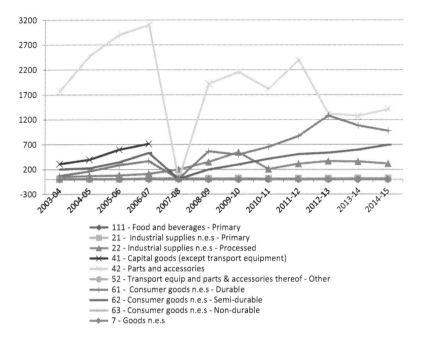

111 - Food and beverages - Primary
21 - Industrial supplies n.e.s - Primary
22 - Industrial supplies n.e.s - Processed
41 - Capital goods (except transport equipment)
42 - Parts and accessories
52 - Transport equip and parts & accessories thereof - Other
61 - Consumer goods n.e.s - Durable
62 - Consumer goods n.e.s - Semi-durable
63 - Consumer goods n.e.s - Non-durable
7 - Goods n.e.s

Figure 4.1 India's imports as per BEC classification(2003–04 to 2014–15)

Source: Directorate General of Foreign Trade, Ministry of Commerce and Industry, Government of India

Note: The values for categories 111, 21, 52, and 63 are insignificant and can be seen as a thick line at the bottom of the graph.

We have used the BEC classification to understand how India's imports have fared over the years from 2003–04 to 2014–15 for the 10 categories of BEC: Figure 4.1 shows the trends. The surge in the imports of "Parts and accessories of capital goods" around 2006–07 and the subsequent fall can be noted from Figure 4.1.

Table 4.3A in Appendix 4.1 shows the imports of intermediate goods classified according to BEC (and using the concordance of BEC, SITC 3, and HS) and the average *ad valorem* duties.[28,29] India's intermediate imports reported in Table 4.3A are based on this classification for 2009–15. From Table 4.3A, we observe that the highest average imports in Category 111 was in "Coffee (excluding roasted and decaffeinated)" (HS 090111), where the *ad valorem* duty was 100%.[30] In Category 121, the highest imports were "Palm oil and its fractions, whether or not refined (excl chemically modified and crude)" (HS 151190).[31] The *ad valorem* duty in this case was 15%. The highest imports in Category 21 were "Non-industrial diamonds unworked or simply sawn, cleaved or bruted (excl. industrial diamonds)" (HS 710231).[32] The *ad valorem* duty was 10%. The highest imports in Category 22 were "Gold, incl. gold plated with platinum, unwrought, for non-monetary purposes (excl. gold in powder form)" (HS 710812). The *ad valorem* duty was 10%.[33] The highest imports in Category 322 were "Natural gas, liquefied" (271111).[34] The highest imports in Category 42 were "Parts of telephone sets, telephones for cellular networks or for other wireless networks and of other apparatus for the transmission or reception of voice, images or other data, n.e.s." (HS 851770).[35,36] Finally in Category 53, the largest imports are in the category, "Parts and accessories, for tractors, motor vehicles for the transport of ten or more persons, motor cars and other motor vehicles principally designed for the transport of persons, motor vehicles for the transport of goods and special purpose motor vehicles, n.e.s." (HS 870899).[37] The *ad valorem* duty is 10%.[38] Some of these duties have been reduced in the Annual Budget 2017–18.[39]

The discussion in this section identifies several important sectors for value chain activity which will be taken up in subsequent chapters. These are automobiles, diamonds, and electronics. The electronics is a sector with limited value chain activity in India. Discussions in the semiconductor microchip or Chapter 10 will focus on some of the problems faced by this sector.

Complexity of India's exports

Examining the exports from India in 2016 using the *Atlas of Economic Complexity*,[40,41] we can note the items that India exported in that year (see Figure 4.1A in Appendix 4.1) and 2006 (Figure 4.2A in Appendix 4.1). The imports for India can be seen in Figures 4.3A and Figure 4.4A, respectively, in Appendix 4.1 for 2016 and 2006. The figures convey the same message as Table 4.1A and show the share of certain sectors in the trade. We note from Figure 4.3A that the category, "Minerals" comprises 26.03% of imports in 2016 and 12.02% of exports in the same year. The figures also show the relative decline (or increase) in exports (imports) of certain categories in 2016 compared to 2006. For example, the largest group of exports in 2016 is the category "Stone and glass." However, this category formed 13.93% of exports in 2006. The decline in the exports of "Minerals" was from 20.46% in 2006 to 12.02% in 2016. An increase in imports can be seen in the category "Electronics" from 7.86% in 2006 to 9.96% of imports in 2016. This categorization in terms of complexity also helps in predicting which sectors hold promise for India in the future. This will be discussed further in Chapter 13.

Conclusion

In this chapter, we discuss the extent of India's participation in GVCs. Examining India's exports and imports, we note that India has a negative trade balance in goods for most of the years. We decompose India's imports using the BEC classification to understand the nature of such imports. For value chain activity, intermediate goods are important. While intermediate goods could be used for further processing for goods to be sold in domestic markets or exported, final goods are purely for consumption. Hence it is important to distinguish between intermediate goods and final goods in the imports of a country. For this, we examine the total imports over the period 2009–15. As we note earlier in the chapter, India's imports are dominated by intermediates. This also corroborates the point by OECD (2013) that India's participation in GVCs is on account of sourcing of intermediates from abroad.

Appendix 4.1

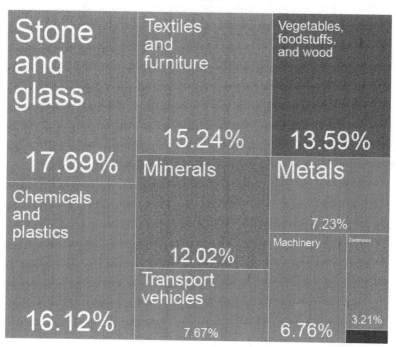

$266B

Stone and glass 17.69%

Textiles and furniture 15.24%

Vegetables, foodstuffs, and wood 13.59%

Minerals 12.02%

Metals 7.23%

Chemicals and plastics 16.12%

Transport vehicles 7.67%

Machinery 6.76%

Electronics 3.21%

Figure 4.1A India's exports to the world in 2016

Source: Atlas of Economic Complexity

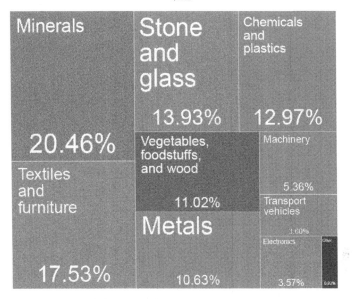

$133B

Minerals 20.46%

Textiles and furniture 17.53%

Stone and glass 13.93%

Vegetables, foodstuffs, and wood 11.02%

Metals 10.63%

Chemicals and plastics 12.97%

Machinery 5.36%

Transport vehicles 3.60%

Electronics 3.57%

Other 0.02%

Figure 4.2A India's exports to the world in 2006

Source: Atlas of Economic Complexity

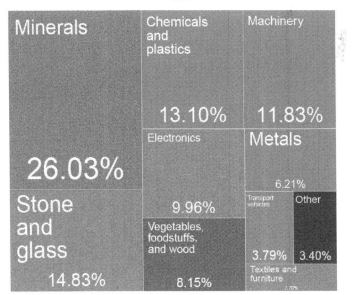

$348B

Minerals 26.03%

Stone and glass 14.83%

Chemicals and plastics 13.10%

Electronics 9.96%

Vegetables, foodstuffs, and wood 8.15%

Machinery 11.83%

Metals 6.21%

Transport vehicles 3.79%

Other 3.40%

Textiles and furniture 2.70%

Figure 4.3A India's imports from the world in 2016

Source: Atlas of Economic Complexity

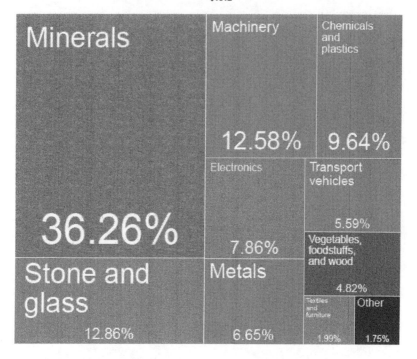

Figure 4.4A India's imports from the world in 2006

Source: Atlas of Economic Complexity

Table 4.1A India's gross exports (X) and imports (M) trade with the world, HS 2007-two digit (value in 1000 USD)

Code	Description		2009	2010	2011	2012	2013	2014	2015	2016
01–05	Live animals; animal products	X	2839939	4262278	6327642	6869453	10264957	11045724	9358368	9589895
		M	135768	289939	351322	224319	113670	162091	162913	156982
06–15	Vegetable products, animal or vegetable fats, and oils and products	X	8085615	9641935	16244444	23330665	22815994	21387411	16545167	15031601
		M	8695210	10388287	13978800	16044757	15296769	17239458	18740476	19247240
16–24	Prepared foodstuffs; beverages, spirits, and vinegar; tobacco and manufactured tobacco products	X	3785873	5303245	7254852	7525391	8097953	6527828	5672447	5871731
		M	1600393	1785272	1060629	1610765	1562422	2018349	2019534	2689096
25–26	Mineral products	X	6853724	8042310	6517867	4927968	4426384	3346762	2443746	3131938
		M	5021072	7350300	9291238	10092810	10864237	10250824	8584255	5912332
27–27	Mineral fuels, mineral oils, and products of their distillation	X	24021691	37984132	56656789	54380880	69571281	62348539	31393703	27715391
		M	82661824	110840658	157356407	185696088	184194009	176948969	104645637	89308777
28–38	Products of chemical or allied industries	X	17177611	22292230	27346363	31281092	35219071	33723702	32976878	33650847
		M	23153322	28565790	36150096	37210568	36729278	38365510	37556117	33757342
39–40	Plastics and articles thereof; rubber and articles thereof	X	3572389	5305698	8048978	7677742	9197375	8161529	7374341	7621031
		M	6716205	10039833	11525612	13166388	13455944	15169320	14260423	14279329
41–43	Raw hides and skins, leather, furskins, and articles thereof	X	1979652	2236947	3039805	3110756	3862940	3914329	3524423	3266485
		M	489064	619401	748804	753940	839388	1020378	1000425	935941
44–49	Wood and articles of wood; pulp of wood or of other fibrous cellulosic material	X	908422	1170784	1472361	1533564	1858883	1808043	1861800	1916368
		M	3971298	5244315	6832267	6848840	7051375	7871765	6948697	6800751
50–63	Textiles and textile articles	X	21912923	27127765	33374091	32682933	40191283	38597568	37161683	35429025
		M	3215916	3914312	4934156	5151070	5410108	5850648	5855277	6080575

(Continued)

Table 4.1A (Continued)

Code	Description		2009	2010	2011	2012	2013	2014	2015	2016
64–67	Footwear, headgear, umbrellas, sun umbrellas, walking-sticks, seat-sticks, whips, riding-crops and parts thereof; prepared feathers and articles made therewith; artificial flowers; articles of human hair	X	1692602	1866609	2342690	2287684	3020182	3315600	3114304	3035819
		M	175291	292795	360095	405727	450097	481217	530752	583232
68–71	Articles of stone, plaster, cement, asbestos, mica, or similar materials; ceramic products; glass and glassware; natural or cultured pearls, precious or semi-precious stones and metals	X	33979729	34135529	51967716	45218409	46794454	43580730	41417644	45331272
		M	43689065	70088534	95522722	83614717	69394316	61898518	61931053	50350950
72–83	Base metals and articles of base metal	X	12390787	21936761	21198929	22078062	25475962	25585088	21239363	19370500
		M	15912478	20370020	26271510	27526013	23865019	26675233	26629810	22697175
84–85	Machinery and mechanical appliances; electrical equipment; parts thereof	X	16791943	16856219	22496600	21832535	24365993	22598459	21167317	21775356
		M	48284515	53317777	67750439	65875338	61732983	63116880	67972856	69521009
86–89	Vehicles, aircraft, vessels, and associated transport equipment	X	10611724	15100921	19765972	18231199	21728990	25899945	22013905	21414973
		M	11474279	11183929	10309034	13563811	14370946	12169590	12990277	13611298
90–99	Miscellaneous manufactured articles	X	10160413	7145130	17528153	6596437	9719685	5703384	7115916	6174681
		M	11205853	15742227	19959659	21191227	20715008	20130712	20916230	20772764

Source: UN Comtrade database

Table 4.2A Normalized revealed comparative advantage[#] of India

HS	Category	2006	2013	HS	Category	2006	2013
1	Live animals	-0.88	-0.94	49	Printed books, newspapers, pictures	-0.43	-0.43
2	Meat and edible meat offal	-0.03	0.33	50	Silk	0.83	0.47
3	Fish & crustaceans, molluscs & other aquatic invertebrates	0.39	0.41	51	Wool, fine/coarse animal hair, horse hair yarn	-0.24	-0.25
4	Dairy products; birds' eggs; natural honey; edible products of animal origin, n.e.s.	-0.46	-0.43	52	Cotton	0.76	0.80
5	Products of animal origin, n.e.s.	-0.17	-0.19	53	Other vegetable textile fibres; paper	0.62	0.65
6	Live tree & other plants; bulbs, roots and the like	-0.31	-0.70	54	Man-made filaments	0.44	0.49
7	Edible vegetables & certain roots & tubers	0.20	0.05	55	Man-made staple fibres	0.54	0.49
8	Edible fruit & nuts; peel of citrus fruits or melons	0.22	-0.04	56	Wadding, felt, & non-woven; yarns; twine, cordage	-0.29	-0.14
9	Coffee, tea, mate, & spices	0.66	0.52	57	Carpets & other textile floor coverings	0.80	0.70
10	Cereals	0.50	0.64	58	Special woven fabrics; tufted textile fabrics	0.16	0.25
11	Products of milling, industry; malt; starches; inulin	-0.51	-0.07	59	Impregnated, coated, cover/laminated textile fabrics	-0.42	-0.34
12	Oil seed, oleaginous fruits; misc. grains	0.17	-0.07	60	Knitted or crocheted fabrics	-0.48	-0.40
13	Lac; gums, resins, & other vegetable saps	0.82	0.90	61	Articles of apparel & clothing accessories knitted or crocheted	0.43	0.26
14	Vegetable plaiting materials; vegetable products n.e.s.	0.66	0.61	62	Articles of apparel & clothing access, not knitted or crocheted	0.56	0.41
15	Animal/vegetable fats & oils, & their cleavage products;	-0.12	-0.32	63	Other made-up textile articles; sets; worn clothing and worn textile articles; rags	0.72	0.59
16	Preparation of meat, of fish, or of crustaceans	-0.19	-0.78	64	Footwear, gaiters & the like; parts of such articles	0.25	0.04
17	Sugars & sugar confectionery	0.37	0.10	65	Headgear & parts thereof	-0.54	-0.58

(Continued)

Table 4.2A (Continued)

HS	Category	2006	2013	HS	Category	2006	2013
18	Cocoa & cocoa preparations	-0.93	-0.82	66	Umbrellas, walking-sticks, seat-sticks	-0.81	-0.94
19	Preparations of cereal, flour, starch/milk	-0.47	-0.44	67	Prepared feathers & down; artificial flowers	0.70	0.43
20	Preparations of vegetable, fruit, nuts or other parts	-0.33	-0.44	68	Articles of stone, plaster, cement, asbestos	0.37	0.19
21	Misc. edible preparations	-0.31	-0.37	69	Ceramic products	-0.44	-0.28
22	Beverages, spirits, & vinegar	-0.84	-0.66	70	Glass & glassware	-0.31	-0.34
23	Residues & waste from the food industry	0.57	0.40	71	Natural/cultured pearls, precious stones	0.75	0.61
24	Tobacco & manufactured tobacco substitutes	0.13	0.15	72	Iron & steel	0.21	0.14
25	Salt; sulphur; earth & stone; plastering materials	0.54	0.41	73	Articles of iron or steel	0.18	0.10
26	Ores, slag, & ash	0.66	-0.32	74	Copper & articles thereof	0.33	0.00
27	Mineral fuels, oils & product of their distillation	0.02	0.10	75	Nickel & articles thereof	-0.85	-0.02
28	Inorganic chemicals; organic or inorganic compounds of precious metals, of rare-earth metals	-0.01	-0.19	76	Aluminium & articles thereof	-0.31	-0.18
29	Organic chemicals	0.28	0.23	78	Lead & articles thereof	-0.44	0.20
30	Pharmaceutical products	-0.02	0.11	79	Zinc & articles thereof	0.47	0.34
31	Fertilizers	-0.92	-0.88	80	Tin & articles thereof	0.02	-0.22
32	Tanning/dyeing extract; tannins & their derivatives	0.23	0.25	81	Other base metals; cermets; articles thereof	-0.62	-0.61
33	Essential oils & resinoids; perfumery, cosmetic	-0.14	-0.13	82	Tool, implement, cutlery, spoon & forks, of base metal	0.09	-0.14
34	Soap, organic surface-active agents	-0.47	-0.35	83	Misc. articles of base metals	-0.27	-0.41
35	Albuminoidal substances; modified starches	-0.19	-0.20	84	Nuclear reactors, boilers, machinery, & mechanical appliances, parts thereof	-0.53	-0.49

Code	Product				
36	Explosives; pyrotechnic products; matches;	**0.06**	**0.04**	−0.62	−0.55
37	Photographic or cinematographic goods	−0.76	−0.86	−0.62	−0.61
38	Misc. chemical products	−0.02	−0.02	−0.50	−0.31
39	Plastics & articles thereof	−0.21	−0.28	−0.94	**0.07**
40	Rubber & articles thereof	−0.01	−0.15	−0.08	**0.14**
41	Raw hides & skins (other than furskins) & leather	**0.45**	**0.36**	−0.66	−0.64
42	Articles of leather; saddlery/ harnesses	**0.55**	**0.31**	−0.67	−0.81
43	Furskins & artificial fur; manufactures thereof	−1.00	−0.99	−0.69	−0.75
44	Wood & articles of wood; wood charcoal	−0.81	−0.75	−0.89	−0.53
45	Cork & articles of cork	−0.86	−0.86	−0.58	−0.57
46	Manufactures of straw, of esparto/other	−0.66	−0.90	−0.63	−0.69
47	Pulp of wood/of other fibrous cellulosic material	−0.99	−1.00	−0.05	−0.09
48	Paper & paperboard; articles of paper pulp	−0.57	−0.52	**0.48**	−0.13

Code	Product		
85	Electrical machinery equipment & parts thereof		
86	Railway/ tramway locomotives, rolling-stock & parts thereof		
87	Vehicles other than railway/ tramway rolling-stock and parts thereof		
88	Aircraft, spacecraft, & parts thereof		
89	Ships, boats, & floating structures		
90	Optical, photographic, cinematographic, measuring, checking precision, medical or surgical instruments and apparatus		
91	Clocks & watches & parts thereof		
92	Musical instruments; parts & accessories thereof		
93	Arms & ammunition; parts & accessories		
94	Furniture; bedding, mattress, mattresses		
95	Toys, games & sports requisites; parts & accessories thereof		
96	Misc. manufactured articles		
97	Works of art, collectors' pieces, and antiques		

Source: Computed with UN Comtrade data using Trade Sift

Note: *RCA > 0 indicates comparative advantage and RCA < 0 indicates comparative disadvantage. Figures in bold indicate comparative advantage.

Note: n.e.s. not elsewhere specified or included

Table 4.3A India's tariff lines and average imports (2009–15) (1000 USD)

BEC category	HS	Average of ad valorem duties	Average imports	BEC category	HS	Average of ad valorem duties	Average imports	BEC category	HS	Average of ad valorem duties	Average imports
111	10190	30	1131	121	20110	30		121	151329	78.8	3961
111	10290	30		121	20210	30		121	151411	75	88837
111	10391	5		121	20311	30		121	151491	75	15438
111	10392	5	34	121	20321	30		121	151521	100	87
111	10410	5	98	121	20410	30	159	121	151550	71.7	2232
111	10420	5	1	121	20421	30		121	151610	30	
111	10511	30	2379	121	20430	30		121	151620	47.5	9058
111	10512	30		121	20441	30		121	160300	30	298
111	10594	30	30	121	20500	30		121	170112	60	2511
111	10599	30	27	121	209	30	1	121	170191	60	15006
111	10611	30		121	30510	30		121	170211	25	35627
111	10612	30	293	121	40210	60	34862	121	170219	2.5	9050
111	10619	30	1	121	40410	30	16962	121	170230	30	2727
111	10620	30		121	40490	30	474	121	170240	30	1290
111	10631	30		121	40811	30	8	121	170250	30	1567
111	10632	30	31	121	40819	30	38	121	170260	30	2749
111	10639	30		121	40891	30	1	121	170290	30	1808
111	10690	30	2962	121	40899	30	2	121	170310	10	2330
111	80111	70	93	121	110100	30	1308	121	170390	10	128
111	80119	70	15	121	110220	30	109	121	180310	30	17397
111	81210	30	18	121	110290	30	259	121	180320	30	232
111	81290	30	39	121	110311	30	14	121	180400	30	13790
111	81400	30	15	121	110313	30	1217	121	180500	30	21561

111	**90111**	**100**	101167	121	110319	30	4	121	180620	30	12113
111	**90112**	**100**	22	121	110320	30	155	121	190190	30	3075
111	1002	0	0	121	110510	30	7	121	190300	30	428
111	1003	0	2395	121	110520	30	1241	121	210210	30	7401
111	100610	80	43	121	110610	30	4	121	210220	30	541
111	100620	80	1	121	110620	30		121	210230	30	81
111	1007	50		121	110630	30	1597	121	**220430**	**150**	50
111	100810	0	119	121	110710	30	1681	121	230210	15	256
111	100830	0	4	121	110720	30	2997	121	230230	30	342
111	100890	0	470	121	110900	30	5763	121	230240	30	13706
111	1201	30	262	121	120810	30	44	121	230250	30	949
111	120300	70	322	121	120890	30	40	121	230700	30	
111	120510	30	0	121	150420	30	1251	121	350710	10	40
111	120590	30	72	121	150430	30		121	50100	30	15507
111	120600	30	729	121	150710	7.5	1466501	121	50210	30	3011
111	120740	30	42109	121	150810	7.5		121	50290	30	891
111	120750	30	380	121	151000	32.5	2600	121	50400	30	1
111	120791	20	37094	121	**151110**	**100**	4705464	121	50510	30	162
111	120799	30	27984	121	151190	15	1305095	121	50590	30	5
111	121010	30	24372	121	151211	41.3	1061792	121	50610	30	259
111	121020	30	3271	121	**151221**	**100**	652	121	50690	30	49
111	121299	30	281	121	151229	57.5		121	50710	30	
111	180100	30	55692	121	**151311**	**100**	6401	121	50790	30	44
111	350211	20	9	121	151319	15	3031	121	50800	25	5015
111	350219	20	452	121	**151321**	**100**	201155	121	51000	30	1154
21	51110	30	193	21	230320	30	25	21	252010	5	68644
21	51191	30	17	21	230330	30	40	21	252100	5	213276
21	51199	26.4	8909	21	230800	30	39	21	252410	10	
21	60110	5	1316	21	240110	30	247	21	252490	10	247766

(Continued)

Table 4.3A (Continued)

BEC category	HS	Average of ad valorem duties	Average imports
21	60120	5	2891
21	60210	5	116
21	60220	5	308
21	60230	5	
21	60240	5	4
21	60290	5	6229
21	70110	30	13
21	1004	0	3295
21	100510	50	44
21	100590	50	8510
21	120400	30	150
21	120799	30	740
21	120910	5	1
21	120921	15	13081
21	120922	15	2
21	120923	15	165
21	120924	15	434
21	120925	15	5626
21	120929	15	56239
21	120930	15	4403
21	120991	5	36
21	120999	5	4403
21	121120	30	36
21	121130	15	
21	240120	30	12943
21	240130	30	3
21	250100	5	2809
21	250200	5	515
21	250300	5	274158
21	250410	5	15328
21	250490	5	1626
21	250510	5	9697
21	250590	5	1974
21	250610	5	168
21	250620	5	98
21	250700	5	20699
21	250810	5	3030
21	250830	5	143
21	250840	5	19933
21	250850	5	3745
21	250860	5	2903
21	250870	5	157
21	250900	5	676
21	251010	5	633737
21	251020	5	440291
21	251110	5	3311
21	251120	5	46
21	251200	5	2411
21	252510	5	192
21	252520	5	244
21	252530	5	67
21	252610	5	328
21	252620	5	1899
21	252910	5	2835
21	252921	5	7455
21	252922	5	46095
21	252930	5	607
21	253010	5	3962
21	253020	5	5
21	253090	5	12651
21	260111	2.5	227250
21	260112	2.5	120398
21	260120	2.5	15
21	260200	2.5	390999
21	260300	2.5	4943521
21	260400	0	25293
21	260500	2.5	15224
21	260600	2.5	55743
21	260700	2.5	47464
21	260800	2.5	44654
21	260900	2.5	1125
21	261000	2.5	36359

21	121140	15	49439	21	251310	5	600	21	261100	2.5	439
21	121190	15	407	21	251320	5	1421	21	261210	2.5	29869
21	121300	30	17	21	251400	5	2	21	261220	2.5	64
21	121410	30	134	21	251511	10	4195	21	261310	2.5	107983
21	121490	30	18496	21	251512	10	189080	21	261400	2.5	3246
21	130120	30	78261	21	251520	10	496	21	261510	2.5	27060
21	130190	29.2	2	21	251611	10	16443	21	261590	2.5	60049
21	130211	30	206	21	251612	10	2479	21	261610	2.5	2178
21	130212	30	2652	21	251620	10	121	21	261690	2.5	46174
21	130213	30	20024	21	251690	10	434	21	261710	2.5	63321
21	130219	15	8113	21	251710	5	16810	21	261790	2.5	14738
21	130220	15	8126	21	251720	5	19	21	261800	2.5	4115
21	140110	30	377	21	251730	5	132	21	261900	5	309
21	140120	30	946	21	251741	5	562	21	262011	5	1594
21	140190	30	9	21	251749	5	139	21	262019	5	31095
21	140420	30	4316	21	251810	5	33411	21	262021	5	
21	140490	30	5	21	251820	5	2332	21	262029	5	17526
21	152200	30	39	21	251830	5	3822	21	262030	5	312
21	180200	30	114	21	251910	5	736	21	262040	5	41659
21	230310	30		21	251990	5	43704	21	631090	5	17516
21	262060	5		21	430190	0	3	21	700100	8.3	63020
21	262091	5	669	21	440121	5	38	21	710110	10	41797
21	262099	5	138	21	440122	5	25011	21	710121	10	18780
21	262110	5	2040	21	440310	5	67	21	710210	10	21704
21	262190	5	578	21	440320	5	4969	21	710221	10	12756641
21	271091	5	18044	21	440341	5	70011	21	710231	10	
21	271099	5	578	21	440349	5	639878	21	710310	10	17832
21	271410	5	18044	21	440391	5	1360	21	710510	10	
21	271490	5		21	440392	5	5664				

(Continued)

Table 4.3A (Continued)

BEC category	HS	Average of ad valorem duties	Average imports	BEC category	HS	Average of ad valorem duties	Average imports	BEC category	HS	Average of ad valorem duties	Average imports
21	284450	7.5		21	440399	5	981742	21	710590	10	353
21	300692	10	8	21	440410	10	21	21	711230	10	104
21	310100	7.5	11491	21	440420	10	643	21	711291	10	24
21	310250	0	1098	21	450110	10	248	21	711292	10	1272
21	310490	7.5	95801	21	450190	10	3229	21	711299	10	3437
21	382510	10	1	21	450200	10	19	21	720410	2.5	45012
21	382520	10	1	21	470710	10	5417	21	720421	2.5	858415
21	382530	10	21	21	470720	10	866	21	720429	2.5	49111
21	382541	10	529	21	470730	10	1484	21	720430	2.5	12303
21	382549	10	21	21	470790	10	576081	21	720441	2.5	52428
21	382550	10		21	500100	30	9	21	720449	2.5	2049382
21	382561	10		21	500300	15	2748	21	720450	2.5	1014
21	382569	10	24	21	510111	5	1554	21	740400	5	780029
21	382590	10	414	21	510119	5	213231	21	750300	2.5	11476
21	391510	7.5	3495	21	510121	5	16914	21	760200	2.5	1137100
21	391520	7.5	47	21	510129	5	80399	21	780200	5	101433
21	391530	7.5	17292	21	510130	5	1019	21	790200	5	90381
21	391590	7.5	86203	21	510211	5	5059	21	800200	5	7
21	400110	70	8033	21	510219	5	950	21	810197	5	223
21	400121		281115	21	510220	5	74	21	810297	5	4
21	400122		385253	21	510310	10	415	21	810330	5	41
21	400129		46611	21	510320	10	629	21	810420	5	408
21	400130		12	21	510330	10		21	810530	5	40
21	400300	10	1064	21	510400	10	9	21	810730	5	
21	400400	10	7560	21	520100	0	326834	21	810830	5	270

21	410120	0	11348	21	520210	0	461	21	810930	5	21629
21	410150	0	5769	21	520291	0	41	21	811020	2.5	516730
21	410190	0	30552	21	520299	0	2506	21	811213	5	
21	410210	0	4367	21	530110	0	504	21	811222	5	
21	410221	0	18822	21	530130	0	314	21	854810	6.7	
21	410229	0	7445	21	530210	30	1	21	890800	2.5	
21	410320	0	15	21	530290	30	2				
21	410330	0	1927	21	530310	7.5	49697				
21	410390	0	1562	21	530390	10	1932				
21	411520	10	3585	21	530500	10	5035				
21	430110	0	15	21	550510	10					
21	430130	0	1547	21	550520	10					
21	430160	0	64	21	630900	10	100975				
21	430180	0	3	21	631010	5	7826				
322	270120	10	401	42	820770	10	20224	42	843699	7.5	5993
322	270220	10	2	42	820780	10	18030	42	843790	7.5	19026
322	270400	10	795267	42	820790	10	159045	42	843890	5	23570
322	270500	10	9	42	820810	10	3823	42	843991	7.5	7521
322	271111	5	6316338	42	820820	10	1232	42	843999	7.5	38474
322	271112	2.5	1486609	42	820830	10	887	42	844090	7.5	1463
322	271113	2.5	2610656	42	820840	10	306	42	844190	7.5	20414
322	271114	5	196	42	820890	10	31948	42	844240	7.5	2007
322	271119	5	695262	42	820900	10	90764	42	844250	7.5	40715
322	271600			42	821194	10	1440	42	844391	7.5	
322	340311	7.5		42	821195	10	102	42	844399	1.7	
322	340319	7.5		42	840140	7.5	11	42	844811	5	11913
322	340391	7.5		42	840290	7.5	113113	42	844819	5	12284
322	340399	7.5		42	840390	7.5	26604	42	844820	5	39419
322	440210	5		42	840490	7.5	26504	42	844831	5	8672

(*Continued*)

Table 4.3A (Continued)

BEC category	HS	Average of ad valorem duties	Average imports	BEC category	HS	Average of ad valorem duties	Average imports	BEC category	HS	Average of ad valorem duties	Average imports
322	440290	5		42	840590	7.5	3351	42	844832	5	24537
42	401011	10	7847	42	840690	7.5	312352	42	844833	5	13605
42	401012	10	8089	42	841090	7.5	16178	42	844839	5	83299
42	401019	10	4804	42	841290	7.5	68962	42	844842	5	9243
42	401031	10	8485	42	841391	8	249548	42	844849	5	38147
42	401032	10	2611	42	841392	7.5	5464	42	844851	5	12804
42	401033	10	1935	42	841490	8.2	451656	42	844859	5	25289
42	401034	10	661	42	841590	10	281284	42	845090	8.8	46815
42	401035	10	1741	42	841690	7.5	61604	42	845190	7.5	13523
42	401036	10	421	42	841790	7.5	113865	42	845230	8.8	13312
42	401039	10	40713	42	841891	7.5	853	42	845290	8.1	12678
42	420500	10	13219	42	841899	7.5	70748	42	845390	7.5	10099
42	590900	10	1993	42	841990	7.5	141734	42	845490	7.5	62449
42	591000	10	6968	42	842091	7.5	3814	42	845530	7.5	116893
42	591110	10	6055	42	842099	7.5	9687	42	845590	7.5	193350
42	591120	10	3962	42	842191	7.5	12858	42	846610	7.5	22961
42	591131	10	3234	42	842199	7.5	237732	42	846620	7.5	7537
42	591132	10	9113	42	842290	7.5	63878	42	846630	7.5	110483
42	591140	10	1184	42	842390	8.8	15933	42	846691	7.5	15315
42	591190	10	38611	42	842490	7.5	94436	42	846692	7.5	12849
42	820220	10	15811	42	843110	7.5	22803	42	846693	7.5	163186
42	820231	10	4422	42	843120	7.5	19567	42	846694	7.5	57759
42	820239	10	17662	42	843131	7.5	61124	42	846791	7.5	2540
42	820240	10	1896	42	843139	7.5	132368	42	846792	7.5	6711
42	820291	10	2066	42	843141	7.5	18400	42	846799	7.5	25511

42	820299	10	26441	42	843142	7.5	11916	42	846890	7.5	14452
42	820713	10	1939	42	843143	7.5	315603	42	847310	7.5	4775
42	820719	10	19184	42	843149	7.5	471988	42	847321	0	1463
42	820720	10	65413	42	843290	7.5	21172	42	847329	0	8576
42	820730	10	112397	42	843390	7.5	13092	42	847330	0	1430667
42	820740	10	20285	42	843490	7.5	2929	42	847340	7.5	75570
42	820750	10	34666	42	843590	7.5	1329	42	847350	0	22689
42	820760	10	9527	42	843691	7.5	4084	42	847490	7.5	142949
42	847590	7.5	29032	42	852990	8.3	946688	42	854110	0	148533
42	847690	7.5	3193	42	853090	7.5	10983	42	854121	0	11819
42	847790	7.5	147394	42	853190	10	71823	42	854129	0	183230
42	847890	7.5	4371	42	853290	0	19198	42	854130	0	47701
42	847990	7.5	365856	42	853310	0	20521	42	854140	0	972865
42	848110	7.5	16347	42	853321	0	15363	42	854150	0	16184
42	848120	7.5	41870	42	853329	0	27314	42	854160	0	47951
42	848130	7.5	16316	42	853331	0	1722	42	854190	0	31175
42	848140	7.5	22669	42	853339	0	8472	42	854231	0	876287
42	848180	7.5	671473	42	853340	0	45924	42	854232	0	136689
42	848190	7.5	220175	42	853390	0	9292	42	854233	0	14353
42	848210	7.5	312826	42	853400	0	278556	42	854239	7.5	518584
42	848220	7.5	117732	42	853510	7.5	5279	42	854290	0	85322
42	848230	7.5	89122	42	853521	7.5	8957	42	854390	7.5	170543
42	848240	7.5	20239	42	853529	7.5	28342	42	854511	7.5	54355
42	848250	7.5	38130	42	853530	7.5	18399	42	854519	7.5	89491
42	848280	7.5	112042	42	853540	7.5	10589	42	854520	7.5	11756
42	848291	7.5	36291	42	853590	7.5	70276	42	854590	7.5	11085
42	848299	7.5	130380	42	853610	7.9	36072	42	854610	7.5	4373
42	848310	7.5	156053	42	853620	7.5	79609	42	854620	7.5	27126
42	848320	7.5	33984	42	853630	7.5	16396	42	854690	7.5	56305

(Continued)

Table 4.3A (Continued)

BEC category	HS	Average of ad valorem duties	Average imports	BEC category	HS	Average of ad valorem duties	Average imports	BEC category	HS	Average of ad valorem duties	Average imports
42	848330	7.5	72406	42	853641	10	37973	42	854890	10	11513
42	848340	7.5	285759	42	853649	7.5	130591	42	870990	10	2576
42	848350	7.5	72051	42	853650	7.5	164707	42	900590	10	16012
42	848360	7.5	96424	42	853661	10	14349	42	900661	10	939
42	848390	7.5	172808	42	853669	10	164982	42	900669	10	2800
42	848410	7.5	27615	42	853690	7.5	331674	42	900791	10	4893
42	848420	7.5	33252	42	853710	7.5	269502	42	900792	10	2734
42	848490	7.5	23508	42	853810	7.5	72331	42	900890	10	785
42	848690	7.5	7153	42	853890	7.5	89951	42	901090	7.5	1785
42	848710	7.5	10365	42	853929	7.5	525804	42	901190	7.5	6845
42	848790	7.5	73816	42	853931	10	28825	42	901290	7.5	5065
42	850300	7.5	503175	42	853932	10	25918	42	901390	3.8	83274
42	850490	7.5	297470	42	853939	10	9716	42	901490	7.5	4465
42	850870			42	853941	10	11503	42	901590	7.5	27507
42	851490	7.5	26051	42	853949	10	1377	42	901790	10	7186
42	851590	7.5	47361	42	854011	10	20057	42	902230	7.5	34076
42	851770	0	3042508	42	854012	10	140091	42	902290	7.5	137431
42	851890	10	26618	42	854020	10	45	42	902490	7.5	9578
42	852210	10	190	42	854040	5	15451	42	902590	7.5	12899
42	852290	10	67821	42	854060	10	1998	42	902690	0	49189
42	852321	10	3487	42	854071	10	806	42	902890	7.5	26281
42	852329	10	28595	42	854079	10	3439	42	902990	7.5	22368
42	852351		219810	42	854081	10	3179	42	903090	7.5	65699
42	852352	0		42			11073	42	903190	7.5	175119

Table (continued). Each group of columns reads: flag | code | rate | value.

Group 1

Flag	Code	Rate	Value
42	852359	5	1156892
42	852380	8.6	124347
42	852910	8.3	346
22	110811	30	1744
22	110812	30	2202
22	110813	30	2559
22	110814	50	3150
22	110819	50	751
22	110820	30	4756
22	130231	30	5297
22	130232	30	7679
22	130239	30	
22	1501	30	28
22	1502	15	1445
22	1503	30	2361
22	150410	30	1
22	150500	15	118
22	150600	30	2730
22	151511	100	134
22	151519	57.5	10661
22	151530	57.5	5895
22	151590	71.7	5487
22	151800	23.6	2505
22	152000	20	1515
22	152110	30	4495
22	152190	30	78978
22	220710	150	2
22	220720	5	
22	230110	30	

Group 2

Flag	Code	Rate	Value
42	854089	10	3131
42	854091	10	12131
42	854099	10	9685
22	270600	10	6278
22	270710	10	52
22	270720	10	23
22	270730	5	27477
22	270740	2.5	38411
22	270750	10	66842
22	270791	10	491
22	270799	10	48621
22	270810	10	25099
22	270820	5	2887
22	271210	5	1959
22	271220	5	60713
22	271290	2.5	77299
22	271311	2.5	431596
22	271312	5	135651
22	271320	5	107034
22	271390	5	400407
22	271500	7.5	2712
22	280110	2.5	318
22	280120	7.5	109763
22	280130	7.5	13934
22	280200	7.5	6715
22	280300	7.5	149264
22	280410	7.5	100
22	280421	7.5	388
22	280429	7.5	18284

Group 3

Flag	Code	Rate	Value
42	903290	7.5	148801
42	903300	7.5	246964
22	281121	7.5	190
22	281122	7.5	27904
22	281129	7.5	2862
22	281210	7.5	10304
22	281290	7.5	4195
22	281310	7.5	14917
22	281390	7.5	3132
22	281410	7.5	931174
22	281420	7.5	657
22	281511	7.5	11313
22	281512	7.5	99231
22	281520	7.5	21597
22	281530	7.5	194
22	281610	7.5	945
22	281640	7.5	686
22	281700	7.5	9598
22	281810	7.5	640
22	281820	6.3	305431
22	281830	7.5	10912
22	281910	7.5	8777
22	281990	7.5	2472
22	282010	7.5	10477
22	282090	7.5	3240
22	282110	7.5	24197
22	282120	7.5	32
22	282200	7.5	3191

(Continued)

Table 4.3A (Continued)

BEC category	HS	Average of ad valorem duties	Average imports	BEC category	HS	Average of ad valorem duties	Average imports	BEC category	HS	Average of ad valorem duties	Average imports
22	230120	5	8978	22	280430	7.5	523	22	282300	7.5	51041
22	230400	15	351	22	280440	7.5	1127	22	282410	7.5	2341
22	230500	15	40	22	280450	7.5	667	22	282490	7.5	211
22	230610	15	21	22	280461	7.5	71764	22	282510	7.5	42993
22	230620	15	134	22	280469	7.5	6225	22	282520	7.5	12135
22	230630	5	9009	22	280470	7.5	67138	22	282530	7.5	6446
22	230641	15	596	22	280480	7.5	956	22	282540	0	5347
22	230649	15		22	280490	7.5	16785	22	282550	7.5	2525
22	230650	15	13016	22	280511	7.5	13347	22	282560	7.5	15098
22	230660	15	431	22	280512	7.5	11780	22	282570	7.5	3566
22	230690	13.5	8169	22	280519	7.5	5922	22	282580	7.5	17939
22	230990	30	195656	22	280530	7.5	3695	22	282590	7.5	14289
22	240399	30	4874	22	280540	7.5	8636	22	282612	7.5	29021
22	252020	5	5402	22	280610	7.5	687	22	282619	7.5	2310
22	252210	5	45269	22	280620	7.5	4	22	282630	7.5	7385
22	252220	5	3162	22	280700	7.5	48473	22	282690	7.5	4189
22	252230	5	247	22	280800	7.5	268	22	282710	7.5	3976
22	252310	10	19527	22	280910	7.5	3727	22	282720	7.5	818
22	252321	10	1674	22	280920	6.3	1510494	22	282731	7.5	622
22	252329	0	51496	22	281000	7.5	9764	22	282732	7.5	249
22	252330	10	3666	22	281111	7.5	2142	22	282735	7.5	326
22	252390	10	4707	22	281119	7.5	13762	22	282739	7.5	17871
22	282741	7.5	43	22	283720	7.5	2938	22	290230	5	267184
22	282749	7.5	2953	22	283911	7.5	504	22	290241	2.5	50201
22	282751	7.5	487	22	283919	7.5	2608	22	290242	5	4676

22	282759	7.5	3359	22	283990	7.5	18011	22	290243	0	671243
22	282760	7.5	8597	22	284011	7.5	28137	22	290244	5	1756
22	282810	7.5	43	22	284019	7.5	6246	22	290250	2	749430
22	282890	7.5	2960	22	284020	7.5	4227	22	290260	5	206
22	282911	7.5	15122	22	284030	7.5	1181	22	290270	5	3172
22	282919	7.5	6287	22	284130	7.5	11862	22	290290	5	49483
22	282990	7.5	1919	22	284150	7.5	225	22	290311	6.3	626
22	283010	7.5	5464	22	284161	7.5	474	22	290312	7.5	42910
22	283090	7.5	2674	22	284169	7.5	1247	22	290313	7.5	9026
22	283110	7.5	2081	22	284170	7.5	72	22	290314	5	101
22	283190	7.5	28	22	284180	7.5	515	22	290315	2	130157
22	283210	7.5	6056	22	284190	7.5	11257	22	290319	5	11443
22	283220	7.5	877	22	284210	7.5	3415	22	290321	2	267030
22	283230	7.5	886	22	284290	7.5	3965	22	290322	7.5	3611
22	283311	7.5	2564	22	284310	7.5	3677	22	290323	5	6883
22	283319	7.5	3088	22	284321	7.5	1642	22	290329	5	6722
22	283321	7.5	234	22	284329	7.5	4176	22	290331	5	764
22	283322	7.5	459	22	284330	7.5	548	22	290339	5	51227
22	283324	7.5	7472	22	284390	7.5	99199	22	290410	5	19535
22	283325	7.5	9263	22	284410	7.5		22	290420	5	14007
22	283327	7.5	8072	22	284420	7.5		22	290490	5	28627
22	283329	7.5	5044	22	284430	7.5	18	22	290511	5	402387
22	283330	7.5	429	22	284440	7.5		22	290512	7.5	60712
22	283340	7.5	1834	22	284450	7.5		22	290513	7.5	50327
22	283410	7.5	7957	22	284510	7.5		22	290514	7.5	59742
22	283421	7.5	430	22	284590	7.5		22	290516	7.5	103567
22	283429	7.5	2443	22	284610	7.5	6544	22	290517	7.5	3672
22	283510	7.5	2541	22	284690	7.5	5658	22	290519	7.5	65796
22	283522	7.5	2426	22	284700	7.5	16496	22	290522	7.5	28746

(Continued)

Table 4.3A (Continued)

BEC category	HS	Average of ad valorem duties	Average imports	BEC category	HS	Average of ad valorem duties	Average imports	BEC category	HS	Average of ad valorem duties	Average imports
22	283524	7.5	2303	22	284800	7.5	284	22	290529	7.5	5395
22	283525	7.5	4747	22	284910	7.5	43267	22	290531	7.5	727396
22	283526	7.5	13295	22	284920	7.5	30650	22	290532	7.5	61128
22	283529	7.5	5590	22	284990	7.5	10655	22	290539	7.5	41983
22	283531	7.5	69566	22	285000	7.5	38046	22	290541	7.5	6303
22	283539	7.5	9742	22	2852	7.5	305	22	290542	7.5	23202
22	283620	7.5	140942	22	285300	7.5	10108	22	290543	7.5	14094
22	283630	7.5	6916	22	290110	2.5	70869	22	290544	20	2583
22	283640	7.5	21956	22	290121	2.5	41801	22	290545	20	29147
22	283650	7.5	58575	22	290122	2.5	2658	22	290549	7.5	11700
22	283660	7.5	3385	22	290123	5	38237	22	290551	7.5	2
22	283691	7.5	4310	22	290124	2.5	5830	22	290559	7.5	2804
22	283692	7.5	2808	22	290129	5	129747	22	290611	7.5	4385
22	283699	7.5	22278	22	290211	5	7196	22	290612	7.5	1171
22	283711	7.5	11261	22	290219	5	76189	22	290613	7.5	7027
22	283719	7.5	2811	22	290220	5	37503	22	290619	7.5	19228
22	290621	7.5	1179	22	291429	5	42893	22	291811	7.5	8787
22	290629	7.5	18933	22	291431	7.5	17	22	291812	7.5	9227
22	290711	7.5	230195	22	291439	7.5	51543	22	291813	7.5	6055
22	290712	7.5	22828	22	291440	7.5	3429	22	291814	7.5	47732
22	290713	7.5	17579	22	291450	7.5	5020	22	291815	7.5	7524
22	290715	7.5	34670	22	291461	2.5	4878	22	291816	7.5	19381
22	290719	7.5	58243	22	291469	7.5	19910	22	291818	7.5	0
22	290721	7.5	13509	22	291470	7.5	47670	22	291819	7.5	39954

22	290722	7.5	41167	22	291511	7.5	7720	22	291821	7.5	17254
22	290723	7.5	49783	22	291512	7.5	29218	22	291822	7.5	161
22	290729	7.5	12180	22	291513	7.5	5213	22	291823	7.5	7288
22	290811	7.5	228	22	291521	7.5	289666	22	291829	7.5	26342
22	290819	7.5	6526	22	291524	7.5	1716	22	291830	7.5	61237
22	290891	7.5	24	22	291529	7.5	48870	22	291891	7.5	302
22	290899	7.5	9674	22	291531	7.5	4312	22	291899	7.5	50239
22	290911	7.5	294	22	291532	10	123748	22	291910	7.5	272
22	290919	7.5	29661	22	291533	7.5	29505	22	291990	7.5	11880
22	290920	7.5	1796	22	291536	7.5	69	22	292011	7.5	594
22	290930	7.5	43172	22	291539	7.5	62209	22	292019	7.5	15336
22	290941	7.5	1486	22	291540	7.5	1673	22	292090	7.5	71804
22	290943	7.5	21876	22	291550	7.5	16068	22	292111	7.5	51142
22	290944	7.5	3898	22	291560	7.5	24095	22	292119	7.5	28974
22	290949	7.5	22860	22	291570	7.5	53459	22	292121	7.5	65494
22	290950	7.5	21498	22	291590	7.5	135262	22	292122	7.5	1940
22	290960	7.5	13001	22	291611	7.5	27874	22	292129	7.5	42969
22	291010	7.5	619	22	291612	6.3	255250	22	292130	7.5	38679
22	291020	7.5	25138	22	291613	7.5	17920	22	292141	7.5	53805
22	291030	2.5	40149	22	291614	7.5	81763	22	292142	7.5	53220
22	291040		1	22	291615	7.5	2700	22	292143	7.5	17713
22	291090	7.5	7425	22	291619	7.5	17450	22	292144	7.5	38284
22	291100	7.5	3991	22	291620	7.5	4299	22	292145	7.5	37091
22	291211	7.5	462	22	291631	7.5	34100	22	292146	7.5	33
22	291212	7.5	821	22	291632	7.5	3960	22	292149	7.5	16977
22	291219	7.5	27114	22	291634	7.5	1231	22	292151	7.5	24953
22	291221	7.5	7151	22	291639	7.5	38927	22	292159	7.5	41798
22	291229	7.5	49753	22	291711	7.5	4905	22	292211	7.5	11198
22	291241	7.5	14204	22	291712	7.5	31467	22	292212	7.5	15293

(Continued)

Table 4.3A (Continued)

BEC category	HS	Average of ad valorem duties	Average imports	BEC category	HS	Average of ad valorem duties	Average imports	BEC category	HS	Average of ad valorem duties	Average imports
22	291242	7.5	5693	22	291713	7.5	1550	22	292213	7.5	7598
22	291249	7.5	23107	22	291714	7.5	53816	22	292214	7.5	39
22	291250	7.5	397	22	291719	7.5	36562	22	292219	7.5	34472
22	291260	7.5	11844	22	291720	7.5	13807	22	292221	7.5	75493
22	291300	7.5	10228	22	291732	7.5	740	22	292229	7.5	121885
22	291411	7.5	101384	22	291733	7.5	94	22	292231	7.5	0
22	291412	7.5	39833	22	291734	7.5	441	22	292239	7.5	10063
22	291413	7.5	33791	22	291735	7.5	61363	22	292241	7.5	49939
22	291419	7.5	23169	22	291736	7.5	745296	22	292243	7.5	27782
22	291422	7.5	34668	22	291737	5	3682	22	292244	7.5	210
22	291423	7.5	23395	22	291739	7.5	107619	22	293943	7.5	
22	292249	7.5	78854	22	293339	7.5	151944	22	293949	7.5	559
22	292250	7.5	100617	22	293341	7.5	48	22	293951	7.5	6727
22	292310	7.5	1365	22	293349	7.5	21696	22	293959		295
22	292320	7.5	8799	22	293352	7.5	1881	22	293961	7.5	295
22	292390	7.5	10434	22	293353	7.5	19	22	293962	7.5	294
22	292411	7.5	131	22	293354	7.5	283	22	293963	7.5	
22	292412	7.5	281	22	293355	7.5	0	22	293969		2301
22	292419	7.5	44871	22	293359	7.5	166688	22	293991	7.5	48
22	292421	7.5	3551	22	293361	7.5	47518	22	293999	7.5	12144
22	292423	7.5	0	22	293369	7.5	47849	22	294000	7.5	20380
22	292424	7.5		22	293371	10	40041	22	294110	7.5	296549
22	292429	7.5	79885	22	293372	7.5	1058	22	294120	7.5	7429
22	292511	7.5	8239	22	293379	7.5	16962				

22	292512	7.5	4	22	293391	7.5	670	22	294130	7.5	34488
22	292519	7.5	4423	22	293399	7.5	140359	22	294140	7.5	6745
22	292521	7.5	3	22	293410	7.5	24367	22	294150	7.5	132229
22	292529	7.5	5864	22	293420	7.5	13588	22	294190	7.5	432785
22	292610	2.5	160183	22	293430	7.5	767	22	294200	7.5	932731
22	292620	7.5	42989	22	293491	7.5	144	22	300120	10	954
22	292630	7.5	6	22	293499	7.5	215779	22	300190	10	35010
22	292690	7.5	95701	22	293500	7.5	39794	22	300210	10	201407
22	292700	7.5	9514	22	293621	7.5	9003	22	300220	10	195350
22	292800	7.5	20675	22	293622	7.5	8245	22	300230	10	12404
22	292910	7.5	299517	22	293623	7.5	7990	22	300290	10	38919
22	292990	7.5	5130	22	293624	7.5	4484	22	300310	10	3362
22	293020	7.5	643	22	293625	7.5	5888	22	300320	10	953
22	293030	7.5	840	22	293626	7.5	18868	22	300331	10	4
22	293040	7.5	90442	22	293627	7.5	7633	22	300339	10	5615
22	293050	7.5	11	22	293628	7.5	11106	22	300340	10	258
22	293090	7.5	115806	22	293629	7.5	15158	22	300390	10	34184
22	2931	7.5	99307	22	293690	7.5	6685	22	300510	10	8593
22	293211	7.5	52821	22	293711	7.5	456	22	300590	10	13243
22	293212	7.5	522	22	293712	7.5	43150	22	300610	10	8878
22	293213	7.5	14016	22	293719	7.5	10087	22	300620	10	2595
22	293219	7.5	10470	22	293721	7.5	37252	22	300630	10	22885
22	293291	7.5	1021	22	293722	7.5	6419	22	300640	10	18794
22	293292	7.5	57	22	293723	7.5	25834	22	300650	10	509
22	293293	7.5	667	22	293729	7.5	49608	22	300670	10	955
22	293294	7.5	13	22	293750	7.5	2388	22	310210	7.5	2019848
22	293295	7.5	24	22	293790	7.5	40708	22	310221	5	6680
22	293299	7.5	84036	22	293810	7.5	5641	22	310229	7.5	373
22	293311	7.5	760	22	293890	7.5	32522	22	310230	7.5	59290

(Continued)

Table 4.3A (Continued)

BEC category	HS	Average of ad valorem duties	Average imports	BEC category	HS	Average of ad valorem duties	Average imports	BEC category	HS	Average of ad valorem duties	Average imports
22	293319	7.5	58205	22	293911	7.5	25440	22	310240	7.5	57
22	293321	7.5	3432	22	293919	7.5	3084	22	310260	7.5	13372
22	293329	7.5	65766	22	293920	7.5	7772	22	310280	7.5	4
22	293331	7.5	22646	22	293930	7.5	2507	22	310290	7.5	2127
22	293332	7.5	1322	22	293941	7.5	655	22	310310	7.5	28231
22	293333	7.5	409	22	293942	7.5	160	22	310390	7.5	2436
22	310420	10	1413329	22	321410	10	33077	22	370239	10	3362
22	310430	5	30259	22	321490	10	18447	22	370241	10	1926
22	310490	7.5		22	321511	10	20946	22	370242	10	6819
22	310510	7.5	1272	22	321519	10	101064	22	370243	10	133
22	310520	5	90660	22	321590	10	40562	22	370244	10	6027
22	310530	5	2634163	22	330112	20	8912	22	370255	10	4182
22	310540	5	149461	22	330113	20	3806	22	370256	10	597
22	310551	5	94469	22	330119	20	4377	22	370310	10	27995
22	310559	5	152584	22	330124	20	832	22	370320	10	57082
22	310560	5	12628	22	330125	20	3546	22	370390	10	9231
22	310590	5	39612	22	330129	20	61054	22	370400	10	378
22	320110	7.5	2824	22	330130	20	3540	22	370510	10	51
22	320120	7.5	22677	22	330190	20	39148	22	370590	10	1085
22	320190	7.5	34463	22	330210	10	32103	22	370610	10	1095
22	320210	7.5	13920	22	330290	10	56604	22	370690	10	913
22	320290	7.5	7197	22	340211	10	44208	22	370710	10	359
22	320300	7.5	12963	22	340212	10	4255	22	370790	10	35167
22	320411	7.5	43612	22	340213	10	33792	22	380110	7.5	8152
22	320412	7.5	7760	22	340219	10	26828	22	380120	7.5	1963

22	320413	7.5	9408	22	340290	10	46970	22	380130	7.5	6829
22	320414	7.5	2195	22	340420	10	4769	22	380190	7.5	24610
22	320415	7.5	48100	22	340490	10	48575	22	380210	7.5	24563
22	320416	7.5	33074	22	340700	10	4264	22	380290	7.5	19260
22	320417	7.5	76915	22	350110	20	253	22	380300	7.5	902
22	320419	7.5	31119	22	350190	20	3318	22	380400	7.5	23629
22	320420	7.5	14755	22	350220	20	5695	22	380510	7.5	23256
22	320490	7.5	16394	22	350290	20	3313	22	380590	7.5	5227
22	320500	7.5	2090	22	350300	20	19346	22	380610	7.5	77139
22	320611	10	299789	22	350400	16.7	19831	22	380620	7.5	2031
22	320619	10	97070	22	350510	20	33542	22	380630	7.5	4312
22	320620	7.5	549	22	350520	20	1256	22	380690	7.5	16552
22	320641	7.5	1444	22	350691	10	51947	22	380700	7.5	195
22	320642	7.5	3385	22	350699	10	57984	22	380910	20	199
22	320649	7.5	50484	22	350790	10	66830	22	380991	7.5	50914
22	320650	7.5	19343	22	360100	10	140	22	380992	7.5	23166
22	320710	7.5	43799	22	360200	10	5672	22	380993	7.5	45871
22	320720	7.5	3488	22	360300	10	4552	22	381010	7.5	17246
22	320730	7.5	1485	22	360410	10		22	381090	7.5	18121
22	320740	5	15539	22	360490	10	1032	22	381111	10	43
22	320810	10	20671	22	360690	10	54	22	381119	10	14405
22	320820	10	30114	22	370110	10	48935	22	381121	10	99170
22	320890	10	80765	22	370120	5	119	22	381129	10	33715
22	320910	10	10882	22	370130	10	10767	22	381190	10	61591
22	320990	10	40243	22	370191	10	822	22	381210	7.5	37029
22	321000	10	13991	22	370199	10	7132	22	381220	7.5	21387
22	321100	10	1766	22	370210	10	30467	22	381230	7.5	140785
22	321210	10	23687	22	370231	10	214	22	381300	10	2265
22	321290	10	25222	22	370232	10	74	22	381400	10	23171

(Continued)

Table 4.3A (Continued)

BEC category	HS	Average of ad valorem duties	Average imports
22	381511	7.5	18968
22	381512	7.5	95326
22	381519	7.5	102647
22	381590	7.5	297126
22	381600	7.5	92995
22	381700	7.5	199418
22	381800	0	109758
22	381900	10	11390
22	382000	10	5939
22	382100	7.5	15405
22	382200	10	255391
22	382311	7.5	18941
22	382312	7.5	8660
22	382313	7.5	3987
22	382319	7.5	179266
22	382370	7.5	72341
22	382410	7.5	6028
22	382430	7.5	21444
22	382440	7.5	40248
22	382450	7.5	5028
22	382460	20	1360
22	382471	7.5	60
22	382472	7.5	0
22	382473	7.5	1
22	390421	7.5	884702
22	390422	7.5	84467
22	390430	7.5	21036
22	390440	7.5	12828
22	390450	7.5	13477
22	390461	7.5	22725
22	390469	7.5	26353
22	390490	7.5	73532
22	390512	7.5	6700
22	390519	7.5	5020
22	390521	7.5	5794
22	390529	7.5	54526
22	390530	7.5	56771
22	390591	7.5	9055
22	390599	7.5	62878
22	390610	7.5	31350
22	390690	7.5	217242
22	390710	7.5	38634
22	390720	7.5	309523
22	390730	7.5	136109
22	390740	7.5	281121
22	390750	7.5	1985
22	390760	7.5	104494
22	390770	7.5	71
22	391710	10	2968
22	391721	10	8567
22	391722	10	1120
22	391723	10	6317
22	391729	10	20838
22	391731	10	12478
22	391732	10	12291
22	391733	10	1324
22	391739	10	25166
22	391740	10	25539
22	391810	10	15955
22	391890	10	13310
22	391910	10	11236
22	391990	10	181331
22	392010	10	63942
22	392020	10	70136
22	392030	10	6074
22	392043	10	9525
22	392049	10	70507
22	392051	10	34212
22	392059	10	6805
22	392061	10	21189
22	392062	10	34294
22	392063	10	3992

22	382474	7.5	756	22	390791	7.5	70317	22	392069	10	42254
22	382475	7.5	0	22	390799	7.5	146519	22	392071	10	3406
22	382476	7.5		22	390810	10	151021	22	392073	10	1434
22	382477	7.5	5	22	390890	10	125315	22	392079	10	3490
22	382478	7.5	3966	22	390910	7.5	4828	22	392091	10	29044
22	382479	7.5	846	22	390920	7.5	16581	22	392092	10	8771
22	382481	7.5	55	22	390930	7.5	56700	22	392093	10	114
22	382482	7.5	2	22	390940	7.5	44596	22	392094	10	585
22	382483	7.5	518	22	390950	7.5	111140	22	392099	10	96624
22	382490	7.5	394908	22	391000	7.5	142164	22	392111	10	1518
22	390110	7.5	1044254	22	391110	7.5	34760	22	392112	10	6562
22	390120	7.5	590178	22	391190	7.5	28131	22	392113	10	16332
22	390130	7.5	200929	22	391211	7.5	8189	22	392114	10	1148
22	390190	7.5	277733	22	391212	7.5	1964	22	392119	10	17201
22	390210	7.5	546779	22	391220	7.5	10406	22	392190	10	127452
22	390220	7.5	18488	22	391231	7.5	29045	22	392210	10	5971
22	390230	7.5	146159	22	391239	7.5	119493	22	392290	10	32236
22	390290	7.5	50520	22	391290	7.5	52292	22	392310	10	36084
22	390311	7.5	7879	22	391310	7.5	7754	22	392321	10	13338
22	390319	7.5	24445	22	391390	7.5	19257	22	392329	10	25700
22	390320	7.5	10950	22	391400	7.5	13754	22	392330	10	23135
22	390330	7.5	120571	22	391610	10	1901	22	392340	10	5518
22	390390	7.5	43016	22	391620	10	10042	22	392350	10	53361
22	390410	7.5	144873	22	391690	10	8945	22	392390	10	51362
22	392510	10	1201	22	410510	10	67797	22	520829	10	3281
22	392520	10	11161	22	410530	10	7128	22	520831	10	6318
22	392590	10	34022	22	410621	10	8781	22	520832	10	23874
22	392610	10	14790	22	410622	10	1498	22	520833	10	1817
22	392630	10	6606	22	410631	10	126	22	520839	10	705

(Continued)

Table 4.3A (Continued)

BEC category	HS	Average of ad valorem duties	Average imports	BEC category	HS	Average of ad valorem duties	Average imports	BEC category	HS	Average of ad valorem duties	Average imports
22	400211	10	13709	22	410632	10	215	22	520841		11259
22	400219	10	424681	22	410640	10	64	22	520842		59922
22	400220	10	151526	22	410691	10	19868	22	520843	10	3137
22	400231	5	164212	22	410692	10	1280	22	520849		525
22	400239	10	113368	22	410711	10	4916	22	520851		3170
22	400241	10	408	22	410712	10	962	22	520852		4956
22	400249	10	51053	22	410719	10	41607	22	520859		1469
22	400251	10	401	22	410791	10	670	22	520911	10	869
22	400259	10	63646	22	410792	10	835	22	520912	10	553
22	400260	10	6172	22	410799	10	40639	22	520919	10	738
22	400270	10	86677	22	411200	10	7120	22	520921	10	4648
22	400280	10	7499	22	411310	10	2623	22	520922	10	335
22	400291	10	7115	22	411320	10	967	22	520929	10	700
22	400299	10	28122	22	411330	10	129	22	520931		8065
22	400510	10	23375	22	411390	10	6467	22	520932		10158
22	400520	10	3565	22	411410	10	496	22	520939		1334
22	400591	10	12122	22	411420	10	1242	22	520941		1851
22	400599	10	14595	22	411510	10	2662	22	520942		26634
22	400610	10	18	22	420600	0	1162	22	520943		410
22	400690	10	2060	22	430211	0	7	22	520949		99
22	400700	10	8142	22	430219	0	1439	22	520951		752
22	400811	10	4130	22	430220	0	49	22	520952		220
22	400819	10	1130	22	430230	0	207	22	520959		1921
22	400821	10	9852	22	481960	10	7069	22	521011	10	709
22	400829	10	8003	22	482010	10	493	22	521019	10	857

22	400911	10	15340	22	482030	10	1777	22	521021	10	1200
22	400912	10	5026	22	482040	10	404	22	521029	10	414
22	400921	10	15257	22	482090	10	169	22	521031	10	6805
22	400922	10	6578	22	482110	10	2169	22	521032	10	229
22	400931	10	11467	22	482190	10	51730	22	521039		263
22	400932	10	8232	22	482210	10	15126	22	521041		2714
22	400941	10	20307	22	482290	10	180	22	521049		196
22	400942	10	33977	22	482320	10	991	22	521051		775
22	401490	10	7661	22	482340	10	14982	22	440500	10	589
22	401511	10	14356	22	482370	10	536	22	440610	10	
22	401693	10	206463	22	482390	10	1334	22	440690	10	49
22	401694	10	1165	22	490600	0	42086	22	440710	10	51812
22	401699	10	223114	22	520812	10	1262	22	440721	10	95
22	401700	10	4618	22	520813	10	3138	22	440722	10	352
22	410411	10	12161	22	520819	10	6825	22	440725	10	128
22	410419	10	129356	22	520821	10	650	22	440726	10	91
22	410441	10	2180	22	520822	10	2306	22	440727	10	17
22	410449	10	103316	22	520823	10	483	22	440728	10	
22	440729	10	57188	22	450490	10	271	22	480530	10	59
22	440791	10	1038	22	470100	5	2175	22	480540	10	13443
22	440792	10	14644	22	470200	5	234705	22	480550	10	443
22	440793	10	322	22	470311	5	13650	22	480591	10	31608
22	440794	10	23	22	470319	5	20639	22	480592	10	10223
22	440795	10	415	22	470321	5	118590	22	480593	10	5505
22	440799	10	25992	22	470329	5	260167	22	480610	10	1741
22	440810	10	11041	22	470411	5	322	22	480620	10	673
22	440831	10	2758	22	470419	5	299	22	480630	10	2534
22	440839	10	19442	22	470421	5	260	22	480640	10	24862

(Continued)

Table 4.3A (Continued)

BEC category	HS	Average of ad valorem duties	Average imports	BEC category	HS	Average of ad valorem duties	Average imports	BEC category	HS	Average of ad valorem duties	Average imports
22	440890	10	35397	22	470429	5	6567	22	480700	10	4875
22	440910	10	6873	22	470500	5	48385	22	480810	10	1481
22	440921	10	507	22	470610	5	1208	22	480890	10	207
22	440929	10	6854	22	470620	5	808	22	480920	10	515
22	441011	10	33128	22	470630	5	503	22	480990	10	4981
22	441012	10	1482	22	470691	5	2335	22	481013	10	73691
22	441019	10	879	22	470692	5	2257	22	481014	10	10595
22	441090	10	13800	22	470693	5	3902	22	481019	10	158743
22	441112	10	18048	22	480100	10	797362	22	481022	10	38381
22	441113	10	12411	22	480210	10	4402	22	481029	10	15121
22	441114	10	23127	22	480220	10	16630	22	481031	10	12101
22	441192	10	21509	22	480240	10	104	22	481032	10	7397
22	441193	10	609	22	480254	10	7760	22	481039	10	33689
22	441194	10	5035	22	480255	10	6847	22	481092	10	3044
22	441210	10	10491	22	480256	10	7314	22	481099	10	26349
22	441231	10	16583	22	480257	10	281917	22	481110	10	2386
22	441232	10	5566	22	480258	10	4304	22	481141	10	27173
22	441239	10	4592	22	480261	10	6596	22	481149	10	16713
22	441294	10	675	22	480262	10	443	22	481151	10	7641
22	441299	10	39867	22	480269	10	602	22	481159	10	24745
22	441300	10	5085	22	480300	10	4852	22	481160	10	17311
22	441510	10	3466	22	480411	10	7147	22	481190	10	101454
22	441520	10	6213	22	480419	10	20479	22	481200	10	2690
22	441600	10	3047	22	480421	10	4673	22	481320	10	3939

22	Code	Rate	Value	22	Code	Rate	Value	22	Code	Rate	Value
22	441700	10	1127	22	480429	10	12645	22	481390	10	10183
22	441810	10	954	22	480431	10	3742	22	481420	10	91
22	441820	10	14333	22	480439	10	26503	22	481490	10	6771
22	441840	10	3272	22	480441	10	2477	22	481620	10	3572
22	441850	10	19	22	480442	10	1409	22	481690	10	352
22	441860	10	726	22	480449	10	7416	22	481910	10	1222
22	441871	10	1014	22	480451	10	2130	22	481920	10	18685
22	441872	10	3227	22	480452	10	197	22	481930	10	8551
22	441879	10	5430	22	480459	10	15239	22	481940	10	5146
22	441890	10	12267	22	480511	10	1323	22	481950	10	6047
22	442190	10	29352	22	480512	10	20	22	490700	10	34473
22	450310	10	282	22	480519	10	3448	22	490810	10	288913
22	450390	10	240	22	480524	10	1410	22	491110	10	2073
22	450410	10	672	22	480525	10	2646	22	491199	10	11574
22	500200	10	84427	22	520534	10	5	22	521214	10	724
22	500400	10	189530	22	520535	10	182	22	521215	10	702
22	500500	10	19232	22	520541	10	24	22	521221	10	14
22	500710	10	3747	22	520542	10	86	22	521222	10	18
22	500720	10	110	22	520543	10	18	22	521223	10	354
22	500790	10	76359	22	520544	10	92	22	521224		160
22	510510	10	5853	22	520546	10	10	22	521225		46
22	510521	10	379	22	520547	10	86	22	530121	0	7684
22	510529	7.5	4773	22	520548	10	1231	22	530129	0	8964
22	510531	10	925	22	520611	10	70	22	530610	10	31016
22	510539	10	331	22	520612	10	221	22	530620	10	50398
22	510540	10	19	22	520613	10	9	22	530710	10	37787
22	510610	10	1237	22	520614	10	10	22	530720	10	1336
22	510620	10	510	22	520615	10	3	22	530810	10	99
22	510710	10	1707	22	520621	10	15	22	530820	10	11

(Continued)

Table 4.3A (Continued)

BEC category	HS	Average of ad valorem duties	Average imports
22	510720	10	620
22	510810	10	89
22	510820	10	156
22	511000	10	12
22	511111		16055
22	511119		492
22	511120		2609
22	511130		1433
22	511190		1164
22	511211		6142
22	511219		1637
22	511220		1143
22	511230		533
22	511290		581
22	511300		155
22	520300	30	443
22	520411	10	453
22	520419	10	132
22	520511	10	5158
22	520512	10	667
22	520513	10	1249
22	520514	10	39
22	520515	10	124
22	520521	10	481
22	520622	10	545
22	520623	10	67
22	520624	10	14
22	520625	10	22
22	520631	10	59
22	520632	10	
22	520633	10	
22	520634	10	12
22	520635	10	
22	520641	10	16
22	520642	10	17
22	520643	10	1
22	520644	10	175
22	520645	10	175
22	520811	10	8166
22	521059		357
22	521111	10	295
22	521112	10	134
22	521119	10	122
22	521120	10	505
22	521131		1116
22	521132		1035
22	521139		588
22	521141		581
22	530890	10	2843
22	530911	10	3506
22	530919	10	12514
22	530921	10	307
22	530929	10	7998
22	531010	10	19670
22	531090	10	537
22	531100	10	7894
22	540110	10	6510
22	540120	10	41710
22	540211	10	7840
22	540219	10	59753
22	540220	10	40480
22	540231	10	3169
22	540232	10	3096
22	540233	10	44488
22	540234	10	542
22	540239	10	19763
22	540244	10	57222
22	540245	10	61097
22	540246	10	4299
22	540247	10	11098
22	540248	10	338
22	540249	10	7185

22	Code	10	Value	22	Code	10	Value	22	10	Code	Value
22	520522	10	496	22	521142	10	4925	22	10	540251	1653
22	520523	10	1673	22	521143	10	111	22	10	540252	2611
22	520524	10	1516	22	521149	10	111	22	10	540259	2893
22	520526	10	365	22	521151	10	213	22	10	540261	1908
22	520527	10	388	22	521152	10	280	22	10	540262	1395
22	520528	10	22987	22	521159	10	121	22	10	540269	11312
22	520531	10	2874	22	521211	10	348	22	10	540310	469
22	520532	10	195	22	521212	10	1708	22	10	540331	71778
22	520533	10		22	521213	10	2893	22	10	540332	4130
22	540333	10	27	22	550190	10	704.387	22	10	551313	5667
22	540339	10	5667	22	550200	10	48155.93	22	10	551319	9951
22	540341	10	9951	22	550311	10	3475.045	22		551321	62
22	540342	10	62	22	550319	10	10639.26	22		551323	52664
22	540349	10	52664	22	550320	10	64798.59	22		551329	2758
22	540411	10	2758	22	550330	10	40530.38	22		551331	473
22	540412	10	473	22	550340	10	704	22		551339	13855
22	540419	10	13855	22	550390	10	6254	22		551341	14702
22	540490	10	14702	22	550410	10	47987	22		551349	463
22	540500	10	463	22	550490	10	16694	22	10	551411	13109
22	540710		13109	22	550610	10	1621	22	10	551412	3330
22	540720	10	3330	22	550620	10	1260	22	10	551419	1551
22	540730	10	1551	22	550630	10	1364	22		551421	3144
22	540741		3144	22	550690	10	686	22		551422	7224
22	540742		7224	22	550700	10	868	22		551423	166
22	540743		166	22	550810	10	3402	22		551429	317
22	540744		317	22	550820	10	399	22		551430	2527
22	540751		2527	22	550911	10	288	22		551441	36149
22	540752		36149	22	550912	10	3090	22		551442	2677
22	540753		2677	22	550921	10	43381	22		551443	7333

(Continued)

Table 4.3A (Continued)

BEC category	HS	Average of ad valorem duties	Average imports	BEC category	HS	Average of ad valorem duties	Average imports	BEC category	HS	Average of ad valorem duties	Average imports
22	540754		7333	22	550922	10	4192	22	551449		43933
22	540761		43933	22	550931	10	4096	22	551511		7240
22	540769		7240	22	550932	10	5861	22	551512		345
22	540771		345	22	550941	10	55832	22	551513		1715
22	540772		1715	22	550942	10	3937	22	551519		801
22	540773		801	22	550951	10	27521	22	551521		756
22	540774		756	22	550952	10	122	22	551522		671
22	540781		671	22	550953	10	382	22	551529		3061
22	540782		3061	22	550959	10	551	22	551591		305
22	540783		305	22	550961	10	43	22	551599		793
22	540784		793	22	550962	10	9	22	551611	10	33
22	540791		33	22	550969	10	953	22	551612		1167
22	540792		1167	22	550991	10	33	22	551613		546
22	540793		546	22	550992	10	238	22	551614		233
22	540794		233	22	550999	10	3074	22	551621	10	278
22	540810	10	278	22	551011	10	8301	22	551622		927
22	540821	10	927	22	551012	10	98	22	551623		2979
22	540822		2979	22	551020	10	50	22	551624		213
22	540823		213	22	551030	10	89	22	551631	10	1385
22	540824		1385	22	551090	10	1740	22	551632	10	128
22	540831		128	22	551211	10	3314	22	551633	10	247
22	540832		3139	22	551219		16790	22	551634	10	23
22	540833		251	22	551221	10	189	22	551641	10	125
22	540834		1383	22	551229		1348	22	551642	10	385

22	550110	10	6202	22	551291	10	122	22	551643		695
22	550120	10	3337	22	551299	10	667	22	551644		41
22	550130	10	22138	22	551311	10	899	22	551691	10	170
22	550140	10	77	22	551312	10	27	22	551692	10	540
22	551693		59	22	580421		10445.99	22	600490	10	8679
22	551694		37	22	580429		20459	22	600521	10	359
22	560121	10	869	22	580430	10	328	22	600522	10	1508
22	560122	10	3294	22	580610	10	4490	22	600523	10	57
22	560129	10	1593	22	580620	10	16571	22	600524	10	23
22	560130	10	12653	22	580631	10	4516	22	600531	10	43125
22	560210	10	2727	22	580632	10	15928	22	600532	10	49185
22	560221	10	93	22	580639	10	11747	22	600533	10	897
22	560229	10	2307	22	580640	10	417	22	600534	10	881
22	560290	10	1379	22	580710	10	20351	22	600541	10	420
22	560311	10	22835	22	580790	10	4586	22	600542	10	2147
22	560312	10	10995	22	580890	10	628	22	600543	10	71
22	560313	10	8431	22	580900	10	11498	22	600544	10	23508
22	560314	10	15791	22	581010	10	157	22	600590	10	133
22	560391	10	3484	22	581091	10	266	22	600610	10	523
22	560392	10	12574	22	581092	10	754	22	600621	10	166370
22	560393	10	4765	22	581099	10	4448	53	401110	10	158718
22	560394	10	33706	22	581100	10	1247	53	401120	10	15884
22	560410	10	1808	22	590110	10	1545	53	401130	3	12547
22	560490	10	2188	22	590190	10	687	53	401140	10	1147
22	560500	10	2220	22	590210	10	986	53	401150	10	2534
22	560600	10	3254	22	590220	10	236787	53	401161	10	4230
22	560721	10	1184	22	590290	10	31631	53	401162	10	4406
22	560729	10	3937	22		10	520	53	401163	10	

(Continued)

Table 4.3A (Continued)

BEC category	HS	Average of ad valorem duties	Average imports	BEC category	HS	Average of ad valorem duties	Average imports	BEC category	HS	Average of ad valorem duties	Average imports
22	560741	10	27521	22	590310	10	110171	53	401169	10	1537
22	560749	10	122	22	590320	10	71971	53	401192	10	105
22	560750	10	382	22	590390	10	128484	53	401193	10	658
22	560790	10	551	22	590500	10	458	53	401194	10	7809
22	560811	10	43	22	590610	10	2124	53	401199	10	46329
22	560819	10	9	22	590691	10	606	53	401211	10	74
22	560890	10	953	22	590699	10	13503	53	401212	10	128
22	560900	10	33	22	590700	10	20939	53	401213	10	2524
22	580110		238	22	590800	10	703	53	401219	10	167
22	580121		3074	22	600110	10	4710	53	401220	10	1667
22	580122		8301	22	600121	10	64	53	401290	10	3690
22	580123		98	22	600122	10	685	53	401310	10	7438
22	580126		50	22	600129	10	531	53	401320	10	734
22	580131		106	22	600191	10	991	53	401390	10	2363
22	580132		253	22	600192	10	9471	53	731600	10	5774
22	580133		179	22	600199	10	929	53	830230	10	31291
22	580136		1059	22	600240	10	410	53	840710	10	193854
22	580190		385	22	600290	10	2984	53	840729	7.5	8179
22	580211	10	2	22	600310	10	60	53	840731	7.5	26
22	580219		2	22	600320	10	461	53	840732	7.5	855
22	580220	10	25	22	600330	10	433	53	840733	7.5	2368
22	580230		347	22	600340	10	374	53	840734	7.5	199904
22	580300	10	5068	22	600390	10	539	53	840810	7.5	43029
22	580410		10446	22	600410	10	12648	53	840820	7.5	594786

53	840910	7.5	19524	53	860791	10	26749
53	840991	7.5	241619	53	860799	10	111742
53	840999	7.5	515103	53	870600	10	22665
53	841111	7.5	26343	53	870710	10	38172
53	841112	7.5	248408	53	870790	10	45363
53	841121	7.5	4187	53	870810	10	40137
53	841122	7.5	30083	53	870821	10	11483
53	841181	7.5	8455	53	870829	10	305488
53	841182	7.5	83469	53	870830	10	125540
53	841191	7.5	61422	53	870840	10	458124
53	841199	7.5	285719	53	870850	10	182898
53	841210	10	647	53	870870	10	107404
53	841520	10	19725	53	870880		55310
53	850710	10	15971	53	870891	10	20982
53	850720	10	121606	53	870892	10	32083
53	850730	10	19795	53	870893	10	76152
53	850740	10	786	53	870894		133958
53	850780	10	265578	53	870895	10	69128
53	871499	20	100017	53	870899	10	1645698
53	871690	10	26185	53	871420	10	7725
53	880310	2.5	7057	53	871491	20	10170
53	880320	2.5	1196	53	871492	20	84876
53	880330	2.5	1122790	53	871493	20	2201
53	880390	10	99181	53	871494	20	4015
53	910400	10	1504	53	871495	20	776
53	940110	10	5845	53	871496	20	654
53	940120	10	28764				
53	851110	7.5	8271				

(Continued)

Table 4.3A (Continued)

BEC category	HS	Average of ad valorem duties	Average imports	BEC category	HS	Average of ad valorem duties	Average imports	BEC category	HS	Average of ad valorem duties	Average imports
53	851120	7.5	5242								
53	851130	7.5	12546								
53	851140	7.5	44200								
53	851150	7.5	41169								
53	851180	7.5	7821								
53	851190	7.5	93191								
53	851210	10	454								
53	851220	9.2	81535								
53	851230	8.8	8257								
53	851240	10	8816								
53	852721	10	41945								
53	852729	10	49689								
53	853910	10	1576								
53	854430	7.5	64189								
53	860711	10	208								
53	860712	10	11137								
53	860719	10	41326								
53	860721	10	5086								
53	860729	10	23967								
53	860730	10	22561								

Source: UN Comtrade database

Notes: (a) Missing entries in the table indicate non-availability of data. (b) Highlights in bold and underlined show the highest import tariffs in each category.

Notes

1 Kowalski et al. (2015) discuss the drivers of GVC participation, which has been measured by the backward and the forward participation ratios. They also discuss the determinants of GVC participation, which has been further categorized into policy and non-policy factors. Policy factors include import tariffs on intermediate imports, import tariffs on intermediates faced in export markets, RTA coverage of intermediates imports and exports, openness to foreign direct investment (FDI), logistics and border procedures, quality of transport infrastructure. and intellectual property protection. Non-policy factors include market size, share of manufacturing in GDP, distance to economic hubs, and distance to key manufacturing hubs.

2 In this chapter we review and present the papers related to measuring GVC trade in India. Hence all approaches such as involvement in RTAs reviewed in Kowalski et al. (2015) are not discussed in great detail here. Some of the issues will be discussed in the next chapter dealing with barriers as they relate to the policy implications for a country. See also Johnson and Noguera (2016).

3 From trade statistics, this distinction is not clear unless the imports are broken down into these categories.

4 The classification by BEC is an international product classification introduced by the UN in the early 1970s. It is a three-digit classification that groups commodities according to their main end use; that is, consumption goods, capital goods, and intermediate goods. The traded commodities are defined in terms of the Standard International Trade Classification, Revision 3 (SITC Rev. 3) and there are 19 basic categories of goods in BEC, eight of which are intermediate goods. The allocation of commodities according to their main use is based on expert judgement in BEC, which could be subjective, and use could differ according to context.

5 Exceptions are Goldar et al. (2017), Banga (2013), and Athukorala (2013), which are discussed later in the chapter.

6 However, in services (not covered in this book), India's participation is driven mainly by use of Indian intermediates in the exports of other countries.

7 Forward linkages occur when a country provides inputs to foreign partners for their export production. Backward linkages occur when countries source foreign inputs for export production.

8 Kowalski et al. (2015) observes that changes in domestic value-added embodied in exports provides a comprehensive indicator of GVC performance since they capture gains associated with exporting and are also related to changes in the measure of sophistication of imported manufacturing intermediate inputs.

9 It was 11% in 1995 to 26% in 2011. FVA or foreign value-added was highest at 65.83 in petroleum products in 2007–08 and lowest in ready-made garments at 16.44. For formula, see Chapter 2 of this book.

10 The paper examines the export performance of India and East Asian countries in seven product categories: "Office machines and automatic data processing machines" (SITC 75), "Telecommunication and recording sound equipment" (SITC 76), "Electrical machinery" (SITC 77), "Road

vehicles" (SITC 78), "Professional and scientific equipment" (SITC 87), and "Photographic apparatus" (SITC 88). It also uses an econometric analysis to explore the determinants of difference in inter-country export using the gravity model to bilateral trade flows of the total manufacturing trade and parts and components trade for the period 1996–2009.

11 Network trade or global production-sharing trade.

12 The reasons for this are discussed further in the chapter on automobiles, Chapter 6.

13 This is only a crude way of examining value chain activity. Also, this is likely to hold for countries with more backward integration.

14 Using data from UN Comtrade. See Table 4.1A in Appendix 4.1.

15 Gross export shares are less meaningful now as countries specialize in specific activities. India's share in value-added exports was around 1.9% in 2009 (OECD 2013).

16 HS refers to the Harmonized System of classification. The Standard International Trade Classification (SITC) and HS are two different trade classifications, the main difference being that the SITC is focused more on the economic functions of products at various stages of development, whereas the HS deals with a precise breakdown of the products' individual categories. (http://legacy.intracen.org/mas/sitchs.htm)

17 HS has been used rather than SITC since the tariffs examined later are in terms of the HS 6 digit classification.

18 www.ihs.com/products/fats-and-oils-industry-chemicals-economics-handbook.html

19 Refer to Chapter 13 of this book.

20 See Chapter 2 and Chapter 5 of this book.

21 As discussed in Chapter 6 of this book.

22 RCA is computed using the following formula:

$$RCAij = (Xij / Xi) / (Xwj / Xw)$$

where Xij represents country i's export of commodity j, Xwj represents world exports of commodity j, Xi represents the total exports of country i, and Xw represents total world exports.

23 RCA proposed by Balassa (1965) is used as a measure of competitiveness in international markets. This measure has been critiqued for it is not easily comparable across goods nor does it lend itself to ordinal ranking. That is, if the value is two times for a product, it does not necessarily mean that the country is twice as competitive in that product. Also, it is an "ex post" measure since it is based on trade flows. However, if it is used to merely indicate whether a country is a significant exporter (and hence must be competitive) by showing a higher export share in its export bundle, it can be used to indicate competitiveness (Kowalski et al. 2015).

24 The connection between intermediate inputs and exports has been analyzed in the case of Chinese firms by Feng et al. (2016). They found that firms that expanded their intermediate input imports expanded the volume of their exports.

25 See also Srivastava and Sen (2015).

26 There is a close correlation between the HS and the SITC system. In Table 4.1, the conversion table between basic headings, sub-groups,

and groups of the HS 2012 Edition, and the SITC, Revision 3 has been used to generate the number of intermediate categories according to HS. The concordance of the UN HS-SITC has been used to match the BEC categories.

27 Sturgeon and Memedovic (2010) analyze the trend of trade in intermediates by combining the BEC categories of consumption and capital goods as "final goods" and the BEC classified intermediates are treated as "intermediates." The paper finds, contrary to what would be expected, the trade in intermediates (as a share of world imports) has actually declined. The authors try to address this problem by further modifying the BEC classification, as they find it to be too aggregative an approach. Thus, the intermediates are split into two categories: generic and true.

28 OECD (2013) notes that tariffs, while low in developed countries, are not always so in developing countries. Tariffs are cumulative when intermediate inputs are traded across borders several times. Tariffs can reach high levels when downstream firms pay tariffs on imported inputs and face tariffs on the full value of their exports.

29 The duty indicates whether it is prohibitive to import an item. The duty adds a margin of cost to the final good, if used to produce for the export market. Indian firms also complain of duty inversion or intermediates being taxed at rates higher than the final goods. However, apart from the duty, the ease of importing also is important. We return to this point in the chapter dealing with barriers.

30 We do not focus on this category in this book. However, it is an important part of the agro-based food value chains.

31 Also not discussed in this book; however, there are several issues related to this item.

32 We focus on this in Chapter 13 of this book. The value-added product is one of India's leading export items.

33 This is a category that is purely for consumption.

34 Natural gas is used as feedstock in the petrochemical industry as well as a fuel. This will be discussed in the chapter on petrochemicals.

35 This sector is very important since the manufacturing capability is absent in the country. We discuss some of the issues related to this sector in the chapter on semiconductor microchips.

36 "n.e.s." means not elsewhere specified.

37 The automobile sector is discussed later in Chapter 6 of this book.

38 Some duties have been reduced in the Union Budget of India 2017–18. See http://indiabudget.nic.in/budget.asp (accessed on 24 August 2017).

39 Items on which duties have been reduced include liquefied natural gas, nickel, vegetable tanning extracts, and certain capital goods (http://pib.nic.in/newsite/PrintRelease.aspx?relid=157851)

40 Hausman et al. (2005) See http://atlas.cid.harvard.edu/explore/tree_map/export/pri/all/show/2015/ (accessed on 2 February 2018).

41 The *Atlas* has been used to identify sectors where a country could develop competence in the future (Hausman et al. 2005). Kowalski et al. (2015) use a measure of import sophistication using Hausman et al.'s (2005) PRODY indicator to identify the comparative advantage weighted per capita GDP of exported products.

References

Athukorala, P.-C. 2013. 'How India Fits into Global Production Sharing: Experience, Prospects and Policy Options,' Working Paper No. 2013/13. Arndt-Corden Department of Economics, Crawford School of Public Policy ANU College of Asia and the Pacific.

Balassa, B. 1965. 'Trade Liberalization and Revealed Comparative Advantage,' *Manchester School of Economic and Social Studies*, 33: 99–123.

Banga, R. 2013. 'Measuring Value in Global Value Chains,' Regional Value Chains Background Paper. UNCTAD.

Feng, L., Li, Z. and D. Swenson. 2016. 'The Connection Between Imported Intermediate Inputs and Exports: Evidence from Chinese Firms,' *Journal of International Economics*, 101: 86–101.

Goldar, B., Das, D.K., Sengupta, S. and P.C. Das. 2017. 'Domestic Value Addition and Foreign Content: An Analysis of India's Exports from 1995 to 2011,' Working Paper 332. ICRIER.

Hausman, R., Hwang, J. and D. Rodrik. 2005. 'What You Export Matters,' Working Paper 11905. Cambridge, MA: National Bureau of Economic Research.

Hummels, D., Ishii, J. and K.M. Yi. 2001. 'The Nature and Growth of Vertical Specialization in World Trade,' *Journal of International Economics*, 54: 75–96.

Johnson Robert, C. and Guillermo Noguera. 2016. 'A Portrait of Trade in Value Added Over Four Decades,' Working Paper 22974. Cambridge MA: National Bureau of Economic Research.

Kowalski, P. et al. 2015. 'Participation of Developing Countries in Global Value Chains: Implications for Trade and Trade-Related Policies,' Trade Policy Paper No. 179, Paris: OECD Publishing.

Mirodout, S., Lanz, R. and A. Ragoussis. 2009. 'Trade in Intermediate Goods and Services.' Trade Policy Paper No. 93. OECD.

OECD. 2013. *Interconnected Economies: Benefiting From Global Value Chains*. Report on global value chains, DSTI/IND (2013) 2 Draft. Paris: OECD.

Srivastava, S. and R. Sen. 2015. 'Production Fragmentation in Trade of Manufactured Goods in India: Prospects and Challenges,' *Asia-Pacific Development Journal*, 22(1): 33–66.

Sturgeon, T. and O. Memedovic. 2010. 'Mapping Global Value Chains: Intermediate Goods Trade and Structural Trade in the World Economy,' Working Paper 05/2010. UNIDO.

5 Integration of developing countries in GVCs and the case of India

Survey findings

Fragmented production is not new: for years, low- and medium- income countries (LMICs) have imported parts from developed countries for the assembly of local goods for the domestic market (Taglioni and Winkler 2016). However, today, value addition takes place on the imported parts (due to the fragmentation of production), which are then exported to other countries. Baldwin and Lopez-Gonzalvez (2013) have coined the term "import to export" to explain this phenomenon. Baldwin (2011) contends that since 1970 seven countries (China, Korea, India, Indonesia, Thailand, Turkey, and Poland) have gained more than 1 percentage point of world manufacturing gross domestic product (GDP). (All the G7 countries are share-losers over this period.) Apart from India, all the manufacturing sectors of these countries are heavily involved in the international supply chains of Japan (the East Asians) or Germany (Poland and Turkey).[1]

For countries that have embraced and integrated into global value chains (GVCs), the challenge is getting the GVC to work for their country's development. For other countries, the challenge is to understand what has to be done to integrate into GVCs. The depth of integration in the South Asian region has barely increased since the mid-1990s, unlike in other income groups, signalling that the region has yet to gain momentum. Moreover, the complexity and quality of exported goods has been modest. Policymakers in such countries could take note of the following factors (which are often ignored): 1. It is not necessary to produce for the entire chain; there are benefits even to specialization or producing for parts of the chain.[2] 2. Competition is fierce and participation is not automatic, as countries face many challenges in entering international production.[3] 3. Imports have to be valued – GVCs have made imports very important and low- and medium-income countries are not only importing parts but absorbing foreign technology and know-how through imports.[4]

From a policy perspective, how GVCs integrate into the economy is critical (Taglioni and Winkler 2016) and the role of the lead firm is very important in this context.[5] The role of the government may be limited if the lead firms make most of the decisions, and linkages with the rest of the economy remain weak (Taglioni and Winkler 2016). For host countries, benefits from technology transfers, knowledge spillovers, and increase in value addition can translate into better jobs, and so on only if links with the rest of the economy are strong.[6] This latter factor is crucial in adjudging the role of GVCs in a country's development. The sector of engagement is also vital since the role of the lead firm varies from sector to sector, as do the types of governance within the chains.[7]

This chapter will provide evidence from India's engagement in GVCs. Why does India lag? This chapter will present broad findings from the sectors surveyed in India, focusing on their strengths and weaknesses. It will list the barriers to integration faced by all the sectors and suggest ways of overcoming them.

Integration into GVCs

As we saw in Chapter 4, India's integration into GVCs remains nascent despite the strong growth in trade flows over the last two decades. The share of foreign value-added embedded in the production of exports is low even compared with the 20% average observed in developing and emerging market economies. The domestic value-added embodied in foreign final demand was 20% for India in 2011, while the foreign value-added in domestic final demand was about 25% for India in the same year.[8] Combining the two measures from the buyer's and seller's perspective gives the GVC participation index.[9] As we have seen in Chapter 4, India's backward and forward participation has been low at 22% and 19%, respectively, in 2009 (OECD 2013b).

GVC participation[10] also depends on attracting foreign investment and internationalizing domestic firms (Blyde 2014). How can countries internationalize their domestic firms? This can be done in two ways: first, countries (and firms) can export to international buyers and, second, firms can become domestic final producers that import intermediates. Thus, identification of tasks becomes important for a country. Participation in GVCs then depends critically on competence and competitiveness in performance of specific tasks, and thus on the education and skills of a country's workforce and its entrepreneurs (OECD 2013a). Since participation in GVCs is not assured (Taglioni and Winkler 2016), countries must compete with each other to enter

GVCs. Some major factors determining successful integration are predictability, reliability, and time sensitivity. These, along with protection of property rights, are essential for attracting foreign investment. Connectivity, too, plays a major role in determining whether an input will be sourced domestically or from abroad. There are a few aspects which further need to be noted in this context and are discussed in the following sections.

Evidence of integration into specific sectors

India's participation in GVC or participation index has been noted previously. Entering a GVC requires answering two questions: first, what tasks will the firm (country) perform in the GVC and, second, what form of governance does the GVC follow? The identification of tasks relates to the three steps that countries need to take: first, identify sectors with revealed comparative advantage (RCA)[11] based on value-added exports; second, analyze the upstream and downstream output of a GVC product; and, third, identify the tasks within a broad sector or value chain that creates the largest domestic value-added. In Chapter 4, we analyze and presented an analysis based on RCA computations. The values of RCAs based on value-added exports have been calculated for India by Gasiorek et al. (2015) for various sectors. Their analysis suggests that for sectors such as manufacturing and recycling (ISIC 37), the RCA values considering both gross exports and value-added exports are positive. This means that this industry has been successful in terms of providing inputs into Indian exports in other industries as well as in terms of direct exports.

Methodology of the study

Sturgeon and Memedovic (2010) argue that the list of true (customized) intermediates can be obtained by field research and vetting of intermediates by experts. For this study, a primary survey was conducted between 2014 and 2015.[12] An extensive questionnaire was designed to capture the elements of value chain activity in India. The pilot survey was conducted between January 2014 and March 2014 in three sectors – apparel, cables, and automotive components – covering about 20 firms. The findings from the pilot were presented in a workshop conducted on 3–4 April 2014.[13] Based on the feedback received at the workshop and interactions with industry associations and other stakeholders, the main survey was conducted between August 2014 and February 2015.

Survey[14]

The main survey[15] was conducted between August 2014 and February 2015 in the five sectors selected. These segments (or sectors) were: passenger cars in the automobile industry, reactive dyes and specialty chemicals in the chemicals industry, semiconductor microchips in information technology (IT), and formulations in the pharmaceutical industry. Table 5.1 presents a snapshot of the main survey.

As noted previously, entering a GVC requires answering two questions: first, what tasks will the firm (country) perform in the GVC and, second, what form of governance does the GVC follow? Based on our survey of firms (and secondary sources), we have tried to identify where India falters in each of the steps outlined previously for the identification of tasks. Table 5.2 indicates that value-added exports occur in most segments, barring the semiconductor microchip, for which only the design is done in India.

Table 5.1 Coverage of the survey

Sector	Segment	Cities covered	Number of firms interviewed
Automotive	1 Passenger cars and auto components	1 Delhi/national capital region (NCR)	8
			9
			3
		2 Chennai	5
		3 Pune	1
		4 Haryana	
		5 Vapi	
Chemicals	1 Reactive dyes	1 Mumbai	10
		2 Ahmedabad	1
	2 Specialty chemicals	1 Mumbai	12
		2 Ankleshwar	4
		3 Surat	2
		4 Vapi	2
		5 Kolkata	2
Electronics	1 Semiconductor microchips	1 Bengaluru	19
Pharmaceuticals	1 Formulations	1 Mumbai	11
		2 Ahmedabad	4
		3 Ankleshwar	3
		4 Vapi	1
Total			97

Source: Authors' compilation based on survey

Table 5.2 Identification of tasks

	Identification of tasks		
	If value-added exports occurring from India	*If upstream and downstream segments are part of GVC*	*Tasks*
Automotives	Yes	Yes	Casting and forging
Chemicals (specialty)	Yes	No	–
Diamond	Yes	No	Cutting of raw diamond
Garments	Yes	No	Embroidery, embellishments
Petrochemicals	Yes	Yes	–
Pharmaceuticals (formulations)	Yes	No	Stabilizing
Reactive dye	Yes	Yes	–
Semiconductor microchip	No	No	Design

Source: Authors' compilation based on survey

Table 5.2 indicates also that, in some cases, notably the specialty chemicals and garments segment, neither the upstream nor downstream outputs are part of the GVC. In the case of garments, most firms are not part of GVCs. Firms that are part of a GVC are adept in certain tasks such as embroidery or embellishments.[16] In the case of specialty chemicals, due to the absence or high costs of certain raw materials, the backward specialization is absent in most sub-segments.[17] Thus it is important to examine specific sectors in great detail to understand where a country may be faltering.

Upgrading and learning

The challenges posed by GVCs are different since countries must not only enter international production, but also must upgrade to higher value-added products. Otherwise, competition can lead to production shifting to lower cost producers and countries. The challenges faced by countries include risks faced in integration in the global trading system, along with complexities and uncertainties associated with organizing production across several locations.

How can countries internationalize their domestic firms? This can be done in two ways: first, countries (and firms) can export to international buyers and, second, firms can become domestic final producers that import intermediates. Thus, identification of tasks becomes important for a country. Participation in GVCs then depends critically on competence and competitiveness in performance of specific tasks, and thus on the education and skills of a country's workforce and its entrepreneurs (OECD 2013a). For participation and upgrading within value chains, investment in innovation and knowledge-based capital, such as research and development (R&D), intellectual property, software, and data, as well as economic competencies such as organizational know-how and branding, are crucial.[18]

The difference in upgrading in several of the sectors that have been surveyed emerges (see Table 5.3) from two factors: first, the nature of the governance of the chain and the role played by the lead firms[19] and, second, the nature of the technology and knowledge in each sector varies. For example, in certain industries such as the chemicals industry, the knowledge and production processes are proprietary and upgrading requires investment in R&D.[20] However, in sectors such as garments, production processes are more standardized and upgrading can come from use of newer raw materials. Policy formulation must take these details into cognizance.

Table 5.3 Evidence of integration and upgrading in India

	Integration	GVC governance	Learning	Upgrading
Automobiles	Yes	Relational	Yes	Yes
Chemicals (specialty)	No	Relational/ modular	No	Limited
Diamonds	Yes	Market	Yes	No
Garments	No	Hierarchy/ captive	No	Limited
Petrochemicals	Yes	Relational/ hierarchy	Yes	No
Pharmaceuticals (formulations)	Yes	Modular/ market	No	Limited
Reactive dyes	Yes	Market	Yes	No
Semiconductor microchips	Yes	Modular	No	No

Source: Authors' compilation based on survey

For participation and upgrading within value chains, investment in innovation and knowledge-based capital, such as R&D, intellectual property, software, and data, as well as economic competencies such as organizational know-how and branding, are crucial.[21] Labour skills score high (particularly in the information and communication technology (ICT), textiles, and apparel and tourism sectors) as a factor influencing investment decisions. In general, countries that are tied in to GVCs generally have higher skill levels than those that are not, and participation in these value chains sharpens that distinction as firms and workers learn (OECD 2014). Evidence shows that over the period 1995–2008 in developing countries, there has been an increase in demand for high-skilled labour driven by an increase in demand for high-skill workers in services, though in some countries (e.g. China, India, and France) manufacturing also added to high-skill demand (OECD 2014). Evidence from surveyed sectors is shown in Table 5.4.

Table 5.4 Role played by lead firms in GVCs – employment generation and skilling by sector

Sector	Role of lead firms	Employment generation	Skilling
Automobiles	Catalyst for innovation, harbingers of technology, financial investment, and skilling workforce	Significant	Significant
Chemicals (specialty)	Heralded innovation and stimulated demand	Low	Moderate
Pharmaceuticals (formulations)	Significant role in establishment of IP compliance	Significant	Significant
Reactive dye	Introduction of environmental standards and greener options	Significant	Moderate
Petrochemicals	Overcoming problems of feedstock access, attracting investment and forward integration	Moderate	Significant
Diamond	Skilling workforce and attracting important investors	Significant	Significant
Garments	Reduction of lead times, standardization of the production process, and preferential transportation and logistics through long-term relationships	Significant	Moderate

(*Continued*)

Table 5.4 (Continued)

Sector	Role of lead firms	Employment generation	Skilling
Paper	Introducers of modern technology	Moderate	–
Semiconductor microchip	Innovation leading to reduction in costs	Significant	Significant

Source: Authors' compilation based on survey

Impediments to integration in GVCs: the case of India

This section focuses on the barriers that have been responsible for developing countries such as India lagging behind in integration into GVCs. It identifies government policy–related, firm-level, and other constraints, which have specifically affected transfer of knowledge and learning capabilities in different sectors. A country's competitiveness can be measured at three levels: capacity to join GVCs, capacity to remain part of GVCs, and capacity to move up the value chain within GVCs. Many barriers or incentives to trade are common to trade in general, but some can be specific to GVC trade (OECD, WTO and World Bank Group 2014). For instance, participation in GVCs requires further opening to imports and an integrated framework of analysis encompassing goods, services, and FDI; or imposing of private standards by a lead firm. Assessing the impact of participation may require assessing the location of specific stages of production (e.g. anti-dumping measures). Such barriers may vary, as GVCs have different shapes and patterns of governance according to sectors and lead firms (Cattaneo et al. 2013).

Business environment

All firms surveyed in this research study were of the opinion that future support should target improving the business environment. Some factors can change the structures of value chains. Gereffi et al. (2005) argued that improved standards, IT, and the capabilities of suppliers can shift governance structures from captive and hierarchal towards relational, modular, and market governance, which offers more opportunities for joining, and upgrading in, a value chain. Suppliers from all sectors ranked lack of access to finance (in particular, trade finance) as a major obstacle in the way of entering, establishing, or moving up value chains.

SMEs in sectors such as dyes and intermediates emphasized the importance of effective support coming via financing[22] (access and incentives for domestic and foreign investment). Lead firms focused trade facilitation and better public-private sector coordination. Labour force training is also recognized as an effective way to increase supply-side capacity.

GVCs ease capacity constraints since a country does not need to develop a fully integrated industry to participate in international trade. Nonetheless, capacities and productivity (and costs) remain important for decisions by foreign investors and lead firms considering various locations for outsourcing and/or off-shoring around the world. Competitiveness and attractiveness for foreign investors is determined by ease of access to efficient services and infrastructure in the host country. This includes access to efficient transportation networks, energy (cheap and reliable), finance, telecommunications, and IT/ITES etc. For instance, high investment in physical infrastructure is considered as an important reason for low trade costs faced by South East Asian countries.

Costs

India, in particular, has faced a gamut of issues, ranging from lack of political will, resource (finance and skill) constraints, mis-management of resources, technological backwardness, and operational issues in the past. These are also reflected in the trade restrictiveness and performance indicators published every year by organizations such as the World Bank and World Economic Forum (WEF).[23] Transportation and shipping costs and inadequate infrastructure were cited as major obstacles. Among lead firms across all sectors, customs procedures rank high as a particular obstacle in bringing developing country suppliers into their value chains (refer to Table 5.5).

Role of FDI

GVC participation also depends on attracting foreign investment. The role of FDI in promoting technological and other spillovers has been studied at length.[24] Decisions to invest and do business in a foreign country can be driven by myriad factors, the first of which are structural variables.[25] Second, tariff/non-tariff measures and business climate/environment influence the competitiveness of domestic companies and determine openness and attractiveness for foreign investors.

The host country's potential for GVC participation can be assessed against the capacity for scale production (includes compliance of demand on production and labour cost, and standards); availability of services necessary to support production and market integration (including complying with demands on production quantity and turnaround time); education and skills of workforce matching the needs of global producers and buyers; capacity for innovation; and investment and tax incentives. Questions related to barriers were directed to firms in different sectors. Firms were asked to rank the main barriers to participation as suppliers in value chains, or as the main drivers of lead firms' decisions to source and invest (i.e. to link them to their value chains). Table 5.1B in Appendix 5.1 shows how India fares with respect to critical factors affecting GVC participation.

Table 5.5 Summary of factors impeding GVC participation in India

	Impeding factor	Evidence of obstacle
Policy related		
Horizontal	Liberalized FDI policy	Electronics
	Trade policy factors	Automobiles
Targeted	Transport and infrastructure/ logistics	All industries
	Institutional and legal frameworks	Electronics/IT
Natural		
	Geography – distance from shipping routes	All industries
	Climate	–
Firm specific		
	Capability to meet international product and quality standards	Clothing, Specialty chemicals, Pharmaceuticals
	Access to finance	Dyestuffs, Electronics, Pharmaceuticals, R&D
	R&D	Dyestuffs, Formulations (pharmaceuticals), Specialty chemicals
	Creating sustainable industrial clusters	Dyestuffs, Specialty chemicals
	Human capital related – low-cost knowledge base	Dyestuffs, Electronics
	Technology	Dyestuffs, IT/electronics

Source: Authors' compilation based on survey

Investment in innovation is considered an important driver of GVCs. With the shift in demand to emerging markets, lead firms are required to define strategies to set up innovation centres in developing countries, which can provide a significant boost to developing countries' exports (Govindarajan and Trimble 2012). For this, it is important that the host developing country be able to develop capacities, which rely on education and skills. It is often observed that the highest proportion of value creation in a GVC is found in upstream activities such as new concept development, R&D, or manufacturing of key parts and components, and in downstream activities such as marketing, branding, or customer service. Such activities involve tacit, non-codified knowledge in areas such as original design, creation and management of cutting-edge technology and complex systems, and management or organizational know-how (OECD 2014). However, these features have been lacking or missing in India's case. As indicated in Table 5.1A, the need for R&D has been emphasized repeatedly by firms, particularly in the pharmaceutical and specialty chemicals segment.

Table 5.5 summarizes the barriers identified in the course of the survey across the various sectors (the format of this table has been taken from ADB-ADBI 2015).

Role of government policy

The role of government policy cannot be emphasized enough. Policies to improve connectivity with global markets could address: traditional barriers to trade (from the negotiation of preferential market access (PMA) to the reduction of domestic tariffs); customs (efficiency and procedures, including rules of origin); logistics; and transportation and telecommunications (regulatory and infrastructure dimensions, with greater focus on telecommunications for off-shoring of services, and transportation for goods).

The OECD (2014) emphasizes that GVCs do not respond to piecemeal approaches to policy changes. Rather, a holistic approach is needed, in co-operation with the international community and businesses (WEF 2012). OECD (2015) discusses how regional co-operation can be an effective strategy to promote integration into value chains by addressing regional bottlenecks.

Many of the barriers have resulted from the fact that India has adopted a largely piecemeal approach to policymaking with regard to value chains till now. Targeted policies have been few and only more recently put into place. The organization of the domestic segment of the value chain should go hand-in-hand with its international counterpart. For example, the benefits of efficient transportation and logistics at the border can be undermined by the inefficiency of domestic links (e.g. the unreliability or high cost of domestic transportation, cold chain for fresh products). This expands to all forms of business organizations, from production clusters to professional associations and export promotion programmes (Cattaneo et al. 2013).

Issues in compliance of standards

Standards are key elements of the functioning of GVCs. Lead firms rely increasingly on global standards to reduce complexities of transactions as they place new demands on value chains. These standards establish rules for information exchange, shape firm behaviour, and ensure quality in GVCs. They enable codification of both product and process specifications to ensure that a range of global suppliers can consistently deliver quality end products. They are industry specific and constantly evolving. These include both process and product, public and private; and these need to be respected throughout the value chain at every stage of production. Where local standards and certification/accreditation meet international standards and best practices, the costs of value chain management are significantly reduced, increasing the attractiveness of the country. GVCs therefore make a strong case for regulatory convergence, harmonization, mutual recognition, and diffusion of international standards.

Failure to comply with these standards can result in exclusion from the GVCs (Gereffi et al. 2011). Demands to comply with standards are on most participants in the GVC, well beyond first-tier providers. Inadequate standards can unduly raise the cost of local production and/or create unnecessary obstacles to trade. Excessively low or badly enforced local standards minimize the backward linkages and positive spillover effects of FDI and offshore production in a country: inputs will have to be imported to meet the lead firm's standards and local tasks be confined to basic transformation/manufacturing. Excessively high local standards are equally prohibitive for intra-GVC transactions and could constitute unnecessary obstacles to trade or protectionism in disguise. The adjustment is a gradual process that takes time. Authors have suggested that there exists is a strong case for multi-stakeholder dialogue and co-operation in enforcement of standards (Lee et al. 2012; Cadot et al. 2012). Public standards, public infrastructure for certification/accreditation, and enforcement by public authorities of health/safety/environmental rules are essential to attract production segments.

On the issue of standards,[26] firms in the pharmaceutical sector pointed out that standards are poor in India, quality checks are not well defined, know-how for standardization is lacking, and there is lack of uniformity between products produced in different states as well as in different seasons. The need for quality control was emphasized.

Logistics

India fares poorly in the various logistics performance and efficiency indices compiled internationally. In various indicators, it ranks behind many developed Asian economies such as Japan, Korea, Taiwan, and even emerging markets such as China, Malaysia, and Thailand, including Taiwan.

In the World Bank's International Logistics Performance Index (LPI) 2016,[27] India ranked 35th among 160 countries with a score of 3.03, suggesting modest performance in the constituent parameters. Other indicators which suggest modest performance in logistics are the "Trading across Border" parameter of the "Ease of Doing Business" indicator[28] published by the World Bank; and the "Trade Facilitation Indicator" developed by the OECD.[29]

India's position had deteriorated significantly in the International LPI ranking between 2012 and 2014 but substantially improved in the last two years. The improvement has come about because of policy reforms taken at the domestic level particularly in automation in customs and enhancing the speed of infrastructure development in highways and airports. Recognizing strong linkages between the performance of logistics services and growth of manufacturing and participation in global production networks and value chains, the Government of India has ambitious plans for the sector's development and improve its ranking in the international indices in the coming years. Business environment in this sector has been gradually liberalized to attract foreign investment. In April 2016, India signed and made commitments to implement the WTO Trade Facilitation Agreement, which contains provisions for expediting movement, release, and clearance of goods, through measures for co-operation between customs and other authorities on trade facilitation and customs compliance issues. Logistics is a key component of this Agreement.

In the near future, in order to keep up with its GDP growth, India needs to develop multi-modal infrastructure to facilitate inter-modal traffic that is flexible and cost-effective. Network growth including expansion of ports, improved hinterland connectivity, increased road and rail capacity, and development of coastal and inland waterways can accelerate performance in logistics.

Regulations

Trade policy factors such as tariff restrictions and lack of harmonization in standards are tackled through multilateral or bilateral forums from time to time. Entry into RTAs can further enhance GVC activity (Orefice and Rocha 2014; Baldwin and Lopez-Gonzalez 2013).[30] It is possible to design, at the domestic as well as international level, supply chain agreements that combine a number of policies useful for facilitation of merchandise and services flows within GVCs, and that can link the private sector to trade and competitiveness strategies (WEF 2012).

Intra-governmental coordination is extremely important to gainful GVC participation. The cost of administrative burdens is magnified in GVCs, where management coordination is a major challenge. Cooperation at the inter-ministerial level helps to ensure that infrastructure, education, investment, and trade policies jointly contribute to development goals.

Table 5.6 highlights some points related to regulations that firms revealed during the survey. The details of this table can be found in Table 5.2A.

India can do a lot to facilitate GVCs simply by coordinating the activities of different policymaking and implementation bodies. Important areas of reform are reduction of cumulative value of tariffs, reduction of administrative burden associated with traceability of products by measures such as increasing the staff, harmonization/ mutual recognition of standards along the value chains, and reduction of barriers at the border, including customs and trade facilitation processes.

The need of the hour is for India to integrate into GVCs, to lift productivity levels across sectors and create jobs. Greater participation in GVCs can help foster structural transformation (for instance, through export diversification) and create the possibility to absorb technology and skills from abroad.

Table 5.6 Summary of barriers based on our survey

Regulatory processes	Incentives	Approvals	Environmental	Others
Multiple checks at ports of same documents: Customs, Central Excise Office, Ministry of Finance/Reserve Bank of India (RBI), Directorate General of Foreign Trade (DGFT) (Dyestuffs)	Incentivize exports (Agrochemicals)	Regulatory approvals are high for agro and pharmaceuticals (Specialty chemicals)	International pollution norms are strict – we can change them to our own benefit (Dyestuffs)	Archaic labour laws (Automobiles)
Government policies are restrictive – need too many permissions (Specialty chemicals)	Inverted duty structure – intermediates and final products – as also voiced by SIAM from time to time. Without high level of localization, companies cannot manage to stay competitive in today's times (Automobiles)	Realization certificate of shipping bills can be recalled on yearly basis (Dyestuffs)	Pollution control and regulations have become more stringent (Dyestuffs)	Taxation structure – 56–57% – highest in the world –> Need for goods and services tax (GST) (Auto-components)
India is not business friendly (Specialty chemicals)			No Objection Certificates (NOCs): Environmental clearances are a problem (Pharmaceuticals, Specialty chemicals)	Bribes are common
Multiple clearances and too many holidays (Automobiles) Regulations are needed for the after-market (Automobiles)				

Source: Authors' compilation based on survey

Notes: The sectors where these barriers were observed are in parentheses.

Conclusion

As has been discussed in this chapter, each country needs to evaluate the following questions in the context of GVCs: What is its capacity to join a GVC? What is its capacity to remain part of the GVC? And, finally, what is the capacity of the country to move up the value chain? Depending on where a country is located with respect to a specific GVC, the answers to these questions will guide the policy that the country needs to take. For example, if a country is at the first stage of GVC activity and looking to join a GVC, then other sets of questions needs to be examined. These include: What tasks will the firm (country) perform in the GVC? What is the governance structure in the GVCs that the country is participating in? The benefits from integrating into GVCs will accrue and be enhanced if the GVC sector is integrated into the rest of the economy; hence, it is vital to examine these linkages. In the case of India, we have examined the tasks that the firms are excelling in the context of the several GVCs that have been examined in this book. Also, as we have noted value-added exports are occurring in most of the segments examined.

Coming to the question of moving up the value chain or upgrading, there are two factors that have to be taken into account. First, what is the role of the lead firm in the governance of the chain and, second, what is the nature of technology in the sector? Again, in the context of India, we have observed that, in the chemicals industry, the knowledge and production processes are proprietary and upgrading requires investment in R&D, while, in garments, production processes are more standardized and upgrading can come from use of newer raw materials. The role of the lead firm is of paramount importance in upgrading. In a quasi-hierarchical chain, buyers imposed their conditions concerning product design, marketing, and branding on garment producers (Giuliani et al. 2005). Upgrading is likely to be lowest in such cases compared to a situation where the process is collaborative (Ray et al. 2016). Thus, the process of upgrading is sector specific and efforts to achieve upgrading have to be seen in the context of the sector that is being targeted. Upgrading is neither automatic nor does it provide a country the capability to carry out the entire range of activities to compete in the global economy (Navas-Aleman 2011). This has the following implications for policymakers.

What policymakers need to note

Policymakers in countries could take note of the following factors: 1. It is not necessary to produce for the entire chain; there are benefits even to specialization or producing for parts of the chain. 2. Competition is fierce and participation is not automatic, as countries face many challenges in entering international production. 3. Participation in GVCs also occurs through imports as low- and medium-income countries are not only importing parts but absorbing foreign technology and know-how through imports.

What the government needs to do

Participation in GVCs depends on certain factors, as has been discussed in the chapter. India can do a lot to facilitate GVCs simply by coordinating the activities of different policymaking and implementation bodies. Important areas of reform are reduction of cumulative value of tariffs, reduction of administrative burden associated with traceability of products by measures such as increasing the staff, harmonization/mutual recognition of standards along the value chains, and reduction of barriers at the border, including customs and trade facilitation processes.

Appendix 5.1

Table 5.1A Nature of Indian industry and R&D in sector

Sector	GVC structure	Nature of Indian industry	R&D intensity[*]	R&D in India
Automobiles	Relational	6th largest producer in world	Medium high	Need for more R&D
Chemicals (specialty)	Relational/ modular	7th largest producer in the world (Chemicals)	Medium high	Need for more R&D
Diamond	Market	Full chain not present	Artisanal[#]	None
Garments	Hierarchy/ captive	Large domestics market GVC integration in niche segments	Low tech	Limited
Petrochemicals	Relational/ hierarchy	Due to feedstock problems, capacity low in certain segments	Medium low	Need for more R&D
Pharmaceuticals (formulations)	Modular/market	Largest supplier of generics to the world	High tech	Need for more R&D
Reactive dye	Market	World production share 40%	Medium high	Need for more R&D
Semiconductor microchip	Modular	Full chain not present	High tech	Limited

Source: Authors' compilation based on survey

Notes: [*]Based on OECD 2011. ISIC Rev. 3 Technology Intensity Definition and Ray 2011.
[#]Depends on skill of the worker in cutting gems. Formal R&D conducted in cutting machines in Israel.

Table 5.2A Groups of critical factors (affecting GVC participation)*

Group 1: capability and competitiveness	Group 2: international business	Group 3: access to resources	Group 4: macro conditions
1. Quality of product and conditions New molecules are not coming; scope for process improvements (Specialty chemicals) Quality of Indian construction chemicals is poor, market is only developing in India (Specialty chemicals) Limitations of our technology/ inadequate infrastructure with wide-ranging implications including not fit for introducing all our technology in cars (Automotive) Technology upgradation is needed (Automotive)	1. Foreign rules and regulations India has no duty drawback schemes unlike China (Dyestuffs) India doesn't have crash testing facility (Automotive) No benefits from government – duty drawbacks for intermediates in China (Automotive) Concessions as in China (Automotive)	1. Access to finance India does not have large capital base/funds (Specialty chemicals) Finance is also a problem (Specialty chemicals) In the past many multinational companies (MNCs) did not flourish in India because of funding issues along with no consistent demand (Specialty chemicals) Many MNCs have not stood the test of time in India. There are funding problems, pressure to continually innovate, cannot make huge investments in advance for products whose demand is not there, stock market is volatile (Specialty chemicals)	1. Stable foreign currency exchange China is managing its exchange rate, which can be a problem for India (Automotive)

(Continued)

Table 5.2A (Continued)

Group 1: capability and competitiveness	Group 2: international business	Group 3: access to resources	Group 4: macro conditions
Technology is not there – costs are high (Dyestuffs)	India's rules and regulations in the industry should be on a par with China (Pharmaceuticals)	Lucrative market in chronic diseases. But we have funding problem in developing the ecosystem in the country to tap this market (Pharmaceuticals)	
Technology not well developed – our intermediates emit a lot of pollutants (Dyestuffs)		Scope for improvement in automation (requires higher investment). This will improve quality (Automotive)	
2. Innovation and design	2. Familiarity of foreign business practices	2. Logistics efficiency	2. Cost of inputs
R&D is primarily concentrated in upstream segment (Specialty chemicals)	Foreign suppliers (excluding China) are better than the local suppliers (Automotive)	Power-intensive processes cannot be set up in India (Specialty chemicals)	Feedstock problem, unlike the EU (Specialty chemicals)
R&D and innovation are lacking. Global companies are spending 3–5% on R&D, while India is spending just 0.5%. Plants are not up to world standards compared with countries like Germany (Specialty chemicals)		Transportation problems from PCPIRs (Specialty chemicals)	Cheap imports from China in basic chemicals such as phosphorus are killing our industry (Specialty chemicals)

Westerners – companies like BASF (Germany), Dow (US), Japan. Entry barriers for Indian companies are high (Specialty chemicals)	(Specialty chemicals)	Ethylene Oxide and Propylene Oxide – Reliance (thousands of tonnes of Ethylene Oxide are used in India) (Specialty chemicals)
R&D is a problem (Specialty chemicals)	Infrastructure is poor (Specialty chemicals)	Dependence on China is a real threat in reactive dyes (Dyestuffs)
India is not strong in discovering new molecules. We are not doing discovery (Pharmaceuticals)	Infrastructure bottlenecks: road, water, power, gas for paints (Automotive)	High dependence on China: 30% of product costs (Dyestuffs)
Indian companies' share in R&D is insignificant (Pharmaceuticals)	High proportion of logistics in total cost at 30% (Automotive)	Emerging competition and threat from China in reactive dyes (China produces in bulk volume and offers lower prices in some products) (Dyestuffs)
New molecules are not getting developed in India (Pharmaceuticals)	Infrastructure/supply chain connectivity is not robust. E.g. long waiting hours at ports (Automotive)	China has overtaken India in API and killed the domestic industry; now the threat is emerging in formulations as the Chinese have started focusing on this segment and moving up the value chain (Pharmaceuticals)

(Continued)

Table 5.2A (Continued)

Group 1: capability and competitiveness	Group 2: international business	Group 3: access to resources	Group 4: macro conditions
More R&D expenditure needs to be encouraged (Pharmaceuticals) India is not spending adequately on R&D to develop new molecules, we are just validating and upgrading (Dyestuffs) India is not spending enough on R&D – European and Japanese companies are (Dyestuffs). R&D is lacking (Dyestuffs)		Inappropriate handling at ports (Automotive) Power cost is high (Dyestuffs)	Allopathic: 50% API for India imported from China (Pharmaceuticals) Import dependence and inferior quality of imports from China (Pharmaceuticals) China has an advantage in raw material which can be a problem for India (Automotive)
3. Skilled labour Skill shortage: skilled/semi-skilled plant operators/chemists (Dyestuffs) India is short on skill base in metallurgical engineering (Automotive) Human capital (Automotive) India's improper education system: lack of trained workers; training them is also difficult (Automotive)			

Lack of skills (Dyestuffs, Chemicals, Pharmaceuticals)

Skill shortage (Pharmaceuticals)

4. Competitive advantage

Small-scale operation which does not incentivize exports (China has an edge in this, for example). Cost of production is lower in China, which is its strength (Specialty chemicals)

Scale of manufacturing is small: plant expansion is a problem in India (Specialty chemicals)

India's scale cannot be compared with China's (Automotive)

Threat from China in formulations (Pharmaceuticals)

>80% bulk drugs are imports from China: alarmingly high degree of dependence (Pharmaceuticals)

5. Low-cost production

India needs to have a developed upstream sector. It also needs to take care of the feedstock problem (Specialty chemicals)

(Continued)

Table 5.2A (Continued)

Group 1: capability and competitiveness	Group 2: international business	Group 3: access to resources	Group 4: macro conditions
Indian SSIs do not have the capacity to tap the market: we cannot match the scale of China where they are easily manufacturing these chemicals (Specialty chemicals) Scale is not there (Specialty chemicals) Land availability problem: with the new bill,[31] prices have become prohibitive (Automotive) Cost of land and utilities high (Pharmaceuticals) **6. Ambition of owner** Entrepreneurial spirit is lacking in India, vision is short term, promoters are few, vision is myopic; on the other hand, since there are hundreds of MSMEs, there can be a lot of scope for employment generation (Specialty chemicals)			

Source: Authors' compilation based on survey

Notes: *Based on format of ADB-ADBI (2015).
The sectors where these barriers were observed are in parentheses.

Table 5.3A Questionnaire for firms

I. __Background__

1. Name of the firm: _____

2. Year of inception of the firm: _____

3. Ownership Type:

Private / Public / Partnership

☐   ☐   ☐

4. Please provide the following information:

	2010	2014
(a) Sales turnover in INR 　　(a) 　　(b)		
(b) Proportion of export in sales turnover		
(c) Number of pieces produced		
(d) Number Of factories		
(e) Market Share		
(f) Number of workers 　　Of which		
Contractual		
Permanent		

	2010	2014
Proportion of orders in the domestic 　market from		
Wholesale buyers		
Retailers		
Commission agents		
Total		

(*Continued*)

Table 5.3A (Continued)

II. Products

5. Please specify the products manufactured by your company and share in total turnover:

Product category	% share of total turnover

6. Location of factories/plants/foundries (as applicable):

	Location of factory (city)	Type of product produced	Investment in plant and machinery (in INR million)	Whether presence of R&D facility	Other details
Location 1					
Location 2					
Location 3					
Location 4					
Total					

7. Reasons for choice of location of plant:

Plant	Reason(s)

8. Main buyers:

Segment	Name

9. Please indicate the proportion of your output sold to the following:

	2010	2014
Domestic market		
International market		

10. Who are your major competitors in the market?
    (a) _____
    (b) _____

11. If selling only in the domestic market, have you tried to sell in the export market? What
    problems did you encounter? _____
    _____

12. What is the R&D expenditure as percentage of total turnover for 2013–14? Please put a tick mark.
    (a) Up to 1%
    (b) >1 to 2%
    (c) >2 to 3%
    (d) >3 to 4%
    (e) > 4 to 5%
    (f) > 5%

13. Do you have a testing facility? What quality system standards are your products accredited in? _____
    _____
    _____
    _____

(Continued)

Table 5.3A (Continued)

III. Value chain

14. Please confirm the value chain for manufacturing of your products drawn below and answer the questions that follow:[32]

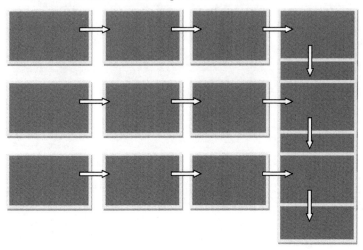

Is this production value chain used in the case of both the export and the domestic market? Yes / No
(a) Export market
(b) Domestic market

If not, describe how the production chain differs from the above diagram in:
(a) Export market
(b) Domestic market

15. For each part of the value chain given above, please make a check mark to indicate where the part is done and in what proportion. *(The answer will help us understand the nature of production in the company – which parts are more critical and are sourced from foreign markets and why? Does this depend on whether the model of car is exported or sold domestically?)*

		Domestic	Foreign
Product 1 Name:_____	R&D		
	Raw materials		
	Manufacturing		
	Marketing		
	Distribution and sales		
	Others (Communication/ desk research etc.)		

Product 2 Name:_____	R&D		
	Raw materials		
	Manufacturing		
	Marketing		
	Distribution and sales		
	Others (Communication/ desk research etc.)		
Product 3 Name:_____	R&D		
	Raw materials		
	Manufacturing		
	Marketing		
	Distribution and sales		
	Others (Communication/ desk research etc.)		
Product 4 Name:_____	R&D		
	Raw materials		
	Manufacturing		
	Marketing		
	Distribution and sales		
	Others (Communication/ desk research etc.)		

16. Please identify the weakest link/least competitive segment in the chains drawn above:
    (The answer will help us understand why India is lagging behind in global integration and what can be done to overcome it.)

    (a) Exports _____
    Reasons _____
    _____

    (b) Domestic _____
    Reasons _____
    _____

17. List in order of importance what can be done to rectify this (please rank 1–5, with 1 most important):
    (With the ranking of these factors, the objective is to prioritize which factor needs to be addressed first.)

(Continued)

Table 5.3A (Continued)

	Rank	*Rectification*	*Rank*	*Rectification*
Improvement in infrastructure				
Patent/copyright issues				
Stringent labour laws				
Improving visibility				
Any other (please specify)				

18. How do you rate Indian vis-à-vis foreign suppliers in terms of quality and reliability of supply
    (e.g. timeliness, low defect rates etc.)?
    (The objective is to understand the reasons for sourcing from India versus sourcing from abroad.)

19. Do you see the above trend in sourcing changing in the next five years? How?
    (The objective is to understand the importance of sourcing sources of the firm and the extent of integration of the firm. Does the firm feel that this sourcing pattern is likely to change and is open ended?)

20. Does your company have foreign collaboration? A) Yes B) No
    <u>Nature of collaboration</u>
    (a) Joint venture
    (b) Technology collaboration
    (c) Export
    (d) Joint R&D facility
    (e) Contract manufacturing
    (f) Other (specify)

*In the case of companies established from abroad, what is the extent of technology transfers taking place from the parent company?

Product or segment	*Technology transfer? Yes/No (Extent in percentage?)*

IV. Inputs and exports

21. For the processes involved in manufacturing your main product (refer to figure above), please give an estimate of time taken (in days) to execute these and whether they are done in-house or outsourced:

	Production process (name)	Time taken (in days)	Whether outsourced or done in-house
1			
2			
3			
4			
5			
6			

22. What are the inputs used in the process of manufacturing? For each of the inputs, please list whether they are domestically sourced or imported and the number of input supplier:

	Domestically	Imported (which country)	Number of input suppliers
Input 1			
Input 2			
Input 3			
Input 4			
Input 5			

23. Would you like to increase the use of imported inputs? If yes, what are the constraints to importing inputs? _____
_____
_____
_____
_____
_____
_____

24. Please provide the following information related to exported products:
Major markets for export

(Continued)

Table 5.3A (Continued)

	Products sold	Share of market
Market 1		
Market 2		
Market 3		
Others		
Total		

	2010	2014
Proportion of orders from:		
Wholesale buyers		
Retailers		
Commission agents		
Total		

25. If exporting, has the buyer been specifying the following? Please put a tick mark.

	2010			2014		
Machineries	Source	Quality	Specification	Source	Quality	Specification
Worker Compliance	Minimum wage	Child labour	Health	Minimum wage	Child labour	Health

26. What is the perception of the connectedness of Indian manufacturing with global manufacturing? What is your assessment of this in the next five years?
    (The answer will help understand the changing nature of the global markets and the firm's participation in the global production network. Is the firm examining this for a futuristic time horizon? This question is open ended so that the firm can answer if it has made any plans to address the changes.)

_____
_____
_____
_____
_____

Source: Prepared by authors for survey

Notes

1 All these countries report a high share of intermediate imports in total imports (Taglioni and Winkler 2016).

2 If countries do not produce products for the entire chain, they can import certain parts and components and specialize in other activities or parts. This, however, does not guarantee value capture and upgrading.

3 Different challenges are faced by countries in integrating and then upgrading into the GVC. See also Hernández et al. 2014 and Meine and Trienekens 2012.

4 Taglioni and Winkler (2016) contend that a country's ability to participate in GVCs "depends as much on its capacity to import world class imports efficiently as the country's capacity to export." The indicator of importing to export (I2E) (Baldwin and Lopez-Gonzalez 2013) measures buyer's intermediate imports embodied in gross exports as a percentage of buyer's total intermediate imports.

5 GVCs generally involve a key role for lead firms, often global brands such as Levi's in garments, Carrefour in food retailing, Ford in automobiles, or Ericsson in telecommunications. These lead firms provide product, market, and technical information with the expectation that lower-tier suppliers will maintain and improve performance to meet global competitive standards. Lower-tier suppliers, in turn, invest in equipment, skills, and specialization necessary for producing within the framework of a production network, with the expectation that lead firms will continue to use their outputs – and over time, provide opportunity for upgrading.

6 There is greater sharing of blueprints, technicians, managerial practices, and transfer of tacit knowledge due to vertically integrated production systems (Taglioni and Winkler 2016). However, spillovers of such knowledge will occur only under certain conditions.

7 Taglioni and Winkler (2016); sector analysis of intermediates imports is very important. Lower share of intermediate imports is reported in electrical and electronic equipment for rapidly industrializing countries. As discussed in Chapter 3, there are five governance types – market, modular, relational, hierarchy, and captive.

8 Taglioni and Winkler (2016); based on OECD TIVA database.

9 India's participation index stands at around 40%. The buying side plays a larger role for most countries, including India, except for the resource-intensive countries of Brunei Darussalam, Colombia, Norway, the Russian Federation, and Saudi Arabia.

10 Four types of firms typically take part in GVCs: first, multinationals, relying on inputs from domestic suppliers; second, domestic suppliers to multinationals in the country; third, domestic suppliers that export; and fourth, domestic producer relying on imported inputs. There is also another group of players – contract manufacturers that produce fully assembled goods for large retailers.

11 Revealed comparative advantage (RCA) – refer to the discussion in Chapter 4 of this book.

12 Ray et al. (2016) conducted a survey of garments for the study "Strengthening the Textile and Clothing Sector in South Asia" in 2012–13. Ray et al. (2014) examine the petrochemicals sector in the study "Study on Petrochemicals Feedstock."

13 A two-day workshop, "Global Value Chains and Trade in Value Added in India" was held on 3–4 April 2014, in New Delhi. The first day of the workshop discussed the concept of trade in value addition vis-à-vis the concept of international trade data. The findings from the pilot survey were presented. The results of the sampled firms surveyed in the garments, optical fibres, brakes, and automotive tyres sectors suggested limited or no integration with the GVC in the chosen industries. The second day of the workshop provided training on the use of the TiVA, WIOD, and Trade Sift databases.

14 The objectives of the survey were: 1. Assess India's engagement in GVCs. 2. Benchmark India's performance against other emerging markets. 3. Assess technical and other regulatory issues that might improve the scope for co-operation for firms (e.g. in terms of voluntary action on standards and conformity assessment and public action). The questionnaire is given in Appendix 5.1, Table 5.3A.

15 The findings of the main survey were presented in a workshop conducted on 16–17 March 2015. The two-day workshop, "Enhancing India's Participation in Global Value Chains: Make in India," was held to discuss the extent of India's integration into GVCs using the WIOD database and the sectoral findings from the survey.

16 More details are presented in Chapter 11 of this book.

17 More details are presented in Chapter 12 of this book.

18 Since GVC trade is often associated with transfers of knowledge and technology, protection of IP is a major determinant for many industries.

19 Role of the governance structure in upgrading; chain governance is one of the factors likely to influence a firm's upgrading chances (Schmitz 2004).

20 In the section on barriers discussed later in this chapter, these differences are exemplified by the responses received in the survey.

21 Since GVC trade is often associated with transfers of knowledge and technology, protection of IP is a major determinant for many industries.

22 Refer to Table 5.1A in Appendix 5.1.

23 See World Economic Forum 2013.

24 See Saggi (2002) for a review of the literature. Ray (2012) can be reviewed in the context of developing countries and Farole and Winkler (2014) in the context of GVCs.

25 Key drivers of FDI include – political and social stability, environment conducive to business, and access to raw materials. See Farole and Winkler (2014).

26 Findings of survey conducted between December 2013 and February 2015.

27 The World Bank follows two approaches in the construction of this index – international and domestic. The International LPI approach compiles logistics performance at the gateways of countries (such as ports or borders), while the Domestic LPI approach enables assessment of the same within countries. The International LPI 2016 allows for comparisons across 160 countries, whereas the domestic LPI covers more than 125 countries across all income groups. The international LPI is the weighted average of the country scores, ranging from one (lowest) to five (highest), on six parameters relevant for policy regulation, indicating key inputs to the supply chain and supply chain performance outcomes.

28 Each year, the World Bank publishes its "Ease of Doing Business" indicator. It is a measure of the friendliness of the regulatory environment in economies to the starting and operation of business firms. The "Ease of Doing Business 2016" index benchmarks across 190 world economies. Rankings are determined by sorting aggregate distance to frontier scores on 10 parameters. Higher rankings (a low numerical value) indicate better, usually simpler, regulations for businesses and stronger protections of property rights. The "Trading Across Border" parameter under this index records the time and cost (excluding tariffs) associated with the logistical process of exporting and importing goods, with three sets of procedures – documentary compliance, border compliance, and domestic transport. The survey covers two Indian cities, Delhi and Mumbai; and one city in the UK, London. India's overall rank in this parameter is a low 143 with a score of 57.61 (out of 100). The World Bank Group, Doing Business. http://www.doingbusiness.org/data/exploretopics/trading-across-borders.

29 The OECD has developed a set of trade facilitation indicators that correspond to the main provisions of the WTO Trade Facilitation Agreement and reflect the state of regulatory framework in different countries. The indicators are developed based on a regulatory database covering border procedures contained in the TFA with inputs from public sources, governments, and the private sector, and fact-checked by covered countries. These cover the full spectrum of border procedures for countries and help governments identify areas for action to help governments boost trade flows by reducing trade costs and introducing other reform measures. (OECD, Trade Facilitation Indicators)

30 The duty inversion that results from joining RTAs has been alluded to by several firms in our survey. The role of RTAs in facilitating GVC has not been analyzed in this book. See Mikic (2011), Hoda and Rai (2014), Das (2015), and Tewari et al. (2015).

31 The Right to Fair Compensation and Transparency in Land Acquisition, Rehabilitation, and Resettlement (Amendment) Bill, 2015. www.pmindia.gov.in/en/news_updates/the-right-to-fair-compensation-and-transparency-in-land-acquisition-rehabilitation-and-resettlement-amendment-ordinance-2015/ (accessed on 01 February, 2017). http://pib.nic.in/newsite/PrintRelease.aspx?relid=122149 (accessed on 26 March, 2018)

32 If the selected products are being manufactured by the same company, the information would be required for all of them. The surveyor can fill up separate questionnaires or the same questionnaire as per the details that follow from this question onwards.

References

ADB-ADBI. 2015. *Integrating SMEs into Global Value Chains: Challenges and Policy Actions in Asia*. Philippines: Asian Development Bank.

Baldwin, R. 2011. 'Trade and Industrialization after Globalization's 2nd Unbundling: How Building and Joining a Supply Chain are Different and Why it Matters,' Working Paper 17716. Cambridge, MA: National Bureau of Economic Research.

Baldwin, R. and J. Lopez-Gonzalez. 2013. 'Supply-Chain Trade: A Portrait of Global Patterns and Several Testable Hypotheses,' NBER Working Paper No. 18957.

Blyde, Juan, S. (ed.). 2014. *Synchronized Factories, Latin America and the Caribbean in the Era of Global Value Chains.* Washington, DC: Inter-American Development Bank.

Cadot, O., Malouche, M. and S. Sebastián. 2012. *Streamlining Non-Tariff Measures: A Toolkit for Policy Makers.* Directions in Development Trade. Washington, DC: World Bank.

Cattaneo, O., Gereffi, G., Miroudot, S. and D. Taglioni. 2013. 'Joining, Upgrading and Being Competitive in Global Value Chains: A Strategic Framework,' World Bank Policy Research Working Paper No. 6406.

Das, R.U. 2015. 'Towards "Make in South Asia" Evolving Regional Values Chain,' Discussion Paper#199. New Delhi: Research and Information System for Developing Countries.

Farole, T. and D. Winkler (eds.). 2014. *Making Foreign Direct Investment Work for Sub-Saharan Africa Local Spillovers and Competitiveness in Global Value Chains.* Washington, DC: International Bank for Reconstruction and Development, The World Bank.

Gasiorek, M., Azubuike, B. and M. Mendez-Parra. 2015. 'India: Trade, Employment and Global Value Chains,' Paper Presented at ICRIER-IA Workshop on Enhancing India's participation in Global Value Chains: Enabling 'Made in India'? New Delhi.

Gereffi, G., Fernandez-Stark, K. and P. Psilos. 2011. *Skills for Upgrading: Workforce Development and Global Value Chains in Developing Countries.* Durham: Duke University Center on Globalization Governance & Competitiveness.

Gereffi, G., Humphrey, J. and T. Sturgeon. 2005. 'The Governance of Global Value Chains,' *Review of International Political Economy*, 12(1): 78–104.

Giuliani, E., Pietrobelli, C. and R. Rabellotti. 2005. 'Upgrading in Global Value Chains: Lessons from Latin America clusters,' *World Development*, 33(4): 549–573.

Govindarajan, V. and C. Trimble. 2012. *Boston Reverse Innovation Create Far from Home.* Win Everywhere: Harvard University Press.

Hernández, René A., Martínez-Piva, Jorge Mario and Nanno Mulder (eds.). 2014. *Global Value Chains and World Trade: Prospects and Challenges for Latin America.* Santiago, Chile: United Nations Economic Commission for Latin America and the Caribbean and German Cooperation (GIZ).

Hoda, A. and D. Rai. 2014. 'Trade and Investment Barriers affecting International Production Networks in India,' Working Paper 281. New Delhi: ICRIER.

Lee, J., Gereffi, G. and J. Beauvais. 2012. 'Global Value Chains and Agrifood Standards: Challenges and Possibilities for Smallholders in Developing Countries,' *Proceedings of the National Academy of Sciences*, 109(31): 12326–12331.

Meine Pieter van Dijk and Jacques Trienekens (eds.). 2012. *Global Value Chains: Linking Local Producers from Developing Countries to International Markets*. Amsterdam: Amsterdam University Press.

Mikic, M. 2011. 'Are India's Regional Agreements Deep Enough to Support Networks?,' Chapter 5 in *India: A New Player in Asian Production Networks?*, Studies in Trade and Investment 75, Chapter 5, pp. 120–136. United Nations Economic and Social Commission for Asia and the Pacific (ESCAP).

Navas Aleman, L. 2011. 'The Impact of Operating in Multiple Value Chains for Upgrading: The Case of Brazilian Furniture and Footwear Industries,' *World Development*, 39(8): 1386–1397.

OECD. 2011. 'ISIC Rev. 3 Technology Intensity Definition, OECD Directorate for Science,' Technology and Industry 7 July 2011 Economic Analysis and Statistics Division. OECD.

OECD. 2013a. 'Mapping Global Value Chains, TAD/TC/WP(2012)6/FINAL,' Trade Policy Paper No. 159. OECD.

OECD. 2013b. *Interconnected Economies: Benefiting from Global Value Chains*. Report on global value chains. DSTI/IND (2013) 2 Draft 14 February]. Paris: OECD.

OECD. 2014 *Global Value Chains: Challenges, Opportunities, and Implications for Policy*.

OECD, WTO and World Bank Group. 2014. *Report Prepared for Submission to the G20 Trade Ministers Meeting*. Sydney: OECD.

OECD. 2015. 'The Participation of Developing Countries in Global Value Chains: Implications for Trade and Trade-Related Policies,' OECD Trade Policy Paper No. 179, OECD Publishing.

Orefice, G. and N. Rocha. 2014.' Deep Integration and Production Networks: An Empirical Analysis,' *World Economy*, 37: 106–136.

Ray, S. 2011. 'International Technology Diffusion and Productivity in Low and Medium Tech Sectors in India,' Chapter 13 in *Knowledge Transfer and Technology Diffusion*, P. Robertson and D. Jacobson (eds.). Cheltenham, UK and Massachusetts: Edward Elgar.

Ray, S. 2012. 'Technology Transfer and Technology Policy in a Developing Country,' *Journal of Developing Areas*, 46(2): 371–396.

Ray, S., Mukherjee, P. and M. Mehra. 2016. 'Upgrading in the Indian Garment Industry: A Study of Three Clusters,' SOUTH Asia Working Paper Series No. 43. ADB.

Ray, S., Goldar, A. and S. Saluja. 2014. 'Feedstock for the Petrochemical Industry,' Working Paper 271. New Delhi: ICRIER.

Saggi, K. 2002. 'Trade, Foreign Direct Investment, and International Technology Transfer: A Survey,' *World Bank Research Observer*, 17: 191–235.

Schmitz, H. (ed.). 2004. *Local Enterprises in the Global Economy: Issues of Governance and Upgrading*. Cheltenham: Edward Elgar.

Sturgeon, T. and O. Memedovic. 2010. 'Mapping Global Value Chains: Intermediate Goods Trade and Structural Trade in the World Economy,' Working Paper 05/2010. UNIDO.

Taglioni, D. and D. Winkler. 2016. *Making Global Value Chains Work for Development*. Washington, DC: World Bank Group.

Tewari, M., Veeramani, C. and M. Singh. 2015. 'The Potential for Involving India in Regional Production Networks: Analyzing Vertically Specialized Trade Patterns between India and ASEAN,' Working Paper No. 292. New Delhi: ICRIER.

World Bank. 2016. *Connecting to Compete 2016 Trade Logistics in the Global Economy – The Logistics Performance Index and Its Indicators*, https://wb-lpi-media.s3.amazonaws.com/LPI_Report_2016.pdf (accessed on 04 January 2017).

The World Bank Group, Doing Business. www.doingbusiness.org/data/exploretopics/trading-across-borders (accessed on 06 March 2017).

World Economic Forum. 2012. *The Shifting Geography of Global Value Chains: Implications for Developing Countries and Trade Policy*. Geneva: World Economic Forum.

World Economic Forum. 2013. *Enabling Trade: Valuing Growth Opportunities*. Geneva: World Economic Forum.

Others

OECD, Trade Facilitation Indicators, http://www2.compareyourcountry.org/trade-facilitation (accessed on 20 December 2016).

Part III
Integration across sectors

Introduction to Part III

Part III will discuss the experience of India in integrating in GVCs. In Chapter 5, we discussed the framework for evaluating the potential of a country in integration in GVCs and staying within a GVC once a part of it. This is answered through three questions: first, what is the capacity of a country to join a GVC? Second, what is its capacity to remain part of the GVC and finally what is the capacity of the country to move up the value chain? The capacity to join a GVC is identified through the identification of tasks within a GVC that a country can specialize in. The ability of a country to stay in a GVC and move up a value chain depends on the nature of upgrading and learning the country engages in. The framework used in this book draws on the role of the governance types (i.e. modular, hierarchical, captive, relational etc.) in fostering learning (and innovation depending on the institutional set up) in a developing country with a large domestic market. The governance of the GVC influences how learning takes place, and hence different mechanisms emerge in different chains (Pietrobelli and Rabellotti 2011).

In Part III of this book, we present examples of insertion of Indian firms in a GVC and upgrading in certain sectors. This part contains two sub sections: sub Section 1 summarizes the results of the sector case studies covering automobiles (Chapter 6), reactive dyes (Chapter 7), petrochemicals (Chapter 8), pharmaceuticals (Chapter 9), and semiconductor microchips, (Chapter 10). These are cases where there is successful integration by Indian firms. Sub Section 2 focuses on the lagging sectors where India has limited integration or has failed to integrate into GVCs. Apparel is covered in Chapters 11 and 12 focuses on specialty chemicals.

The reasons for successful integration or failure to do so are discussed in the context of each chapter. Each chapter presents an overview of the sector, the state of the industry in India, the nature of the value chain and whether or not Indian firms are integrated in the GVC. The scope of upgrading, learning and the barrier to integration are discussed. Discussion of the governance structure in each case brings out what role the lead firm plays (or does not play) in the process of upgrading within each sector. The discussion on the barriers to integration brings out the policy dimension in each case and the role that the government can play in smoothening such obstacles.

6 Integration in the automobile value chain

The case of India

The automobile industry is one of the largest manufacturing sectors in the world, with more than 90 million vehicles produced in 2014 (Sturgeon et al. 2016). It is dominated by producer-driven (or manufacturer-driven) value chains. This means that producers (lead firms) coordinate the global value chain (GVC) process. In the case of the automobile, which is a complex machine, production involves several stages including vehicle design and development; parts, component, module, and sub-system production; and systems integration and final assembly.[1] All these activities are divided among different enterprises and spread over several geographical locations. Manufacturers own car brands whose value is maintained by large investments.[2]

The largest market segment is that of passenger[3] vehicles (nearly 80% of the world market), followed by light and heavy commercial and industrial vehicles for on- and off-road use (about 20%), and finally buses (less than 1%). The Indian passenger car industry is one of the most successful cases of GVC integration. Strong supporting factors have been consistent policy support from the government, foreign direct investment (FDI), the large growing size of the Indian market, new investments in infrastructure, and other favourable demand drivers in the economy.

Nature of the industry

GVCs in this industry are typically relational[4] and captive[5] by nature with less of modularity.[6] The industry is a complex assembly sector with a tiered supply chain structure, meaning that there are multiple supplier-buyer relations within a single supply chain. There are strong agglomeration economies. Lead firms are few and drive supplier co-location[7] at regional, national, and local levels for operational (just-in-time delivery and design collaboration) or political reasons. For ease of export, lead firms locate production close to end markets, creating additional pressure for suppliers to co-locate within regional-scale production systems (Sturgeon and van Biesebroeck 2010). The automobile industry is a capital- and technology-intensive industry with huge investments made in sales and marketing, after-sales services, and quality assurance. The value chain is mainly automaker driven. Conceptualization and design are critical stages in the manufacture of a car and entail high value addition. These functions are generally performed at the company's headquarters, for multinational companies (MNCs), especially in the premium segment. Assembly of engines, electronic and technologically advanced parts, and marketing also involve significant value addition to the final product but are undertaken at the local level.

The auto-component market develops simultaneously as MNC car manufacturers use small and medium enterprises (SMEs) in developing countries as sources for automotive parts. As car manufacturers establish their base, existing SME suppliers in developing countries need to adapt to the demands of these large international manufacturers. They increasingly rely on a limited number of first-tier suppliers that are able to provide auto components on a global scale to original equipment manufacturer (OEM)[8] standards (UNCTAD 2001).[9] As this sourcing trend continues, first-tier suppliers increase in scale and become MNCs in their own right (Jurgens 2003). This change creates a new dynamic in the industry and smaller local suppliers are forced to adapt. Technology accumulation is generated by designing, building, and operating complex production systems, or occurs in the research and development (R&D) laboratories of MNCs and universities.

According to Sturgeon et al. (2016), since centrally designed vehicles are manufactured in multiple regions, buyer-supplier relationships typically span multiple production regions. Automakers increasingly demand that their largest suppliers have a global production presence as a precondition to being considered for new parts.[10] Also, many automotive parts tend to be heavy and bulky, efforts to reduce inventory have driven firms to employ just-in-time delivery to reduce costs and increase quality, and there are (physical) limits to how far apart parts production and final assembly can be. As a result, regional parts production tends to feed final assembly plants producing largely for regional and national markets.

The inception of the passenger car industry in India occurred in the 1920s with General Motors establishing an assembly line for completely knocked down trucks and cars in Bombay. After Independence, the industry went through three or four phases: the first, from 1945 to 1965, was the protectionist phase with a thrust on indigenization; the second phase was between 1966 and 1979, when the regulatory regime was tightened. From 1980 to 1990, regulatory policies were relaxed, and, from 1991 onwards, there was liberalization. The major clusters are in Delhi-NCR (Gurgaon, Manesar), Pune-Aurangabad, and Chennai-Coimbatore.

Before the 1980s, the passenger car sector in India had been stagnant and there were only a few indigenous manufacturers. One significant event occurred in 1983, when the Government of India and Suzuki Corporation of Japan entered into a joint venture arrangement and started manufacturing small cars in the country. The venture was a huge success and gave a huge growth impetus to the industry. In the early 1990s, the Indian economy was liberalized and the large size of the market attracted significant foreign direct investment (FDI) from abroad, enabling a virtuous cycle of development in the sector. Major manufacturers of the world such as General Motors, Hyundai, Fiat, Honda etc. set up manufacturing bases in India.

Today, the industry comprises more than 20 large players (including MNCs) and hundreds of allied ancillary units.[11,12] According to Athukorala 2013, various automakers have established assembly plants in India and even started using India as an export platform for their global production networks. There are two reasons for the expansion of this sector: First, the low value-to-weight nature of products of the automobile industry does not make air transport feasible, which leads to location of industries in regions of high demand. Second, there are a handful of automakers purchasing components from a number of manufacturers, which makes it feasible to locate the parts and component manufacturing close to assemblers in order to secure position. Over the years, the passenger vehicle companies have increased their footprint in global markets and their exports have grown at a compound annual growth rate (CAGR) of approximately 6.6% in the period between fiscal year 2010–11 and 2015–16.

Value chain in the automobile industry

Figure 6.1 illustrates the global automotive value chain and simplified relationships among key players within these chains. A single passenger vehicle is made with thousands of parts manufactured by hundreds of suppliers. Usually component sourcing and parts integration are high-value activities; R&D, design, marketing, and distribution are medium-high–value activities; and material supply is low value-added activity.

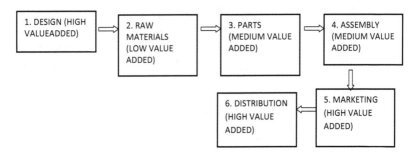

Figure 6.1 Value chain for a passenger car
Source: Authors' compilation based on survey

The value chains comprise the following players: standardizers, material suppliers, component specialists, integrators, assemblers, and distributors (Veloso and Kumar 2002) (shown in Table 6.1A in Appendix 6.1).[13] These are often organized into OEMs (assemblers and final customers in manufacturing), Tier one firms (typically large firms that play the role of integrators and supply critical components), Tier two firms (suppliers of individual parts to Tier ones and OEMs), and Tier three firms (raw material providers).

The concentrated structure has given way for lead firms to have a degree of power over the suppliers, leading to a more captive relationship.[14] The governance pattern is also partially modular[15] since information exchange is complex but may not be fully codifiable.[16] Further, value chain integration is driven by complexity of transactions (seeking just-in-time supply and product differentiation by suppliers), capability of suppliers, and the evolving quality standards with accompanying certification processes and agencies (ISO 9000 and TS 16949). Sourcing of parts, components, and modules represent the largest cost area, accounting for 50–70% of the price of an average car. The second- and third-largest cost areas are R&D and marketing and distribution. The lowest costs are mostly incurred in assembling and materials, and could be around 10% of the total price. However, in terms of value-added, R&D and marketing and distribution account for the highest proportion, followed by assembling and materials, and then sourcing of parts and components.

Regulations

The automobile industry is a fully de-licensed industry with free imports of automotive components allowed and presence of foreign players in all segments. With deep backward and forward linkages, the sector is recognized as one of the key drivers of GDP, exports, and employment in both direct and indirect terms. In the 1990s, the Government of India also put into place a phased manufacturing programme (PMP) for localization of components, under which domestic original equipment manufacturers (OEMs) had to increase the proportion of domestic inputs over a specific period.[17] In 1991, the government introduced a Memorandum of Understanding (MoU) system that continued to emphasize localization of components. Beginning in mid-1991, the Government of India made some broad-ranging changes in its economic and industrial policies towards further liberalization. Mass emission regulatory norms for vehicles were also introduced in this decade as well as a National Highway Policy announced.

In terms of aligning technically with international safety and environment standards, the industry has taken the path of following global trends, primarily in line with EU standards, and has made significant progress.[18] Vehicle technology has evolved to meet the emission and safety regulations in the Auto Fuel Policy specifying the emissions roadmap and safety regulations according to the Safety Road Map adopted by the Central Motor Vehicles Rules-Technical Standing Committee (CMVR-TSC). Today, Indian safety standards are being aligned with Global Technical Regulations (GTRs) and UN Regulations. India is a signatory to the UN WP 29 1998 agreement which develops GTRs. It actively participates in the UN WP 29 body and contributes significantly so that the GTR reflect the driving conditions and requirements of the developing countries.[19]

Regulations are needed for the after-market and there is a need to check for penetration of spurious parts in the country.

Integration into GVCs

A combination of size, growth, potential, and protection has made India one of the most attractive passenger car markets and a formidable manufacturer in the segment, globally. The country is also a key participant in the GVCs.

The domestic value chain has evolved into a multi-tiered structure with a high degree of outsourcing. The automaker-supplier relationship is a hierarchy of suppliers (Tier one, Tier two, Tier three suppliers) with automakers directly dealing only with first-tier suppliers which coordinate with the second tier, and so on. This structure has paved the path for close collaboration between automakers and their suppliers (relational governance) (Sturgeon and Biesebroeck 2011). The local parts manufacturers became world leaders by first acquiring technical and managerial skills from leading OEMs established in the country, which helped them serve customers in competitive export markets (Saraf 2016). Sturgeon et al. (2016) observe that about 46% of the value of international trade was of parts and components in 2014, up from about 41% in 2007. Bodies and drive-train subassemblies, which made up about 5% of trade in 2014, tend to be produced by the in-house manufacturing facilities of automakers; from this, it can be estimated that final vehicles directly account for about 49% of total exports. In India, power-train constitutes 50% of auto-component sales (Edelweiss 2014).

India is a net exporter of cars and exports of intermediates have come down from 93 to 91%. India's imports are dominated by intermediates. The major items of import are in the category, "Parts and accessories, for tractors, motor vehicles for the transport of 10 or more persons, motor cars and other motor vehicles principally designed for the transport of persons, motor vehicles for the transport of goods and special purpose motor vehicles, n.e.s." (HS 870899), followed by "Instrument panel clocks and clocks of a similar type for vehicles, aircraft, vessels and other vehicles" (HS 910400).[20] India's component imports are mainly in two categories: one, high-tech parts which come mainly from Germany, Japan, Korea, and Thailand; and, two, after-market parts which usually originate in China. For multinational enterprises (MNEs), at the time of setup, parts such as engines, brake pads, clutches, and fuel pumps/filters are imported.

Indian manufacturers' top export destinations are the US and Europe (countries such as Germany, the UK, Turkey, and Italy). They also export products such as engine parts, gear boxes, and steering parts to these countries. Some companies have warehouses in the UK and the US which cater to other parts of the world. India exports polished metal to transmission producers and bearings to the Philippines.

Learning and upgrading

Participation in GVCs over the last few decades has induced learning and upgrading in the industry in a significant way. Globalization has pushed automakers to upgrade technology, enlarge product range, and enhance efficiency by cutting costs and boosting productivity.

According to the framework developed by Sturgeon et al. (2016), there have traditionally been four types of industrial policy strategy for upgrading in the automotive GVCs.[21] India's policy approach has included attracting FDI to serve the local market and instituting local content requirements to stimulate assembly and the local supply base. At the same time, the government encouraged the development of national brands and suppliers, which has been the second strategy. Today, the industry is capable of end-to-end production and many companies use 100% local content for many of their brands.

Technology acquisition through collaborations and alliances has been a preferred route followed by Indian firms. Firms such as Hyundai, Maruti Suzuki, and Tata Motors have created a comparative advantage in the production and export of small and compact cars around the world. Though home-grown lead firms have played a key role in propelling growth, it can be said that this segment has benefitted significantly from foreign collaboration.[22] The joint venture model of operation for foreign firms which was popular in the 1990s has gradually given way to a 100% foreign ownership and management model in the last decade.

The prime focus has been on improving operational efficiency. Competitive pressure has caused manufacturers to ensure quality for both growth and survival, as well as to implement formal quality-improvement programmes. The entry of multinational enterprises encouraged the firms to upgrade by adopting programmes like just-in-time, 5-S, Kaizen, total quality management (TQM), total productivity management (TPM), and Six Sigma. The number of firms complying with ISO, QS, and automotive industry-specific TS 16949 certifications, as well as receiving quality awards such as Deming and the Japanese quality medal, also rose over time.

FDI in R&D and design in India has followed FDI in manufacturing. The R&D activities of foreign firms have made the environment conducive for domestic firms to take up innovation activities matching the high-quality standards of MNCs or OEMs. Many academic and research institutions have become proactive in promoting innovations, coming up with schemes for promoting ventures using home-grown technologies. Many domestic companies are seeking active collaboration with premier Indian institutions.[23]

India's strength lies in end-to-end production, especially in the small-car segment. India has also been traditionally strong in the casting and forging segment and is a base for many iron and steel foundries which cater to the sector. India is also good at manufacturing engines, though they are designed elsewhere (Ray and Miglani 2016a). Factors such as having a component base nearby and strategic geographic location are conducive to trade. The metals used in this industry (iron, aluminium, and steel) are also available locally. Lightweight materials,[24] like magnesium composites,[25] which are not locally available are imported.[26]

Role of lead firms

The role of lead firms in the automobile industry has been in upgrading technology through innovations and acquisition of technology.[27] Indian industrial policy encouraged lead firms and capabilities developed in design, product development, and engineering (Sturgeon and Biesebroeck 2010). A number of such strategic moves with few competitors to reckon with have made Maruti Udyog Limited (MUL) India's largest automobile company in terms of sales in the passenger vehicles segment and have helped it emerge as a lead firm propelling the industry's growth in domestic and export markets.[28] The key success factors for this company's growth have been its constantly upgrading models with the latest technologies, affordable pricing with a focus on the middle-income consumer segment, and a large distribution and supplier network. Among foreign firms, the role of Hyundai Motors India Limited (HMIL), local subsidiary of Korea's parent Hyundai Motor Company (HMC), has been noteworthy as a lead firm. It was the first to introduce many innovative concepts in India, including the multi-point fuel injection (MPFI) engine, Common Rail Direct Injection (CRDI) technologies, and the Fluidic Sculpture 2.0 design language to the country. Some of the other companies which have played significant leading roles in the automobile market are the indigenous Tata Motors and Mahindra & Mahindra.[29] These companies, though initially specialized in the manufacturing of commercial and utility vehicles, later on developed capabilities to serve the passenger car segment and emerged among market leaders in the same.

Barriers to integration

Despite fast development in manufacturing over the past few years, the Indian passenger car industry is yet to develop to its fullest potential.[30] There is a greater need for a strong Tier two and Tier three support to Tier one and OEMs for companies in R&D to become globally competitive.[31] Physical infrastructure is often a key differentiator when compared with China that may otherwise have similar strengths.[32] Many industry players feel that logistics-related barriers contribute to fragmentation of the industry and raise operational costs.[33]

Lopez-Acevedo et al. (2016) mention that policies such as high import tariffs on CBUs of passenger cars, which helped attract market-seeking OEMs in the last two decades, are now slowing down the spread of world-class managerial good practices. Moreover, only a few OEMs are "competing" behind even higher import tariffs on both completely built units (CBUs) and auto-parts. A gradual reduction of import tariffs would prove to be a catalyst to the industry's global success. The authors mention that there is a need to spread world-class firm capabilities throughout the industry, from OEMs and Tier one to Tier two and Tier three suppliers. Large productivity gaps persist in the sector with most OEMs (together with their suppliers) having subscale/fragmented operations with low capacity utilization, quality levels, and investments in skills below international benchmarks. A related challenge is moving up the GVC through greater innovation, investment in R&D, and commercialization of new products which remain below global average, with local suppliers primarily relying on build-to-print models. Providing small and medium enterprise (SMEs) assistance to develop linkages to value chains, improve operations, and support programmes for innovative design and R&D activities will enable India to fulfil its potential.

Despite significant development in manufacturing in the past few years, absorption of global best practices has lagged behind in the country. This is probably since India has, from the start, relied more than any other developing country on home-grown lead firms to propel its industry (Sutton 2004). A large part of production capacity is served by after-markets and commoditized parts markets, which have typically less demanding quality standards. The sector is still largely characterized by a few large players producing at export quality, while functioning in a broadly fragmented and unorganized industry.

Absence of strong in-house R&D efforts and efforts to enhance absorptive capacity is a reason companies in India have not moved very far with respect to technology capability. Process upgrading including increasing the efficiency of and between individual links in the chain is also a requirement of the sector.[34] Due to the large investments needed in this sector, new players hesitate to enter, compromising growth with only large and big players among the MNCs dominating the segment. Small companies are not able to meet global demands, which require higher levels of technology. The fact that small firms are cautious about making investments in technology makes the industry lag behind global players. This affects the Tier two/Tier three support to the industry to upgrade and operate at globally competitive levels.

For firms such as General Electric (GE), the extraordinary talent base in India, China, Brazil, and Germany helped drive decisions to base innovation centres there (WEF 2012). Although levels of investment in R&D remain low, a few leading global manufacturers are now moving their R&D centres to India. Yet, indigenization remains the key to further cost competitiveness. This needs establishment of a technologically capable, innovation-driven supplier base and for large automakers (OEMs) and the SMEs to adapt to local conditions.[35]

However, the industry still needs to mature and take steps to improve the skill level of the workforce in terms of developing team spirit, flexibility, and learning capabilities, in the opinion of many experts. Converging towards international safety standards and having domestic crash testing facilities would further encourage firms to adopt (and contribute to) international good practices.

Many independent local suppliers have not managed to either link with global sourcing partners or upgrade their capabilities to reach OEM standards. While this has left some local SMEs behind, opportunities to become local suppliers in second-tier sourcing have emerged. Local suppliers need to upgrade and respond to expectations of MNCs and their OEM partners in terms of quality, supply, and delivery times to maintain competitiveness, domestically and internationally (UNCTAD 2010; Helper and Kuan 2016).

Conclusion

A combination of size, growth, potential, and protection has made India one of the most attractive passenger car markets and a formidable manufacturer in the segment, globally. The country is also a key participant in the GVCs. India's policy approach has included attracting FDI to serve the local market and instituting local content requirements to stimulate assembly and the local supply base. At the same time, the government encouraged the development of national brands and suppliers, which has been the second strategy. India's strength lies in end-to-end production, especially in the small-car segment. India has also been traditionally strong in the casting and forging segment and is a base for many iron and steel foundries which cater to the sector. India is also good at manufacturing engines, though they are designed elsewhere.

A few studies (Sturgeon et al. 2016) and experts in the industry contend that the global automotive industry is in the midst of a transition, from geographic and technological points of view. The automotive sector in India, as in the entire South Asian region, is making a move from a "domestic growth under protection" model to a more sustainable "productivity-driven global growth" model (Saraf 2016). As Bhattacharya (2014) also points out, the direction of the assembler-supplier relationship is changing radically at two broad levels. This is also true for developing countries such as India. First, suppliers are being given greater responsibility for product design and development, and, second, assemblers are focusing on fewer suppliers and deepening collaboration practices with them.[36] These developments make it important for the Indian SME-oriented suppliers to become more innovative, adopt modern technologies, and improvise on their supply chain best practices.

Appendix 6.1

Table 6.1A Value chain of the Indian automotive industry

	First assembly			CKD units		
Function	R&D and design[⟶]	Material supply[⟶]	Component sourcing[⟶]	Parts integration[⟶]	Assembling[⟶]	Marketing and distribution
		• Glass • Rubber • Plastic • Steel • Textile • Electronics	• Body panel chassis • Steering, brakes, and suspension • Electronics • Wheels, tyres, and seats • Engines • Transmission	• Air conditioning • Electrical equipment and installations • Control equipment and instrument panels	• Welding, painting, assembling – Panes – Accessory packaging – Other body work	
Cost for automakers	Medium high	Low	High	High	Low	Medium high

Source: Authors' survey, Veloso and Kumar (2002), UNCTAD (2010)

Notes

1 The automotive value chain is shown in Appendix 6.1, Table 6.1A.
2 The related component value chain consists of a complex mixture of firms of different sizes, types, and geographic scope, producing an enormous variety of products from simple parts to technologically complex systems.
3 We focus on the passenger car segment in this chapter. Globally, passenger cars include automobiles and taxis, sports utility vehicles and light duty pick-up trucks.
4 In this network-style GVC governance pattern, we see mutual dependence regulated through reputation, social and spatial proximity, family and ethnic ties, and the like. Since trust and mutual dependence in relational GVCs take a long time to build up, and since the effects of spatial and social proximity are, by definition, limited to a relatively small set of co-located firms, the costs of switching to new partners tends to be high. https://globalvaluechains.org/concept-tools (accessed on 19 February 2017)
5 In this network-style GVC governance pattern, small suppliers tend to be dependent on larger, dominant buyers. Depending on a dominant lead firm raises switching costs for suppliers, which are "captive." Such networks are frequently characterized by a high degree of monitoring and control by the lead firm (Gereffi, G., Humphrey J. and T. Sturgeon 2005).
6 This is the most market-like of three network-style GVC governance patterns. Typically, suppliers in modular value chains make products or provide services to a customer's specifications.
7 There is a large literature on agglomeration economies focusing on production-driven reasons for co-location of manufacturing – see Rosenthal and Strange (2004) for an overview of empirical evidence from the urban economics literature.
8 The term OEM refers to a manufacturer that supplies equipment to other companies to resell or incorporate into another product using the reseller's brand name.
9 The automobile manufacturers require validation and enter into medium- to long-term contracts with these firms.
10 This has the advantage of the part being replaced quickly in case it is faulty or recalled.
11 The Indian automotive sector is one of the top five industries in the economy in terms of factory gross value. It is the sixth largest producer of vehicles globally, attracted USD 12.3 billion of cumulative FDI between 2000 and 2015, and supported 19 million people in direct and indirect employment in 2012 (Saraf 2016). In 2013, India produced 4,187,000 units and in 2014, 4,024,000 units (Sturgeon et al. 2016).
12 The automobile sector accounts for 7% of GDP, 4% of exports and employs 2.2 million directly and 17 million indirectly.
13 According to Veloso and Kumar (2002), standardizers, often automakers, conduct marketing research, develop the vehicle concept and design the specifications of the vehicle including its key modules and systems, heavily investing in R&D and process engineering. A first-tier supplier could be a standardizer by cooperating with automakers in designing components and modules. Material suppliers provide raw materials (such as steels and

metals, textiles, glasses, plastics, rubbers, and chemicals) to automakers and their suppliers for component production. Components specialists manufacture according to the specifications and requirements of standardizers, and deliver the goods to integrators or assemblers for module and system production or final assembly of vehicles. Components specialists can be further categorized into first-tier suppliers that deliver components directly to assemblers, and, lower-tier suppliers that provide components to other suppliers or integrators. The lower-tier suppliers – the smaller enterprises – tend to manufacture simpler and more labour-intensive parts later to be incorporated by higher-tier suppliers (Veloso and Kumar 2002). Integrators design and assemble key modules and systems for final assembly and are typically first-tier suppliers. Examples include integrating key elements into an engine and air-conditioning system. As integrators must deal with a number of lower-tier suppliers, they must possess a high degree of supply chain management skills and invest in R&D and process engineering. Distributors supply vehicles to consumers in the local market, conduct sales and marketing activities and provide after-sales services. As the demand for automobiles grows in all countries in the sub-region, the need for dealership and repair services rises alongside. Dealership networks have been set up by major automakers in all countries, except Myanmar, where dealership development is underway.

14 As competence to design complex parts and sub-systems is shifting from OEMs to suppliers, the need for co-design has meant that the captive GVC linkages have become possible.

15 See Simona and Axele (2012) in the context of Poland.

16 Industry level standards for vehicle parts and sub-systems have allowed the devising of codification schemes for modular GVC linkages. Linkages between lead firms and suppliers in the industry require tight coordination in design, production and logistics (Humphrey 2003).

17 Efforts to establish an integrated auto-components industry in India were initiated in the 1950s. Until about the mid-1980s, this sector, too, was protected by high import tariffs and production mainly catered to demands of local automobile manufacturers.

18 At the policy level, the focus of the Indian automotive industry has been to develop it as a manufacturing hub till few years back. The aspect of developing 'design capability' only got included in the Automotive Mission Plan in 2006.

19 www.siamindia.com/technical-regulation.aspx?mpgid=31&pgidtrail=33 (accessed on 04 August 2017)

20 Average imports from 2009 to 2013.

21 1. Developing a fully vertical industry with national brands and suppliers is generally not feasible for many developing countries 2. Attracting FDI to serve the local market and instituting local content rules to encourage employment and the local supply base (e.g. China, South Africa, and Thailand) 3. Attracting FDI for assembly and/or parts manufacturing as a low-cost portion of regional production systems 4. Specializing in one or a few parts and sub-systems for export either for use in final assembly for parts sold as replacement parts after-markets and to repair shops.

22 As noted by Sturgeon and van Biesebroeck (2010), every aspect of vehicle development and production, including design and engineering, existed in local firms from the beginning, which allowed the Indian industry to surge

forward. (This is in contrast to China (see also Ray, S. and S. Miglani. 2016a)).

The improvement in the breadth and depth of local capabilities was aided, most notably, by joint ventures with foreign players and acquisitions abroad

23 www.nistads.res.in/images/projectreports/Executive_Summary.pdf (accessed on 23 April 2017).

24 Lightweight materials are used to improve efficiency and reduce emissions. Auto OEMs are looking to shift from basic iron and steel to high-strength steel, aluminium, magnesium, and plastics.

25 Highly inflammable and requires strict establishment of safety norms.

26 See also Ray, S. and S. Miglani. 2016b, *Start your Engines: Automobile Exports, Comparing India and China*, www.theigc.org/blog/start-your-engines-automobile-exports-comparing-india-and-china/

27 Table 5.4 has discussed the role of lead firms in the industry. In each of the cases, we present the role played by lead firms in the Indian context.

28 Its market share in the passenger vehicles segment was close to 80% in the 1980s and has remained around 45% in the last decade in this segment.

29 The most valuable Indian brand is that of Tata. See https://howmuch.net/articles/most-valuable-brands-2017 (accessed on 28 August 2017).

30 Scale remains a problem.

31 Some exceptions are Bharat Forge and Motherson Sumi see BCG. 2015. *Dueling with Dragons 2.0: The Next Phase of Global Corporate Competition.*

32 WEF (2012) Road, water, power shortages.

33 Logistics costs are 30% of the total costs in some cases. Waiting time at ports is high and multiple clearances are required.

34 There are four types of upgrading in value chains (UNCTAD 2010). One, process upgrading, which involves increasing the efficiency of and between individual links in the chain. This can be achieved, for instance, through improvements in logistics or adoption of best practices and standards. Second, product upgrading involves the ability to produce components and sell new, competitive, and innovative products developed by firms. The third is functional upgrading, which seeks to increase the value-added by changing the mix of activities conducted within the firm by resorting to outsourcing or focusing on activities in which they specialize. Fourth, chain upgrading, which allows suppliers to move altogether to a new value chain.

35 http://airccse.org/journal/mvsc/papers/5214ijmvsc06.pdf (accessed on 12 June 2017).

36 Maruti has asked its vendors to use local materials such as steel alloys and local machine tools. Until 2011, Maruti used imported dies from Japan. These are now being designed in India (Bhattacharya 2014).

References

Athukorala, P. C. 2013. 'How India Fits into Global Production Sharing: Experience, Prospects and Policy Options,' Working Paper No. 2013/13. Arndt-Corden Department of Economics, Crawford School of Public Policy ANU College of Asia and the Pacific.

BCG. 2015. *Dueling with Dragons 2.0: The Next Phase of Global Corporate Competition.* The Boston Consulting Group, Inc.

Bhattacharya, S. 2014. 'Supply Chain Management In Indian Automotive Industry: Complexities, Challenges And Way Ahead,' *International Journal of Managing Value and Supply Chain*, 5(2).

Edelweiss. 2014. *Auto Components: The Future – Mega Trends, Mega Factors*. Mumbai: Edel Invest Research.

Gereffi, G., Humphrey J. and T. Sturgeon 2005. 'The Governance of Global Value Chains,' *Review of International Political Economy*, 12(1): 78–104.

Helper, S. and J. Kuan. 2016. 'What Goes on Under the Hood? How Engineers Innovate in the Automotive Supply Chain,' NBER Working Paper No. 22552.

Humphrey, J. 2003, 'Globalization and Supply Chain Netheks: the Auto Industry in Brazil and India,' *Global Networks*, 3(2): 121–141.

Jurgens, U. 2003. 'Characteristics of the European Automotive System: Is There a Distinctive European Approach?' Berlin: WZB (mimeo).

Lopez-Acevedo, G., Medvedev, D. and V. Palmade. 2016. *South Asia's Turn: Policies to Boost Competitiveness and Create the Next Export Powerhouse. South Asia Development Matters'*. Washington, DC: World Bank, https://openknowledge.worldbank.org/handle/10986/25094 (accessed 04 June 2017).

Make in India, www.makeinindia.com/web/mii/sector/automobile-components (accessed on 23 April 2017).

Ray, S. and S. Miglani. 2016a. *Innovation (and upgrading) in the Automobile Industry: The Case of India*. Working Paper 320. New Delhi: ICRIER.

Ray, S. and S. Miglani. 2016b, *Start your Engines: Automobile Exports, Comparing India and China*, www.theigc.org/blog/start-your-engines-automobile-exports-comparing-india-and-china/ (accessed on 18 August 2017).

Ray, S. and S. Miglani. 2016c. 'The role of FDI in fostering growth in the automobile sector in India' Asia-Pacific Tech Monitor, April-June 2016. 5 August (accessed on 04 July 2017).

Rosenthal, S. S. and W. C. Strange. 2004. 'Evidence on the Nature and Sources of Agglomeration Economies,' *Handbook of Regional and Urban Economics*, 4: 2119–2171.

Saraf, P. 2016. *Automotive in South Asia: From Fringe to Global*. Washington, DC: World Bank.

Simona, G.L. and G. Axele. 2012. 'Knowledge Transfer from TNCs and Upgrading of Domestic Firms: the case of the Polish Automotive Sector,' *World Development*, 40(4): 796–807.

Sturgeon, T., Daly, J., Frederick, S., Bamber, P. and G. Gereffi. 2016. *The Philippines in the Automotive Global Value Chain*. Durham, NC: Duke CGGC.

Sturgeon, T. and J. van Biesebroeck. 2010. 'Effects of the Crisis on the Automotive Industry in Developing Countries: A Global Value Chain Perspective' in O. Cattaneo, G. Gereffi and C. Startiz (eds.), *Global Value Chain in a Post-Crisis World: A Development Perspective*. Washington, DC: The International Bank for Reconstruction and Development/The World Bank.

Sturgeon, T. and J. van Biesebroeck. 2011. 'Global Value Chains in the Automotive Industry: An Enhanced Role for Developing Countries?,' *International Journal Technological Learning, Innovation and Development*, 4(1/2/3).

Sutton, J. 2004. *The Auto-component Supply Chain in China and India – A Benchmarking Study*. London: London School of Economics and Political Science.

UNCTAD. 2001. *Promoting Linkages*. World Investment Report, New York and Geneva: United Nations.

UNCTAD. 2010. *Integrating Developing Countries' SMEs into Global Value Chains*. New York and Geneva: United Nations.

Veloso, F. and R. Kumar. 2002. 'The Automotive Supply Chain: Global Trends and Asian Perspectives,' ERD Working Paper Series No. 3. Asian Development Bank.

WEF. 2012. *The Shifting Geography of Global Value Chains: Implications for Developing Countries and Trade Policy*. Geneva: World Economic Forum.

7 India in the chemical GVCs

In a growing economy, the demand for chemicals is directly proportional to the level of economic activity because the chemicals industry is a key enabler for other industries. According to the World Development Indicators 2015, the contribution of the chemicals sector is 14% of manufacturing value-added in 2010. With a large number of products (both final and intermediates) and production processes, the chemicals industry is, perhaps more than other industries, characterized by the presence of a multitude of different global value chains (GVCs) (OECD 2013a). The chemical industry can be divided into a number of sub-sectors with different classification systems defining the broad sub-sectors differently (UNEP 2013). The production system in the chemicals industry can be divided into discrete parts production[1] and the process industry[2] (Hubner 2007).[3] Bulk chemicals (also called base chemicals) can be divided into organic and inorganic chemicals (UNEP 2013).

The industry value chain starts with oil and gas, which are transformed into petrochemicals[4] and then used to produce basic chemicals, polymers, specialties, and active ingredients, as shown in Table 7.1. Products in the early stages of the chemicals GVC are of the commodity type, which are produced in high volumes and sold to the mass market at low prices. Towards the end of the chain lie specialty products,[5] typically involving larger degrees of complexity and customization linked to higher research and development (R&D)/marketing investments and branding. The chemicals industry provides raw materials and inputs for many other industries. The industry obtains a large portion of its inputs internally (between chemical sub-industries) and from other industries. Usually, the greater the proportion of domestic sourcing, the greater the average domestic length of the chemicals GVC.[6] Small countries are seen to have relatively more international stages because they rely highly on imports of intermediates. Larger

Table 7.1 Chemicals value chain

	Oil and gas →	Petrochemicals →	Basic chemicals →	Polymers →	Specialties →	Active ingredients
Product category		**Olefins** Ethylene Propylene Butadiene **Polyolefins** PE PP	**Intermediates** Butanediol THF HMDA	**Performance polymers** Polycarbonate ABS/SAN PMMA	**Specialty chemicals** Additives	**Fine chemicals** Pharmaceuticals Vitamins Flavours and fragrance
	Industrial gases	**Inorganics** Ammonia			**Performance chemicals** Pigments Dispersions Coatings	**Agrochemicals**
Applications	Foils Refrigerants	**Fertilizers** Coolants	**Plastic bottles** Plexiglass		Light stabilizer Lotus effect chemicals (Li et al. 2006)	Herbicides Food and nutrition

Source: Based on OECD (2012)

countries, such as China, generally obtain more of their inputs domestically, suggesting that their industry is strongly clustered, geographically, with other supplying industries (OECD 2013a).

Countries such as Korea, China, Malaysia, and Chinese Taipei specialize in making basic chemicals in the earlier stages of the value chain while others such as Germany and Switzerland are more active in specialty (intermediates and final) products. Market evolution driven by factors such as price volatility and the discovery of new products is responsible for the changing geography of the industry on the global map. The chemical chain is illustrated in Table 7.1.

The Indian chemicals value chain

The Indian chemicals industry has been growing and has a strong and diversified base encompassing many areas such as organic and inorganic chemicals, plastics, fibres, dyestuffs, paints, pesticides, insecticides, specialty chemicals, drugs, and pharmaceuticals.

The Indian chemicals industry can be broadly divided into (i) Alkali chemicals – this includes soda ash, caustic soda, and liquid chlorine (Ministry of Chemicals and Fertilizers 2016). (ii) Inorganic chemicals – there are nine products in this group including Aluminium Fluoride, Calcium Carbide, Carbon Black, Potassium Chlorate, Sodium Chlorate, Titanium Dioxide and Red Phosphorous, Hydrogen Peroxide, and Calcium Carbonate.

(iii) Organic chemicals include 21 products: Acetic Acid, Acetic Anhydride, Acetone, Phenol, Methanol, Formaldehyde, Nitrobenzene, Citric Acid, Maleic Anhydride, Pentaerythritol, Aniline, Chloromethanes, Ortho Nitro Chloro Benzene (ONCB), Para Nitro Chloro Benzene (PNCB), Methyl Ethyl Ketone (MEK), Acetaldehyde, Ethanolamines, Ethyl Acetate, Menthol and Ortho-, Nitro Toluene, Isobutyl Benzene. (iv) The fourth group is pesticides (technical grade) and there are 57 products in this category.[7] The final group (v) is dyes and pigments: there are 18 products in this category and include azo dyes, acid direct dyes (other than azo), basic dyes, disperse dyes, oil soluble (solvent dyes), fast colour bases, ingrain dyes, solubilized vat dyes, optical whitening agents, organic pigments, inorganic pigments, pigment emulsions, reactive dyes, sulphur dyes, vat dyes, food colours, napthols, and other dyes.

Bulk chemicals form the largest sub-segment of the Indian chemical industry with a 40% market share, and the fastest growing segment is that of specialty chemicals with a market share close to 19% (FICCI 2014). India's chemical sector, which currently is the largest (in volume

terms) in Asia after China's and Japan's, is expected to grow at a compound annual growth rate of 14% to reach USD 350 billion by 2021.
The "Make-in-India" initiative has further propelled the sector: 100% FDI is now allowed under the automatic route, industrial licenses have been abolished for most sub-sectors and for Petroleum, Chemical, and Petrochemical Investment Regions (PCPIRs) etc.[8]
Examination of the data for the chemicals sector, presented in Table 7.1A in Appendix 7.1 shows that exports of India are dominated by "Medicaments, n.e.s.," put up in measured doses or in forms or packing for retail sale (SITC Rev. 3 54293). Several other categories of medicaments, for example, "Medicaments containing antibiotics derivatives, thereof" (54219), "antisera/bld fra/vaccine" (54163) etc. are among the top 20 items exported from the sector.[9] Other items include "Other organic compounds" (51699), "Xylene" (51124), "Pigments and preparations thereof" (53117), "Reactive dyes" (53116) etc. This table contains exports and imports of final and intermediate goods (unlike the tables for automobiles) since the SITC code for intermediates and final goods are not known.[10] Imports (Table 7.2A) to India include "Diammonium Hydrogenorthophosphate" (56293), "Urea" (56216) etc.[11] Leaving all the fertilizers aside, India's major imports in the chemicals sector are Polyethylene, Styrene, antibiotics in bulk, Phosphoric Acid, and Ammonia etc.

OECD (2013b) notes that it is the one Indian sector that is integrated into GVCs through backward integration.[12]India's participation is strongly related to investments of large pharmaceutical companies, especially from the US. Like Singapore, Belgium, and the Netherlands, India serves as an important port gateway for (basic) chemicals. We discuss in detail in the rest of this book the cases of three prominent value chains in which India has shown much success. In this chapter we discuss reactive dyes. In subsequent chapters, we discuss petrochemicals (Chapter 8), pharmaceuticals (Chapter 9), and specialty chemicals (Chapter 12).

Reactive dyes

The world market for dyestuffs (dyes, pigments, and dye intermediates) is estimated at about USD 27 billion. Reactive dyes account for around 25% while disperse dyes account for 20% of total dyes production. These two dyes have a dominant share in all regions of the world.[13] In terms of market share, production has been growing in the eastern part of the world in recent times, both due to strict environmental regulations in Western countries and growing Asian markets.

Within Asia, China, Korea, India, Japan, and Taiwan are the important countries where this sector is concerned.

In the Asian Region, China, Korea, and Taiwan are strong players in disperse dyes while India leads in the production of reactive dyes because intermediates such as Vinyl Sulphone are easily available in the country (Planning Commission 2011).

India's position in the global reactive dyes industry

India contribution in dyestuffs production is nearly 12.5% worldwide, while in Asia, the country leads in the production of reactive dyes.[14] The overall production capacity of dyestuffs in India is estimated at around 0.2 million tonnes per annum and about 45% of this consists of reactive dyes. India's share in world production as far as this segment is concerned is about 40%. A range of dyes including disperse, reactive, vat, pigment, and leather dyes are now being manufactured in the country. The industry forms an important link in the chain of other chemicals-consuming industries such as textiles, leather, plastic, paper, packaging, printing inks, paints, and polymers. The textile industry is a major consumer of dyestuffs and about 70% of total production is consumed by it.

The industry, primarily started to cater to the needs of the domestic textile industry, now not only meets more than 95% of the domestic market's requirement, but is a significant exporter to other countries. In Western countries, stricter environmental norms and standards, as well as the costs of handling effluents, has necessitated relocation of a large number of companies to the less strict Asian markets of India and China.

Value chain for reactive dyes

This industry is based on chemicals derived from coal tar and the petrochemical industry. The basic raw materials used to make dyestuffs are Benzene, Toluene, Xylene, and Naphthalene. These raw materials are transformed into dye intermediates by nitration, sulphonation, amination, reduction, and other chemical processes. Other processes include formulation, reaction of the intermediates (diazotition), and coupling of the intermediates.

There are close to 700 firms[15] in the industry, but it is highly fragmented and mostly comprises small- to medium-scale companies[16] with sales of less than USD 300 million annually. Investments from international companies have tended to be small-scale on average.[17]

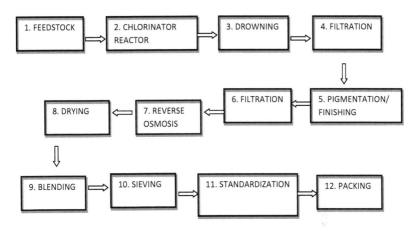

Figure 7.1 Value chain for reactive dyes
Source: Authors' compilation based on survey

The industry has recorded a double-digit growth rate in the past few years. However, it is at an interesting crossroads at present and has the potential to become a trailblazer internationally.

The synthesis of reactive dyes can take up to 12 days depending on the variety of dye required. The value chain of the process can be standardized (Figure 7.1) and India's strength lies in end-to-end production.

India has certain strengths in reactive dye production; for instance, the availability of intermediates such as Vinyl Sulphone locally, a trained workforce, and know-how. The industry is one where there is little dependence on the finished product and Indian colorants have been meeting most of the domestic requirements.

Learning and upgrading

Recently, the focus has been shifting towards the R&D sector. Spending on innovation has increased, primarily because of the increased sales to the automotive and consumer electronics segments. National research institutes such as the National Chemical Laboratory (NCL) and private sector companies are concentrating on developing specialty chemicals and polymeric additives for specific end-user segments such as automobiles and textiles. Some of the units have established joint ventures abroad using indigenous technology (Planning Commission 2011).

To move up the value chain, the industry first needs to develop products in alignment with the world's best standards such as REACH,[18] with respect to manufacture, supply, and use of colorants.[19] This may have strict implications for defaulting players but will, in the long run, encourage consolidation and organized practices, as well as benefit the industry.

Role of lead firms

Indian reactive dyes firms such as Atul, Sudarshan, and Clariant are leaders in reactive dyes and are integrated into GVCs through exports (Avendus 2016). By backward integration, they are catering to their feedstock requirement. Industry leaders are complying with environmental norms and are trying to move to greener options.[20]

Barriers to integration

It is now being recognized that a cohesive approach towards procurement, product development, manufacturing processes, and marketing with risk management and reporting at each step is critical across the value chain. The dyestuffs industry can capitalize on its strengths and consolidate its position on the global map, but there are challenges at present. One, there is insufficient availability of feedstock such as Naphthalene and Benzene.[21] Other issues include infrastructural bottlenecks (power shortages), environmental concerns,[22,23] and multiple taxation requirements.[24] The industry has a number of small and medium enterprises (SMEs) which for long have not been in a position to bear the cost of market development necessary for product promotion. SMEs in sectors such as dyes and intermediates pointed out the importance of effective support coming via financing (access and incentives for domestic and foreign investment). Margins are low in this segment as scale and operational efficiency are important (Avendus 2016).

Investment in R&D with a view to generating intellectual property is generally absent. A change of mindset is needed to invest in R&D to be able to sell value-added products.

Conclusion

The world market for dyestuffs (dyes, pigments, and dye intermediates) is estimated at about USD 27 billion. In terms of market share, production has been growing in the eastern part of the world in recent times, both due to strict environmental regulations in Western countries and growing Asian markets. Within Asia, China, Korea, India,

Japan, and Taiwan are the important countries where this sector is concerned. China, Korea, and Taiwan are strong players in disperse dyes while India leads in production of reactive dyes.

In India, concerted efforts are being put in by the industry and academia to improve the position and competitiveness of the chemicals sector internationally, but focused, consistent work is still needed. Second, research expenditure, which is at low levels (1–2%) currently, should be increased; investment needs to be focused towards product development. The industry is of the view that an enabling environment for organized clusters be provided including proper infrastructure, adequate power supply, and effluent disposal/reuse facilities. With government support and use of better and greener technologies, manufacturers can deliver reliable colorants at competitive prices.

There is a likelihood that some of the advantages that the competing Chinese industry currently enjoys may fade with a strengthening Yuan and stricter standardization (which China is not flexible enough to be able to adapt to easily). This can place India in the unique position of being able to establish itself as a major manufacturing hub of reactive dyes in the near future. The country is already the second largest producer of reactive dyes in the world. China's captive consumption is large, which leaves the global market open for Indian exports. By undertaking a consistent campaign and establishing its credentials, India has the potential to establish a reliable "Made in India" brand in colorants.

Appendix 7.1

Table 7.1A India's top 20 export items in chemicals sector, SITC Rev. 3 (value in 1000 USD)

Product code	Product description	2016	2015	2014	2013	2012	2011	2010	2009	2008	2007
54293	Medicaments, n.e.s., put up in measured doses or in forms or packings for retail sale	9798207	9330569	8288881	8375464	6631679	5282830	3954777	2925700	2605582	2037385
51699	Other organic compounds	1131335	1301232	1205413	1611034	2571148	2554242	2216190	2185373	2390950	1975214
54219	Antibiotics n.e.s. retail	931336	976389	911596	839679	873003	871746	572588	498979	823155	570120
54163	Antisera/bld fra/vaccine	772900	682654	630643	589971	404089	374557	170107	281295	81739	152166
57433	Polyethylene Terephthalate	761144	594010	517747	735701	356139	530244	458378	281200	389654	340471
54139	Other antibiotics (bulk)	651819	679028	680511	761967	685408	672778	464389	385761	335377	228376
51124	Xylenes	592269	722387	1376970	1701267	1552867	1412199	926311	661433	893761	1029763
53117	Synthetic organic pigments/ preparations	570989	573548	613988	621166	535238	529366	435145	289614	369819	291575
57511	Polypropylene	561352	739177	1209475	1538483	853399	1187199	799951	370054	302676	502803
53116	Reactive dyes/preparations	524728	529790	683609	541046	359323	254286	251487	214060	266885	232619
51577	N-hetero atom cmpds n.e.s.	510841	440133	446980	345803	246049	164554	69250	57850	38022	25883
51579	Other heterocyc compounds, n.e.s.	451207	433435	397929	429865	160011	143268	71344	93493	55843	59159
51574	Unf pyridine ring compounds	445393	356832	343747	353584	192922	142750	202813	176901	155687	151008
51122	Benzene	438985	512819	616465	818248	766331	604001	418882	305128	384233	311559
54213	Penicillin/strept retail	417634	441206	608708	558494	314758	376395	259771	200804	259951	205517
59149	Pesticides retail pack	407358	481621	455972	523744	363477	262896	383099	284939	187727	81692
51576	Pyrimidine ring compound	348657	284795	248005	259044	166450	139097	153520	79539	66925	28206
58226	Polycarb/etc., film etc.	315980	344363	393619	395947	359730	412390	310963	215110	217647	231902
51389	Other polyacids etc./derivatives	304605	194929	145252	156025	140420	154288	114569	69850	128916	66240
55135	Essential oil concentrate	301688	287875	250634	262853	303586	270059	187661	139392	162779	131967

Source: UN Comtrade database

Table 7.2A India's top 20 import items in chemicals sector, SITC Rev. 3 (value in 1000 USD)

Product code	Product description	2016	2015	2014	2013	2012	2011	2010	2009	2008	2007
56293	Diammonium Phosphate fer	1690541	3102343	1824174	1752648	3398943	3584507	2572233	2204292	6294714	1220035
52234	Phosphoric acids etc.	1626174	1578474	1251024	1364448	1735802	1914306	1349395	1406101	2493538	1033916
56216	Urea (fertilizer)	1455590	2617927	2103064	2667358	2644195	1831427	1183602	1091363	2385852	1696345
57111	Polyethylene sg<0.94	1042653	1201108	1349834	1073212	1117880	875046	1082257	610439	434437	331660
57312	PVC n.e.s. non-plasticized	992532	916560	1292154	1173469	1028698	745720	626731	409581	235890	227261
56231	Potassium chloride fertilizer	983422	1186353	1329788	1163057	1164798	1205751	1659933	2183620	2479701	683939
51124	Xylenes	958816	677059	931753	1165234	900269	656991	474187	289637	425248	515147
51221	Ethylene Glycol	791841	798164	941694	827431	694157	750257	655234	424839	312814	241200
51125	Styrene	775863	756791	1008246	963685	875954	669903	541021	430409	529929	565839
52261	Ammonia, anhydrous/solution	753612	1044010	1121351	986491	1196885	1093175	596689	484215	788950	569152
57112	Polyethylene sg>0.94	726155	766730	808620	548093	581015	425301	589697	411795	301199	255058
59899	Other chemical products, preparations, n.e.s.	605480	492287	508525	501740	453620	451633	371467	239480	277833	231707
51699	Other organic compounds	587661	909397	866843	1064120	1107565	982073	910473	688648	636431	502645
54139	Other antibiotics (bulk)	585577	620513	607738	592523	586995	588640	566457	439449	412530	350476
54293	Medicaments n.e.s. retail packs	583530	517714	566247	489393	475297	549830	632720	569254	503685	385639
57511	Polypropylene	575429	646937	693897	578755	538774	459216	465049	444824	224320	233165
54163	Antisera/bld fra/vaccine	524522	534250	526325	460909	440706	393828	267004	241110	155945	123017
51389	Other Polyacids etc./ derivatives	486353	810988	1181614	1232092	876228	1114653	866801	413150	303536	201571
53311	Titanium Dioxide pigment	475498	445745	494451	447251	458912	448410	292204	191042	170682	136090
57311	PVC not mixed other subs	472916	366534	174935	113589	81088	78345	117920	81702	102624	107655

Source: UN Comtrade database

Notes

1 Countable objects are modified or assembled in a sequence of production steps (Hubner 2007).
2 Substances are extracted, transformed, purified, or mixed (Hubner 2007).
3 Kline (1976: Hubner 2007) define the following segments: true commodities which are identified by their chemical structure and are produced by several suppliers and examples, including Hydrochloric Acid, Hydrogen Peroxides, Ethylene Glycol; pseudo commodities are defined by the chemical structure and their application characteristics are optimized. Examples include fertilizers, solvents, and elastomers. Fine chemicals have complex production processes and are high value-added. Examples include amino acids and pharmaceutical active ingredients. Specialty chemicals are developed to solve specific application problems and there are 33 primary segments and 350 secondary segments. These include textile chemicals, plastics additives, synthetic dyes, cosmetics chemicals, water-soluble polymers, specialty paper chemicals, food additives, specialty coatings, printing inks, catalysts, specialty surfactants, industrial and institutional cleaners, flavours and fragrances, specialty polymers, electronic chemicals, advanced ceramic materials, pesticides, active pharmaceutical ingredients etc.
4 Petrochemicals have been discussed in Chapter 8 of this book.
5 The specialty chemicals sector has been discussed in Chapter 12 of this book.
6 See Chapter 2 of this book for a discussion on the length of GVCs.
7 DDT (Dichlorodiphenyltrichloroethane), Malathion, Parathion (Methyl), Dimethoate, Dichlorvos or 2,2-dichlorovinyl Di-Methyl phosphate (DDVP), Quinalphos, Monocrotophos, Phosphamidon, Phorate, Ethion, Endosulphan, Fenvalerate, Cypermethrin, Anilophos, Acephate, Chlorpyriphos, Phosalone, Metasystox, Abate, Fenthion, Triazophos, Lindane, Temephos, Deltamethrin, Alphamethrin, Profenofos Technical, Pretilachlor Technical, Lambda Cyhalothrin, Phenthoate, Permethrin Tech, Imidacloprid Tech, Captan and Captafol, Ziram (Thio Barbamate), Carbendazim (Bavistin), Calixin, Mancozeb, Copper Oxychloride, Hexaconazole, Metconazole, 2, 4-D, Butachlor, Ethofumesate Technical, Thiamethoxam Technical, Pendimethalin, Metribuzin, Triclopyr Acid Technical, Isoproturon, Basalin, Glyphosate, Paraquat, Diuron, Atrazin, Fluchloralin, Zinc Phosphide, Aluminium Phosphide, Methyl Bromide, and Dicofol.
8 See Government of India, Make in India: Sector Survey – Chemicals, www.makeinindia.com/article/-/v/make-in-india-sector-survey-chemicals
9 These items relate to formulations in the pharmaceutical category and will be discussed in that chapter.
10 Sturgeon and Memedovic (2010) sort products as defined by the BEC into customized and generic products. Customized intermediate products are most likely to be used in specific final products or a narrow class of products (most auto and aircraft parts and electronic components). However, generic intermediates (including chemicals and plastics) are likely to be used in a wide range of products. There is need for industry experts to vet which are true (customized) intermediates and which are generics, in such cases.

11 Examining the average over the period 2004–14.
12 About four percent overall GVC participation by industry in 2009.
13 Market for direct vat dyes and others has remained more or less stagnant.
14 Reactive dyes, vat dyes, and azo dyes are required mainly for dyeing and printing cotton fibre. Disperse dyes are consumed mostly in the dyeing of synthetic fibres. Acid dyes are consumed in leather and woolen products. Many special dyes and pigments are used in printing inks. Some also have multiple uses in different applications (India Chemical and Petrochemical Industry Business, Investment Opportunities Handbook, Volume I). The key difference between dyes and pigments are their size and solubility: while dyes are soluble, pigments form a suspension (Avendus 2016)
15 The dyestuffs industry provides employment to about 10,000 people. http://planningcommission.gov.in/aboutus/committee/wrkgrp12/wg_chem0203.pdf (accessed on 07 May 2017). Most units are located in Gujarat or Maharashtra.
16 Small- and medium-scale enterprises defined at www.rbi.org.in/scripts/faqview.aspx?Id=84 (accessed on 07 May 2017).
17 Different feedstock is used depending on the end product: Naphthalene and Toluene are imported.
18 REACH is the Regulation on Registration, Evaluation, Authorisation, and Restriction of Chemicals. It entered into force on 01 June 2007. It streamlines and improves the former legislative framework on chemicals of the EU. The main aims of REACH are to ensure a high level of protection of human health and environment from the risks that can be posed by chemicals, promotion of alternative test methods, free circulation of substances on the internal market, and enhancing competitiveness and innovation.
19 The industry has many SME-sized manufacturing units which lack best standards. Increased concerns for safety, health, and environment have led to banning of several hazardous substances in the recent past. (ERM. 2016. *An Environmental Agenda for the Growth of India's Chemical Sector*, authored by R. Raja and J. Sathaye. ERM.)
20 See HDFC Bank Investment Advisory Group, India's Chemical Sector: Sector Update.
21 According to some industry sources, India is almost fully dependent on China for naphthalene supplies.
22 The colorant industry is considered to be one of the most polluting industries in the country.
23 Some industry players perceive that the industry is unnecessarily labelled as polluting and this has kept the government from giving it attention and entrepreneurs regularly face bureaucratic impediments.
24 Introduction of comprehensive goods and services tax (GST) from 1 July 2017 has meant that many of the taxes will now be subsumed in the GST.

References

Avendus. 2016. *Specialty Chemicals in India*. Avendus Capital Private Limited.
ERM. 2016. *An Environmental Agenda for the Growth of India's Chemical Sector*, authored by R. Raja and J. Sathaye. ERM.
FICCI. 2014. *Spurting the Growth of Indian Chemical Industry – Handbook on Indian Chemicals and Petrochemicals Sector*. FICCI.

Hübner, R. 2007. *Strategic Supply Chain Management in Process Industries: An Application to Specialty Chemicals Production Network Design.* Heidelberg: Springer.

Kline, C. 1976. 'Maximizing Profits in Chemicals,' *Chemtech*, 6: 110–117.

Li, J., Zhang, Z., Xu, J. and C. P. Wong. 2006. *Self-Cleaning Materials – Lotus Effect Surfaces.* Kirk-Othmer Encyclopedia of Chemical Technology.

Ministry of Chemicals & Fertilizers. 2016. *Chemicals and Petrochemicals Statistics at a Glance.* Statistics and Monitoring Division, Department of Chemicals & Petrochemicals, Government of India.

OECD. 2012. *Mapping Global Value Chains.* Sydney: Trade and Agriculture Directorate Trade Committee, OECD.

OECD. 2013a. 'Mapping Global Value Chains,' OECD Trade Policy Paper No. 159. TAD/TC/WP(2012)6/FINAL. OECD.

OECD. 2013b. *Interconnected Economies: Benefiting From Global Value Chains.* Report on global value chains DSTI/IND (2013) 2 Draft 14 February. Paris: OECD.

Planning Commission. 2011. *Report of Working Group on Chemicals.* Government of India.

Sturgeon, T. and O. Memedovic. 2010. 'Mapping Global Value Chains: Intermediate Goods Trade and Structural Trade in the World Economy,' Working Paper 05/2010. UNIDO.

UNEP. 2013. *Global Chemicals Outlook – Towards Sound Management of Chemicals.* United Nations Environment Programme.

Others

Government of India, Invest India, www.investindia.gov.in/chemicals-sector/ (accessed on 2 June 2017).

Government of India, Make in India: Sector Survey – Chemicals, www.makein india.com/article/-/v/make-in-india-sector-survey-chemicals (accessed on 23 November 2017).

HDFC Bank Investment Advisory Group, India's Chemical Sector: Sector Update, 29 June 2016 www.hdfcbank.com/assets/pdf/Chemical_Sector_Update_June_2016.pdf (accessed on 15 May 2017).

8   Integration in the petrochemicals sector in India

The petrochemical industry plays a crucial role in development and growth of an economy. Petrochemicals constitute a very important segment of world chemicals market, with a share of nearly 40%. The total output of the global petrochemical industry was valued at USD 550 billion in 2014. Petrochemicals products are the building blocks of many industries including polymers, synthetic rubber, synthetic fibres, fibre intermediates, and basic chemicals. The investment requirement in this sector is huge, often running into millions of rupees. The Indian domestic petrochemical market is dominated by Polyolefins (Polyethylene and Polypropylene), which make up 73% of the commodity resins[1] consumed in 2015–16. The future prospects for this industry depend on the upgrading in this sector. As the oil-producing countries of the Gulf integrate production downwards, they are likely to offer stiff competition to players in India.

Nature of the industry

Petrochemicals are produced from various chemical compounds, mainly from hydrocarbons which are derived from crude oil and natural gas. Products manufactured by the petrochemical industry include polymers, synthetic fibres, elastomers, synthetic detergents intermediaries, a broad range of basic chemicals and intermediates, and performance plastics (Planning Commission 2012). The products are used extensively in almost every sector including agriculture, housing, clothing, healthcare, construction, furniture, automobiles, household appliances, toys, horticulture, packaging, and medical appliances. Consumption of petrochemicals has a positive correlation with gross domestic product (GDP) growth.

The petrochemical industry is among the most important sectors of the economy for two important reasons. First, petrochemicals has backward linkages with other industries in petroleum refining (the basic raw material being naphtha, which is a product of refining) and natural gas processing (such as ethane and propane extracted from natural gas), as well as forward linkages with industries that deal in a variety of downstream products such as plastics, synthetic fibres, synthetic rubber, synthetic detergents, and chemical and pharmaceutical intermediates. Second, petrochemical downstream processing units contribute to employment generation and entrepreneurial development in the small and medium enterprise (SME) segment, serving a vital need of the economy.[2]

The raw materials used to manufacture petrochemicals are known as feedstocks, which come from the refinery. The important feedstocks used in the petrochemical industry are petroleum gases, naphtha, kerosene, and gas oil, which are produced by distillation of crude oil, as well as ethane and natural gas liquids, which are obtained from natural gas.

Value chain of the petrochemical industry

The petrochemicals industry uses a variety of hydrocarbon feedstock such as different cuts of naphtha from refinery and natural gas (natural gas liquids or NGL, ethane, propane, butane, liquid petroleum gas or LPG), most of which is imported. Of the total Ethylene capacity in the country, nearly 67% is naphtha based and 33% is gas based (Ray et al. 2014). The industry is growing at 5.3% per annum (Industry estimates, Draft Report of the Working Group on Chemicals and Petrochemicals 12th Five-Year Plan).

Petrochemical manufacturing involves the cracking and conversion of carbon building blocks into intermediates. Figure 8.1A in Appendix 8.1 shows the value chain for the petrochemical industry.

Basic petrochemicals fall into two major categories: Olefins and aromatics. The olefins comprise Ethylene, Propylene, Butadiene, and Alpha Olefins such as Butene, Octene, and Hexene. Ethylene and Propylene are two major building blocks for downstream products. Addition to the capacity in the upstream segment has meant that India is self-sufficient in building blocks such as Ethylene, Propylene, Butadiene, and aromatics.[3] Aromatics[4] comprise Benzene,[5] Toluene,[6] and Xylene.[7] Olefins and aromatics are the major building blocks from which most petrochemicals are produced.[8] The domestic Indian market is dominated by Polyolefins (Polyethylene and Polypropylene), which make up 73% of the commodity resins consumed in 2015–16 (CPMA 2016). Since demand exceeds production, India imports the

Table 8.1 Performance of basic petrochemicals (2007–08 to 2014–15) (1000 MT)

Group	2007–08	2008–09	2009–10	2010–11	2011–12	2012–13	2013–14	2014–15
Synthetic fibres/yarn								
Production	2660	2479	2835	3123	3105	3124	3144	3527
Exports	396	350	404	576	734	776	906	806
Imports	141	132	98	121	142	147	155	224
Polymers								
Production	5304	5060	4791	5292	6211	6424	6784	6533
Exports	631	357	658	822	1163	1113	1188	903
Imports	1152	1275	2160	2500	2435	3180	3125	3787
Synthetic rubber								
Production	105	96	106	105	100	96	105	172
Exports	14	16	15	15	22	11	13	26
Imports	342	290	376	446	493	520	580	578
Synthetic detergent intermediates								
Production	585	552	618	638	623	627	597	596
Exports	130	90	95	134	75	50	33	28
Imports	49	76	91	79	107	127	124	134
Performance plastics								
Production	733	804	990	976	969	945	783	766
Exports	272	290	294	366	310	348	475	409
Imports	89	131	112	192	175	250	311	395
Total basic petrochemicals								
Production	9386	8991	9340	10135	11008	11216	11412	11594
Exports	1444	1104	1466	1913	2304	2298	2614	5068
Imports	1733	1904	2837	3338	3353	4223	4295	2253

Source: Compiled from Ministry of Chemicals and Fertilizers (2015)

balance. Imports were 33% in 2014–15. India is one of the largest net importers of petrochemicals intermediates, with imports of USD 5.6 billion in 2013.[9] Table 8.1 shows the performance of the major petrochemicals in the country from 2007–08 to 2014–15.[10]

Table 8.1 shows that India's production of synthetic fibres, polymers, and performance plastics is strong, but it relies on imports for synthetic rubber and synthetic detergent intermediates. However, in these categories there are some exports too.

Integration into GVCs

Examination of the feedstock for petrochemicals shows that both naphtha and natural gas are imported by India (Ray et al. 2014). Imports of naphtha and natural gas were 858 kilo tonnes (KT) and 19520 MMSCM in 2014–15 (for all sectors; that is, fertilizers and petrochemicals). The consumption of naphtha was 9517 KT and that of natural gas was 2890 MMSCM in the petrochemicals sector in 2014–15. The refining capacity of the country stands at 230 metric tonnes per annum (MTPA) with the commissioning of the Indian Oil Corporation Limited (IOCL) refinery at Paradip.[11]

Table 8.2 shows the production and consumption of basic petrochemicals in the country. As we note from Table 8.2, in "Synthetic fibres/yarn"[12] (and to some extent in "Performance plastics"), India's production exceeds its consumption.[13] However, for all the other categories of basic petrochemicals, India is an importer, as consumption exceeds production (Planning Commission 2012).

Table 8.3 shows the net exports (exports minus imports) of basic petrochemicals from 2007–08 to 2014–15. The net imports were high for "Fibre intermediates"[14] (INR 1,216,318), "Polymers"[15] (INR 2,383,518), "Synthetic rubber"[16] (INR 724,457), "Synthetic detergent intermediates"[17] (INR 109,457), and "Performance plastics"[18] (INR 320,864) in 2014–15. In all other items (i.e. synthetic fibres, aromatics, and olefins), exports exceeded imports (Ministry of Chemicals & Fertilizers 2015).

Combining all the items, we note that the highest exports were of "Synthetic fibres/yarns" and the highest imports were of "Polymers." Of the former, the category "Polyester Filament Yarn" and "Polyester Stable Fibre" stood out among the exports,[19] while in the latter category, "High Density Polyethylene (HDPE)" and "Linear Low Density Polyethylene (LLPDE)" stood out among imports.[20] Categories in which India lacks significant manufacturing capability (or is not using the latest technology) include "Styrene," "Acrylonitrile," and "Propylene Oxide."[21]

Table 8.2 Production and consumption of petrochemicals (2007–08 to 2014–15) (1000 Metric Tonnes/MT)

Group	2007–08	2008–09	2009–10	2010–11	2011–12	2012–13	2013–14	2014–15
Synthetic fibres/yarn								
Polyester Filament Yarn (PFY)	1474 (1341)	1387 (1276)	1562 (1385)	1804 (1446)	1874 (1394)	1878 (1351)	1811 (1210)	2179 (1603)
Nylon Filament Yarn (NFY)	28 (29)	28 (32)	30 (35)	33 (49)	30 (51)	22 (44)	24 (47)	32 (58)
Nylon Industrial Yarn (NIY)	95 (97)	77 (78)	99 (107)	97 (105)	97 (102)	95 (103)	104 (108)	101 (103)
Polypropylene Filament Yarn (PPFY)	10 (11)	9 (10)	9 (9)	6 (6)	7 (8)	6 (6)	6 (5)	5 (4)
Acrylic Fibre (AF)	85 (89)	78 (85)	91 (95)	76 (75)	76 (70)	75 (85)	94 (96)	90 (89)
Polyester Staple Fibre (PSF)	919 (790)	843 (723)	980 (834)	1037 (916)	953 (822)	974 (833)	1010 (847)	1021 (920)
Polypropylene Staple Fibre (PPSF)	3 (3)	3 (3)	3 (3)	4 (3)	4 (4)	8 (6)	23 (9)	25 (15)
Polyester Staple Fibrefil (PSFF)	45 (45)	51 (51)	54 (54)	53 (53)	49 (49)	51 (51)	56 (56)	57 (57)
Polyester Industrial Yarn (PIY)	0 (0)	2 (2)	5 (5)	13 (13)	14 (14)	15 (15)	15 (15)	17 (17)
Total	2660 (2404)	2479 (2260)	2835 (2528)	3123 (2668)	3105 (2513)	3124 (2496)	3144 (2393)	3527 (2864)
Polymers								
Linear Low Density Polyethylene (LLDPE)	837 (981)	817 (1013)	683 (1059)	897 (1467)	1033 (1474)	1012 (1529)	1037 (1523)	910 (1450)
High Density Polyethylene (HDPE)	974 (1094)	942 (1115)	856 (1303)	887 (1268)	1119 (1302)	1177 (1657)	1195 (1657)	1156 (1947)
Low Density Polythene (LDPE)	198 (269)	191 (273)	193 (348)	179 (363)	194 (379)	187 (434)	190 (428)	184 (489)
Polystyrene (PS)	274 (212)	240 (194)	270 (232)	296 (262)	288 (257)	290 (252)	270 (224)	281 (247)
Polypropylene (PP)	1978 (1825)	1771 (1901)	1617 (1478)	1684 (1527)	2209 (1791)	2421 (2091)	2648 (2184)	2590 (2475)
Polyvinyl Chloride (PVC)	998 (1349)	1051 (1388)	1110 (1738)	1278 (1939)	1296 (2144)	1257 (2389)	1367 (2574)	1330 (2622)
Expandable Polystyrene (EPS)	44 (51)	49 (53)	63 (66)	71 (78)	72 (77)	81 (82)	77 (78)	81 (79)
Total	5304 (5824)	5060 (5977)	4791 (6293)	5292 (6970)	6211 (7483)	6424 (8491)	6784 (8722)	6533 (9367)
Synthetic rubber								
Styrene Butadiene Rubber (SBR)	17 (122)	13 (104)	19 (157)	12 (195)	9 (214)	8 (207)	12 (244)	57 (263)
Poly Butadiene Rubber (PBR)	74 (103)	72 (94)	73 (122)	76 (123)	79 (145)	77 (147)	81 (167)	108 (176)
Nitrile Butadiene Rubber (NBR)	13 (25)	11 (17)	13 (25)	6 (22)	0 (9)	0 (26)	1 (30)	0 (27)
Ethyl Vinyl Acetate (EVA)	0 (115)	0 (88)	0 (78)	11 (100)	12 (95)	11 (118)	11 (125)	6 (145)
Total	105 (433)	96 (371)	106 (467)	105 (537)	100 (571)	96 (604)	105 (672)	172 (724)

(Continued)

Table 8.2 (Continued)

Group	2007–08	2008–09	2009–10	2010–11	2011–12	2012–13	2013–14	2014–15
Synthetic detergent intermediates								
Linear Alkyl Benzene (LAB)	471 (390)	434 (420)	464 (461)	475 (420)	454 (486)	455 (532)	406 (497)	411 (517)
Ethylene Oxide (EO)	114	117	154	164	169	172	191	185
Total	585 (504)	552 (538)	618 (615)	638 (583)	623 (655)	627 (704)	597 (687)	596 (702)
Performance plastics								
ABS (Acrylonitrile Butadiene Styrene) Resin	78 (90)	68 (88)	84 (114)	90 (131)	89 (134)	91 (147)	102 (165)	107 (177)
Nylon 6 and Nylon 66	17 (43)	16 (47)	18 (58)	21 (77)	18 (86)	19 (97)	20 (119)	21 (137)
Poly Methacrylate (PMMA)	3 (5)	2 (3)	3 (4)	3 (15)	3 (10)	3 (11)	2 (12)	1 (7)
Styrene Acrylonitrile (SAN)	61 (68)	58 (64)	72	82 (74)	77 (87)	80 (82)	88 (86)	89 (93)
Polyethylene Terephthalate (PET)/polyester chips	573 (340)	657 (440)	812 (553)	774 (448)	773 (518)	747 (502)	564 (227)	547 (338)
Polytetrafluoroethylene (PTFE) (Teflon)	1 (3)	2 (2)	2 (3)	6 (3)	9 (4)	6 (3)	6 (2)	2 (-3)
Total	733 (550)	804 (646)	990(808)	976 (801)	969 (835)	949 (846)	783 (619)	766 (752)
Total basic petrochemicals	9386 (9716)	8991 (9791)	9340 (10711)	10135 (11559)	11008 (12057)	11216 (13141)	11412 (13093)	11594 (14409)

Source: Compiled from Ministry of Chemicals and Fertilizers (2015)

Note: *The figures in parentheses denote consumption, while the other figures are production.

Table 8.3 Net exports (exports minus imports) of basic petrochemicals (2007–08 to 2014–15)

Group	2007–08	2008–09	2009–10	2010–11	2011–12	2012–13	2013–14	2014–15
Synthetic fibres/yarn								
Polyester Filament Yarn (PFY)	68709	66668	79900	82215	117640	116702	146075	79995
Nylon Filament Yarn (NFY)	–953	–3776	–6153	–26299	–39815	–47055	–47248	–52509
Nylon Industrial Yarn (NIY)	–3423	–2102	–11798	–12649	–9650	–14465	–7763	–4098
Polypropylene Filament Yarn (PPFY)	–1421	–1016	–274	–351	–814	21	1757	2232
Acrylic Fibre (AF)	–3148	–6632	–4123	11269	9860	–15894	–5666	–1783
Polyester Staple Fibre (PSF)	68709	66668	79900	82215	117640	116702	146075	79995
Polypropylene Staple Fibre (PPSF)	482	687	245	495	357	2162	15653	11401
Total	157418	141406	185504	348904	535343	565587	778633	623875
Polymers								
Linear Low Density Polyethylene (LLDPE)	–85905	–128398	–226172	–363633	–299873	–395498	–400190	–505664
High Density Polyethylene (HDPE)	–75431	–117688	–266647	–224747	–139001	–340264	–442014	–760138
Low Density Polyethylene (LDPE)	–39569	–51253	–94719	–120547	–132819	–189456	–219149	–271864
Polystyrene (PS)	39566	28126	17495	17113	17886	22746	42387	19070
Polypropylene (PP)	74630	–60624	45861	61746	253834	189163	357316	30795
Polyvinyl Chloride (PVC)	–18325	–21717	–33324	–33375	–40459	–45244	–47104	–54140
Expandable Polystyrene (EPS)	–4793	–3045	–2140	–5130	–4460	–747	–269	2048
Total	–250959	–504177	–828375	–994803	–783543	–1401318	–1452757	–2383518

(Continued)

Table 8.3 (Continued)

Group	2007–08	2008–09	2009–10	2010–11	2011–12	2012–13	2013–14	2014–15
Synthetic rubber								
Styrene Butadiene Rubber (SBR)	17 (122)	13 (104)	19 (157)	12 (195)	9 (214)	8 (207)	12 (244)	57 (263)
Poly Butadiene Rubber (PBR)	74 (103)	72 (94)	73 (122)	76 (123)	79 (145)	77 (147)	81 (167)	108 (176)
Nitrile Butadiene Rubber (NBR)	13 (25)	11 (17)	13 (25)	6 (22)	0 (9)	0 (26)	1 (30)	0 (27)
Ethyl Vinyl Acetate (EVA)	0 (115)	0 (88)	0 (78)	11 (100)	12 (95)	11 (118)	11 (125)	6 (145)
Total	105 (433)	96 (371)	106 (467)	105 (537)	100 (571)	96 (604)	105 (672)	172 (724)
Synthetic detergent intermediates								
Linear Alkyl Benzene (LAB)	471 (390)	434 (420)	464 (461)	475 (420)	454 (486)	455 (532)	406 (497)	411 (517)
Ethylene Oxide (EO)	114	117	154	164	169	172	191	185
Total	585 (504)	552 (538)	618 (615)	638 (583)	623 (655)	627 (704)	597 (687)	596 (702)
Performance plastics								
ABS Resin	78 (90)	68 (88)	84 (114)	90 (131)	89 (134)	91 (147)	102 (165)	107 (177)
Nylon 6 and Nylon 66	17 (43)	16 (47)	18 (58)	21 (77)	18 (86)	19 (97)	20 (119)	21 (137)
Poly Methacrylate (PMMA)	3 (5)	2 (3)	3 (4)	3 (15)	3 (10)	3 (11)	2 (12)	1 (7)
Styrene Acrylonitrile (SAN)	61 (68)	58 (64)	72	82 (74)	77 (87)	80 (82)	88 (86)	89 (93)
PET/polyester chips	573 (340)	657 (440)	812 (553)	774 (448)	773 (518)	747 (502)	564 (227)	547 (338)
PTFE (Teflon)	1 (3)	2 (2)	2 (3)	6 (3)	9 (4)	6 (3)	6 (2)	2 (-3)
Total	733 (550)	804 (646)	990(808)	976 (801)	969 (835)	949 (846)	783 (619)	766 (752)
Total basic petrochemicals	9386 (9716)	8991 (9791)	9340 (10711)	10135 (11559)	11008 (12057)	11216 (13141)	11412 (13093)	11594 (14409)

Source: Compiled from Ministry of Chemicals and Fertilizers (2015)

Note: *The figures in parentheses denote consumption, while the other figures are production.

Regulations

The New Industrial Policy announced on 24 July 1991 exempted the petrochemical sector from licensing requirements, thus allowing market forces to determine investment in and growth of the sector. The National Policy on Petrochemicals recognized the need for sustained and continuous growth of the sector.[22] There is no limit on foreign direct investment (FDI) in petrochemicals and 100% is allowed through the automatic route.[23] The Government of India has approved four Petroleum, Chemical, and Petrochemical Investment Regions (PCPIRs) in the States of Andhra Pradesh (Vishakhapatnam), Gujarat (Dahej), Odisha (Paradip), and Tamil Nadu (Cuddalore and Nagapattinam) to promote investment and industrial development in these sectors.[24] The PCPIR is envisioned to reap the benefits of co-siting, networking, and greater efficiencies through the use of common infrastructure and support services. Each PCPIR is a specifically delineated region of area not less than 250 sq. km, wherein 40% of the area has to be for processing activities.[25] The PCPIR scheme will provide a sustained, transparent, consistent, and investment-friendly policy and facilitation regime that would encourage production for both the domestic and the world market. These regions are expected to boost manufacturing, augment exports, and generate employment by providing a conducive and competitive business environment that would reap the benefits of networking and greater efficiency through the use of common infrastructure and support services together with state-of-the-art infrastructure. The infrastructure facilities will include power, adequate water availability, common effluent treatment facility, good roads, transport, and state-of-the-art ports. According to industry experts, there is a structural difference between the PCPIRs and special economic zones (SEZs). While SEZs are for export promotion and entail giving tax breaks for goods exported, Petroleum, Chemicals, and Petrochemicals Investment Regions (PCPIRs) imbibe the principles of collective prosperity. The main objective behind the designing of PCPIRs is that the industry would be more clustered and common infrastructure could be provided.[26]

The general budget 2017–18 has announced a reduction in the basic customs duty for liquefied natural gas (LNG) owing to its use as a fuel and as a feedstock for the petrochemicals sector (Government of India 2017). Other reductions in customs duty have been announced for Medium Quality Terephthalic Acid (MTA) and Qualified Terephthalic Acid (QTA).

Upgrading

Chemicals are globally tradable and cost is the most important criterion for remaining competitive. Innovations in additives, alloys, blends, compounds, composites, and high-grade reinforcement materials such as glass, nano-clays, carbon nano-tubes, and carbon fibres require attention via technology development. New developments in the field of bio- and photo-degradable plastics are also taking place all over the world (Ministry of Chemicals and Fertilizers 2015). The main institutions or companies where significant research is carried out are the Indian Institute of Petroleum (IIP), National Chemical Laboratory (NCL), Indian Institute of Chemical Technology (IICT), National Institute for Interdisciplinary Science and Technology (NIIST), North East Institute of Science and Technology (NEIST-Jorhat), Reliance Industries Limited (RIL), Oil and Natural Gas Corporation (ONGC), Hindustan Petroleum Corporation Limited (HPCL), Chennai Petroleum Corporation Limited (CPCL), Indian Oil Corporation Limited (IOCL) etc. Of all these institutions, IIP has contributed a lot to the petrochemical sector in research (Planning Commission 2012).

Some segments of petrochemicals in which India needs to increase its capacity are HDPE, LLDPE, SBR, PVC. There are plans to set up a Technology Upgradation Fund (TUF) for the petrochemicals domestic downstream plastic processing industry, similar[27] to the one that exists for the textile industry. An advisory body, the Plastics Development Council, with members from industry, academia, and the government, has been constituted under Schedule 19 (4) of the Industries (Development and Regulation) Act, 1951, which will work for the sustained development of the plastics processing sector, including the development of technology and R&D initiatives.

Role of lead firms

Exxon-Mobil and Sumitomo Chemicals have played an important role in the cluster development of Singapore's Jurong Island Chemical Complex (KPMG 2014). Some of the problems that the Indian petrochemical industry faces now have been faced by other countries like China and Singapore in the past (McKinsey and Company 2015a). The role of the lead firms is critical to overcoming these problems of feedstock access, attracting investment, and forward integration with downstream companies.[28]

Barriers to integration

Energy and feedstock costs comprise 60–70% of the cost in chemicals production. In petrochemicals, feedstock costs range from 40 to 60% (Ray et al. 2014). Given India's dependence on imports for both natural gas and naphtha, feedstock costs remain high.[29] The reduction in import duty for natural gas announced in the budget 2017–18 to 2.5% is a welcome move (Government of India 2017). However, other segment-specific problems remain because the value addition is low and costs are high.[30] The petrochemicals sector is a highly cyclic industry and follows a pattern of six to eight years between two peaks or troughs. With an eye on emerging usages, research and development efforts should focus on the need to modernize and upgrade the existing manufacturing processes, improve the quality of existing products, and make it safe for environment and human health.

The constraints vary from segment to segment: for example, where acrylic acid is concerned, the technology is known to four to five manufacturers and attempts at joint ventures have not succeeded. Investments by multinationals in this sector have been cautious, owing to the perception of delays in operationalizing projects (McKinsey and Company 2015b). In other segments, co-location is required. It is difficult to transport Ethylene over long distances.

Conclusion

The petrochemical industry plays a crucial role in development and growth of an economy. Petrochemicals products are the building blocks of many industries including polymers, synthetic rubber, synthetic fibres, fibre intermediates, and basic chemicals. Due to the various uses associated with each segment, the petrochemical industry truly connects with the rest of the economy.

The petrochemicals sector is a highly cyclic industry and follows a pattern of six to eight years between two peaks or troughs; the ability to withstand the troughs of low profitability when margins are shrunk is also necessary for the long haul. The investment requirement in this sector is huge, often running into millions of rupees. Capital financing is one important aspect of investment in petrochemicals. Other important aspects are feedstock tie-ups and the ability to withstand cyclicality. Investment in the petrochemical industry depends on many factors and some important ones are: availability of feedstock, in particular, natural gas; and high duty on feedstock, in particular on LNG and natural gas.[31] Since feedstock costs dominate in this industry, and crude price determine the landed costs of imported naphtha, all petrochemical prices have felt the impact of low crude prices in recent times. The lack of capital financing is attributed to the rising trend in interest rates, slowdown in industrial output, and high cost of borrowing.[32]

The future prospects for this industry depend on the upgrading in this sector. As the oil-producing countries of the Gulf integrate production downwards, they are likely to offer stiff competition to firms in India.

Appendix 8.1

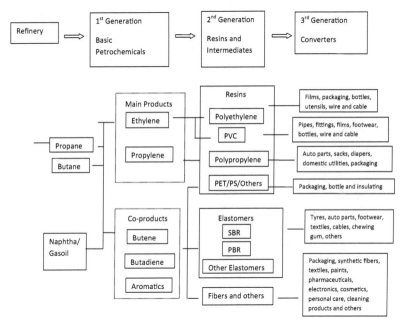

Figure 8.1A Petrochemicals value chain

Source: Author's drawing based on Brakesem: Petrochemical Industry
www.braskem-ri.com.br/petrochemical-industry (accessed on January 24, 2017)

Notes

1 Commodity resins are inexpensive and easy-to-process plastics. They are used in all kinds of applications, including toys, packaging, and consumer products. www.apisolution.com/basic-resin-guide.php (accessed on February 11, 2017).

2 The size of the industry depends on the category being examined – 75% of units are small in the downstream plastic processing industry, which is fragmented, and there are 22,000 units in the tiny-, small-, and medium-scale sector. 0.634 million employment and indirect employment of 2.38 million is provided by this segment (11th Five-Year Plan). The number of persons working in industry division 20 of NIC 2008 (manufacture of chemical and chemical products, excluding pharmaceuticals, which are covered in division 21) was 1.23 million in 2011–12 (Ministry of Chemicals and Fertilizers 2015).

3 As of 2013. See McKinsey and Company (2015a)

4 Products made from aromatics include unsaturated polyester resins, phenolic resins, drugs, dyes, pesticides, polymers, detergents, solvents, inks, paints, other Polyurethanes, as a carrier solvent for wide range of chemical specialties, Oil Field Chemicals to Food Acids (Planning Commission 2012).

5 Phenol derived from Benzene is used for thermoplastic resins and nylon. Phenol is produced by Hindustan Organics Limited (HOC) Ltd. and Schenectady International. Benzene is produced by Mangalore Refinery and ONGC Petro Additions Limited or OPAL (both subsidiaries of ONGC).

6 Used in the pharmaceutical industry, specialty chemicals, dyes, and pigments. Toluene Di-isocyanate (TDI)-grade Toluene is produced by Reliance.

7 Paraxylene is used for the production of intermediates for synthetic fibres. Xylene is produced in India by Reliance and MRPL. Ortho-xylene is also produced by Reliance.

8 These include synthetic fibres, plastics, elastomers etc. Polymers are used in packing of food articles, moulded industrial and home appliances, furniture, extruded pipes etc. Synthetic rubbers are used for making tyres and non-tyre rubber goods and supplement natural rubber. Surfactant intermediates are used to make detergents.

9 Intermediates are Ethylene Oxide, Propylene Oxide, Polyols, Phenol, Acrylic Acids, Styrene and rubber derivatives. India has no capacity in Acetic Acid, Vinyl Acetate, Acrylic Acid, Acrylic Acid Ester, Superabsorbent Polymers, Polycarbonate, and Styrene (McKinsey and Company 2015a).

10 For a break-up of different categories within "Synthetic fibres/yarn" etc., refer to Table 8.2.

11 'India's crude oil refining capacity: a snapshot' 2016. *Business Standard.* February 20.

12 Synthetic fibres are used in both apparel and non-apparel applications. Paraxylene (PX) is mainly used in the manufacture of Purified Terephthalic Acid (PTA) and Di-Methyl Terephthalate (DMT). The DMT market is shrinking globally. PTA and DMT are inputs for Polyester. Paraxylene is produced by Reliance, Indian Oil Corporation (IOC) for its captive PTA

unit. Expansion has been planned by ONGC Mangalore. IOC has already invested in the polyester feedstock chain, PX-PTA-MEG (Monoethylene Glycol), at Panipat and has further plans in Gujarat. MRPL has planned a PX-PTA complex as part of its downstream investment with Mangalore refinery. Besides its use in making PTA, MEG is used to manufacture polyester and antifreeze agents and other chemicals. Reliance is one of the largest manufacturers of polyester. Nearly 85% of MEG produced by RIL goes into captive polyester production. Other major producers of MEG are IOCL and India Glycol Ltd.

13 This is interesting as we have noted in the garments chapter that India's upgrading can take place if non-cotton–based fabrics are used.

14 Synthetic fibres include Polyester Filament Yarn (PFY), Nylon Filament Yarn (NFY), Nylon Industrial Yarn (NIY), Polypropylene Filament Yarn (PPFY), Acrylic Fibre (AF), Polyester Staple Fibre (PSF), and Polypropylene Staple Fibre (PPSF).

15 Polymers include Linear Low Density Polyethylene (LLDPE), High Density Polyethylene (HDPE), Low Density Polythene (LDPE), Polystyrene (PS), Polyvinyl Chloride (PVC), and Expandable Polystyrene (EX-PS). LLDPE is used in mono and multi-layered films, roto moulding, wire and cables, and master batch compounds. HDPE is used in raffia, blow moulding, film, pipes, and injection moulding. LDPE is used to make general purpose film, heavy duty film, liquid packaging, injection moulding, extrusion coating, wire and cables, and adhesive lamination. Polystyrene is of three types – General Purpose Polystyrene (GPPS), High Impact Polystyrene (HIPS), and Expandable Polystyrene (EPS). GPPS is used for disposable containers, cutlery, CD storage cases, co-extrusion for gloss layer, toys, stationery, and refrigeration components. HIPS is used to make electronics, household appliances, disposable containers, toys, and refrigeration components. The uses of EPS include building insulation, sound insulation, packaging materials, and disposable containers. PVC is used in pipes, calendared products, wires and cables, films and sheets, profiles, footwear, and medical and healthcare. Polypropylene is used to produce homopolymers, which are used for packaging and lifestyle products. Copolymers (also from Polypropylene) are used for automotive and appliances (Planning Commission 2012).

16 The synthetic rubber category comprises Styrene Butadiene Rubber (SBR), Poly Butadiene Rubber (PBR), Nitrile Butadiene Rubber (NBR), and Ethyl Vinyl Acetate (EVA). Butadiene is used to produce SBR, PBR etc. Butadiene is produced in India by Reliance and Haldia Petrochemicals. OPAL and IOC, Panipat, both have Butadiene extraction units. BR is used mainly in tyres and as an impact modifier of polymers such as High Impact Polystyrene (HIPS). Nitrile rubbers are used mainly in the manufacture of hoses, gasket seals, and fuel lines for the automobile industry as well as in gloves and footwear (Planning Commission 2012). Due to its excellent abrasion resistance, SBR is widely used in automobile and truck tyres. *Source:* www.petrochemistry.eu/about-petrochemistry/products. html (accessed on 28 January 2017).

17 Also known as surfactants. These include Linear Alkyl Benzene (LAB) and Ethylene Oxide (EO). LAB is used to manufacture detergents. LAB is produced in India by Reliance, TPL, Nirma, and IOC (Planning Commission

2012). EO is used in the production of surfactants and other derivatives such as Glycol Ethers, Polyethylene Glycol, Polyether Polyols, dye intermediates, drug intermediates, and Ethanol Amines. EO is produced by Reliance and India Glycols (Planning Commission 2012).

18 Performance plastics include ABS Resin, Nylon 6 and Nylon 66, Poly Methacrylate (PMMA), Styrene Acrylonitrile (SAN), PET/Polyester chips, and PTFE (Teflon). Acrylonitrile (CAN) is produced by Reliance at Vadodara. ABS is a tough, heat-resistant thermoplastic. It is widely used for appliances and telephone housings, luggage, sporting helmets, pipe fittings, and automotive parts. ABS is produced in India by INEOS ABS and Bhansali Polymer. SAN can be produced by the same process as ABS. (Report of the Working Group on Chemicals and Petrochemicals for the 12th Five-Year Plan, 2012). SAN is mainly used in the automotive, electrical and electronics industry, and is also used in household applications and building products (www.petrochemistry.eu/about-petrochemistry/products.html – accessed on 28 January 2017). PET is used to make bottles, sheets, strapping, and injection moulded products.

19 The largest value of Acrylic fibre was exported to Iran, Nylon Filament Yarn to Spain, Polyester Filament Yarn to Turkey, Polyester Staple Fibre to the US, Polypropylene Filament Yarn to Bangladesh, and Nylon Industrial Yarn to Thailand in 2014–15 (Ministry of Chemicals and Fertilizers 2015).

20 The imports of HDPE and LLDPE were highest from Saudi Arabia in 2014–15 (Ministry of Chemicals and Fertilizers 2015)

21 Planning Commission (2012). Styrene was imported from Singapore, Saudi Arabia, Kuwait, Indonesia, and Malaysia in 2014–15. Acrylonitrile was imported from Brazil, Republic of Korea, the US, the Netherlands, and Russia in 2014–15. Propylene Oxide was imported from Saudi Arabia, Republic of Korea, Singapore, Thailand, and Taiwan in 2014–15 (Ministry of Chemicals and Fertilizers 2015)

22 In 2007, the government approved the National Policy on Petrochemicals to increase investments and competitiveness both in the upstream and downstream sectors, encourage modernization of downstream processing units, promote research and development, develop adequate skilled manpower etc. to achieve an environmentally sustainable and healthy growth of the petrochemical sector. Subsequently, three schemes were formulated and implemented. These were the institution of National Awards for Technology Innovations in the Petrochemicals and Plastic Processing Industry, setting up of centres of excellence in polymer technology, and setting up of dedicated plastic parks to promote a cluster approach to the development of plastic applications. A National Programme on Petrochemical Development was proposed during the 11th Five-Year Plan. The programme aimed to improve existing petrochemical technology through research in upstream and downstream sectors, particularly domestic plastic processing and fabrication technology, to improve quality, and to promote new applications of polymers and plastics (Government of India. Planning Commission. 2007). The scheme also included waste management and promotion of recycling options through the development of degradable and bio-degradable polymers and reduces the overall impact of plastics on the environment (life cycle initiatives).

23 www.makeinindia.com/sector/chemicals (accessed on 04 June 2017).
24 http://chemicals.nic.in/sites/default/files/PCPIRPolicy.pdf (accessed on 01 March 2017).
25 http://chemicals.nic.in/sites/default/files/Annual%20report2014-15.pdf
26 Example of Jurong cluster in Singapore (see McKinsey and Company 2015b).
27 www.business-standard.com/article/companies/tuf-proposed-for-plastic-processing-industry-113091200596_1.html
28 In the case of Singapore, lead firms gradually turned away from commodity petrochemicals towards high-value specialties. For this companies invested heavily and expanded their technological prowess and energy efficiency. Despite having no natural energy resources, feedstock exposure has been reduced through technological advancement through support to R&D science parks (KPMG 2014).
29 India can focus on alternative feedstocks such as coal bed methane, bio-feedstocks, and domestic shale gas. For details, see TSMG (2014).
30 The value addition from petrochemicals to monomers is 6%, while from plastic resins to synthetic rubber, paints, and synthetic fibres is 2%; the value addition from plastic resins to plastic products is 4% (Planning Commission 2012)
31 As discussed, customs duty on LNG has been reduced in the current budget announcements.
32 A survey by Confederation of Indian Industries (CII) (Northern Region) in September 2011 suggested that around 89% of the industry felt that rising interest rates were mainly responsible for declining investment.

References

CPMA. 2016. *Indian Petrochemical Industry – Review of 2016–17 & Outlook for 2017–18, Country Paper From India*. New Delhi: Chemicals & Petrochemicals Manufacturers' Association.

Government of India. 2017. *Budget 2017–2018 Speech of Arun Jaitley*. New Delhi: Minister of Finance.

Government of India. Planning Commission. 2007. Report of the Working Group on Chemicals and Petrochemicals, 11th Five Year Plan (2007–08 to 2011–12). Volume I, Main Report.

KPMG. 2014. *Asia-Pacific's Petrochemical Industry: A Tale of Contrasting Regions*. KPMG Global Energy Institute.

McKinsey & Company. 2015a. *Solving the Puzzle of India's Petrochemicals Intermediates Shortfall*. McKinsey Group.

McKinsey & Company. 2015b. *Building a Self-sufficient Petrochemicals Intermediates Industry in India by 2025*. McKinsey Group.

Ministry of Chemicals & Fertilizers. 2015. *Chemicals and Petrochemicals Statistics at a Glance*. New Delhi: Statistics and Monitoring Division, Department of Chemicals & Petrochemicals, Government of India.

Planning Commission. 2012. *Report of the Sub-group on Petrochemicals for the 12th Five Year Plan*.

Ray S., Goldar, A. and S. Saluja. 2014. *Feedstock for the Petrochemical Indus-
try.* Working Paper 271. ICRIER.
TSMG. 2014. *Petrochem Feedstock Overview, Presentation at India Petro-
chem 2014.* Tata Strategic Management Group.
'TUF Proposed for Plastic Processing Industry,' 2013. *Business Standard.*
September 12.

Others

Autronic Plastics, Inc. www.apisolution.com/basic-resin-guide.php (accessed
on 11 February 2017).
Brakesem: Petrochemical Industry, www.braskem-ri.com.br/petrochemical-
industry (accessed on 24 January 2017).
Government of India, Make in India: Chemicals and Petrochemicals, www.
makeinindia.com/sector/chemicals (accessed on 04 June 2017).
Government of India, Policy Resolution for Promotion of Petroleum, Chemicals and Petrochemical Investment Regions (PCPIRs), http://chemicals.nic.
in/sites/default/files/PCPIRPolicy.pdf (accessed on 01 March 2017).
'India's Crude Oil Refining Capacity: A Snapshot,' 2016. *Business Standard.*
20 February.
Petrochemicals Europe, www.petrochemistry.eu/about-petrochemistry/products.
html (accessed on 28 January 2017).

9 Integration in the pharmaceutical value chain

The case of formulations in India

The Indian pharmaceutical industry has made tremendous progress over the years and is considered as a reliable source for supplies globally. The firms have unique strengths and growth models that keep them ahead of international competitors. The sector has been one of the foremost recipients of foreign investment. The relationship between buyers and suppliers in the GVCs could be both modular and market based depending on the segment.[1] However, knowledge transfer has been limited and the industry is facing serious obstacles to upgrading. Improved regulations and a favourable policy environment are needed along with concerted efforts by the firms if the industry is to enhance integration and move up the value chain.

Nature of the industry

The Indian pharmaceutical market is one of the fastest growing markets globally, with a turnover of approximately USD 36.7 billion in the year 2016. It was growing at an 18% compound annual growth rate (CAGR) during 2005–16 with the market increasing from USD 6 billion to USD 36.7 billion in the same period (IBEF 2017). It is ranked third in the world, contributing to 10% of the global market in terms of volume and 14th (accounting for 1.4% of global market) in terms of value (Deloitte 2014).[2]

Pharmaceutical products may be classified into bulk drugs[3] and formulations.[4] Bulk drugs consist of the actual compound responsible for the effect of the medicine. A bulk drug is also known as the "active pharmaceutical ingredient" (API). The bulk drugs (API) component of the industry is worth around USD 7 billion and constitutes around 60% of the domestic market and about 9% of the global market by volume, and 2% by value.[5] The bulk drugs and formulations may each be further classified into generics[6] and patented products.

Formulations are compounds made out of combining bulk drugs. A pharmaceutical formulation is a process in which different chemical substances are combined to produce the final medicinal product; in this chapter we focus on this segment. Most medicines in the market are examples of formulations and these accounts for 65% in terms of value, while bulk drugs account for 35% (Abrol 2014). Around 85% of the formulations produced in India are sold domestically.[7] As of 2009, India had around 2,389 bulk drug-producing companies and 8,174 companies producing formulations.[8] The domestic pharmaceutical formulation market has grown from USD 10.3 billion in 2010 to about USD 15 billion in 2015 (OPPI).[9] Of the USD 34 billion market, the domestic formulations market is worth about USD 10.9 billion (or INR 660.7 billion).

In 2010, the Indian pharmaceutical companies produced 20–22% of the world's generic drugs in terms of volume and offered 600 finished medicines and nearly 400 bulk drugs in formulations. Indian firms manufactured products for nearly 60,000 generic brands, covering 60 key therapeutic areas. Approximately 80% of this domestic production consisted of formulations, while the remaining 20% comprised bulk drugs (Frost and Sullivan 2012). The Indian Pharmaceutical Industry is highly fragmented with about 15,000[10] players, mostly in the unorganized sector. Out of these, about 300–400 firms belong to the medium and large organized sector. The top 10 participants accounted for nearly 37% of the market share and the top five participants for 22% of the market share in 2010 (Frost and Sullivan 2012).

According to OPPI 2015, 69% of formulations fell into the acute therapeutic category and 31% were in the chronic therapeutic category in 2015.[11] However, organized players dominate the formulations market, in terms of sales. In the formulations category, 78% of the firms are Indian and 22% are multinational companies (MNCs) (OPPI 2015). In 2013–14, the top 10 formulations companies accounted for 42.3% of the total sales of formulations. Multinational pharmaceutical companies had a market share of 20–24% as of March 2014 (ASSOCHAM-YES BANK 2015). While India today leads the world in the production of generic drugs[12] at affordable prices, it lacks an advantage in developing patentable medicines in the world market. The intellectual property rights regime in India may be one of the reasons for the weaknesses of the pharmaceutical sector of India.[13]

Goa, Mumbai, Pune, and Hyderabad have been favoured locations for formulation companies,[14] but upcoming clusters in Baddi, Himachal Pradesh, Pantnagar, and Haridwar in the state of Uttarakhand are attracting manufacturers from across the country because of fiscal incentives offered by the government (IBEF 2017).

The pharmaceutical sector is one of the highest recipients of FDI. In the past, high growth in the domestic market attracted many multinationals for both brownfield and greenfield investments in production and capacity building. While the cumulative investment (between years 2000 and 2015) is worth USD 13.4 billion,[15] much of it has been brownfield by nature; that is, of the kind where existing assets are acquired, rather than where new assets are created and technology upgraded.[16]

India is the largest exporter of formulations with a 14% market share. It ranks 12th in the world in terms of export value.[17,18] India is a global market leader in the export of generic drugs to countries such as the US and Japan, as well as to countries in Africa and Europe (Frost and Sullivan 2012). The key drivers in this sector are knowledge, skills, low production costs, and quality.

Table 9.1A in Appendix 9.1 shows the exports and imports of formulations for the period 2006–07 to 2015–16.[19] Note that exports exceed imports in all the years.

Value chain in the pharmaceutical industry

The value chain of the industry differs for capsules, tablets, and creams/ointments.[20] This is applicable to both the allopathic and ayurvedic categories. The major therapeutic categories of export are anti-infectives, anti-asthmatics, and anti-hypertensives (Kallumal and Bugalya 2012). The steps involved in making a formulation are shown in Figure 9.1.

Regulations

One of the most important features of the pharmaceutical industry is the necessity of high standards since the products concern the lives of people. On the basis of established regulations and patent laws, the global pharmaceutical industry can be broadly classified into regulated and semi-regulated markets. Regulatory bodies impose regulations to ensure that drugs meet the safety and quality standards. Regulatory bodies not only ensure that pharmaceutical companies meet the set quality standards, but also ensure that the pharmaceutical companies do not charge customers unreasonable prices. The stringency of regulatory procedures varies across countries. Regulated markets include the US, the EU, and Japan, which have established systems of patent laws and sophisticated regulatory systems for controlling drug quality. Semi-regulated markets include countries such as China, India, and South Africa, which have less stringent systems of patent laws and less

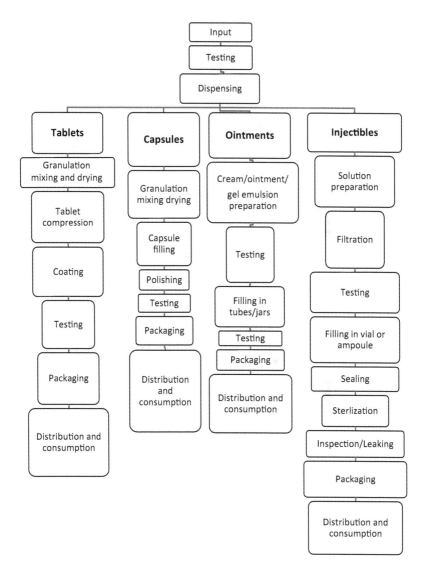

Figure 9.1 Steps in a formulation process
Source: Authors' compilation based on survey

sophisticated regulatory systems for drug quality control. However, there is no single harmonized protocol for drug approval across countries. Each country has its own regulatory authority and drug approval mechanisms.

The Drugs and Cosmetics Act, 1940 (Drugs Act) and Drugs and Cosmetic Rules, 1945 (Drug Rules) regulate the import, manufacture, distribution, and sale of drugs in India. Under the provisions of these Acts, the Centre appoints the Drugs Technical Advisory Board (DTAB) to advise the central government and the state governments on technical matters. The responsibility for enforcing the Drugs Act is entrusted to both the central government and the state governments. Under the Drugs and Cosmetics Act, state authorities are responsible for regulating the manufacturing, sale, and distribution of drugs, while central authorities are responsible for approving new drugs and clinical trials, laying down the standards for drugs, controlling the quality of imported drugs, and co-coordinating the activities of the state drug control organizations. The Drugs Controller General of India (DCGI) is the central body and it co-ordinates the activities of the state drug control organizations, formulates policies, and ensures uniform implementation of the Drugs and Cosmetics Act throughout India. It is also responsible for approval of licenses of specified categories of drugs, such as blood and blood products, intravenous (IV) fluids, vaccines, and sera. In the Indian pharmaceuticals industry patents, price and quality are the parameters regulated.

India is primarily a branded-generics (molecular copies of an off-patent drug with a trade name) market. However, it is important to note that generic versions of molecules which still had patent protection in the rest of the world were produced (by reverse engineering) and marketed in India by domestic market participants until 2005, since India did not follow any patent protection laws up to then. Hence, the Indian generic market size includes the sales value of generic drugs sold by both big pharmaceutical companies (generic copies of the innovator's molecule sold under a different trade name) as well as Indian generic companies such as Ranbaxy, Lupin, and Sun Pharma.

In January 2005, India complied with regulations laid down by the World Trade Organization (WTO) to follow the product patent regime (sale of re-engineered products (for drugs patented after 1995) is restricted). However, enterprises, which had made significant investments and were producing and marketing the concerned product before 1 January 2005, and which continue to manufacture the product covered by the patent on the date of grant of the patent, are protected, and the patentee cannot institute infringement suits against them, but would be entitled to a reasonable royalty.

The key policy instruments include:

1   *Trade restrictions and anti-dumping:* The Import Policy Schedule lists items that are restricted and items that are restricted. Import restrictions are not applicable to this sector (as of 2014) (WTO

2015). India is one of the largest users of anti-dumping measures among the WTO's members. Between 2011 and 2014, India initiated 82 instigations against 23 trading partners. The largest initiation, by product, was in the chemicals category (49.4%) (WTO 2015).[21]

2 *Intellectual property protection:* A significant number of patents have been filed by India in pharmaceuticals (20.4% in patent applications by fields of technology, 1999–2013) (WTO 2015) and it recently amended its Intellectual Property Rights Policy in 2016.[22] The policy has seven objectives including human capital development. For the pharmaceutical sector, it notes that it will "encourage research and development (R&D) including open-source based research drug discovery by CSIR for new inventions for prevention, diagnosis and treatment of diseases, especially those that are life-threatening and those that have high incidence in India."[23]

3 *FDI regulations:* 100% foreign direct investment (FDI) is allowed under the automatic route for greenfield pharma and 100% FDI is allowed under the government route for brownfield pharma. Up to 74% of FDI is under automatic route and beyond 74% is under government approval route.[24]

4 *Drug Price Control Order:* The Drug Price Control Order (DPCO) fixes the ceiling price of some APIs and formulations. APIs and formulations falling under the purview of the legislation are called scheduled drugs and scheduled formulations. The National Pharmaceutical Pricing Authority (NPPA) collects data and studies the pricing structure of APIs and formulations, and accordingly makes recommendations to the Ministry of Chemicals and Fertilizers.[25]

5 *Compulsory licensing:* India has implemented the special compulsory license regime for exports and Section 92A of the Indian law states that compulsory licenses shall be available for manufacture and export of patented products to any country having insufficient or manufacturing capability for public health reasons (WTO 2015). All WTO member countries are eligible to import under this provision but some countries choose not to do so. There has been only one instance of compulsory licensing in the country.[26]

Integration into GVCs

Indian drugs are exported to around 200 countries with about 40% of total production being exported (OPPI 2014). The major therapeutic categories exported are anti-infectives, anti-asthmatics, and anti-hypertensives (Planning Commission 2011). The value chain of an anti-infective drug is shown in Appendix 9.1.

As noted by Joseph 2012,[27] formulations account for the majority of exports to the US. Formulations constituted 89% of exports in 2009.[28] Chaudhuri (2005) showed that in 2001–02 formulations constituted 52% of exports, with bulk drugs constituting the balance.

While the Indian drugs/pharmaceutical companies manufacture a wide range of generic drugs (branded and non-branded), intermediates, bulk drugs, and active pharmaceutical ingredients (API), they also account for 92% of the imports of the chemicals sector. A large part of these imports is bulk drugs.[29] About 84% of APIs of all drugs manufactured in India are imported: 60% from China alone, according to officials in the Central Drugs and Standards Control Organization (CDSCO).[30,31] This indicates the extent of India's integration into this GVC.[32]

This sector has been driven by acquisitions: Lupin acquired Gavis Pharmaceuticals LLC and Novel Laboratories Inc. in 2015. Earlier, Sun acquired Taro Pharmaceuticals Industries Limited. Dr Reddy's Laboratories acquired UCB in 2016. Earlier in 2006, Dr Reddy's Laboratories acquired BetapharmArzneimittel GmbH (Furtado 2017). Zydus Cadila bought the Brazilian company Quimica e Farmaceutica Nikkho do Brasil Ltd (Nikkho), which is purely into the market of "branded generics," in 2007–08.

Upgrading

Before 2005, the regulatory system in India focused only on process patents. Indian pharmaceutical companies thrived during the process patent regime. They would re-engineer products of global innovator companies, which were unavailable in India, and launch them in the country as generics, as India did not recognize the product patents. In this manner, Indian companies gained process chemistry skills, but did not focus on R&D for new drug discovery.[33]

The Department of Pharmaceuticals has a vision for development of the industry: "To make India the Largest Global Provider of Quality Medicines at Reasonable Prices." The vision sees potential developing human resources for the pharmaceutical industry and drug R&D, promoting public-private partnerships, promoting "Brand India" through international co-operation, environmentally sustainable development, and enabling availability, accessibility, and affordability of drugs. To realize these goals, the Department has set specific goals for the 12th Five-Year Plan Period (2012–17).[34] These include achieving a production size of USD 60 billion and an export size of over USD 25 billion, upgradation of SMEs to WHO-GMP,[35] and training of professionals therein, establishment of pharmaceutical growth clusters, developing pharmaceuticals infrastructure, and catalysing drug discovery and innovation, among other measures.[36]

The industry has the potential to grow as an efficient and cost-effective source for generic drugs, especially the drugs going off-patent in a few years, and as an excellent centre for clinical trials. It already has USFDA/WHO-compliant manufacturing facilities.[37]

In January 2005, India complied with regulations laid down by the World Trade Organization (WTO) to follow the product patent regime and, since 2005, India's IPR regime has been TRIPS compliant. However, the discovery of new drugs is lacking in the country. The issues faced by this industry relate to the length of time needed for clinical trials (sometimes two years) and the weakness of the patent regime in India. No new molecules are being discovered in the country and that is the only way to go up the value chain.

Role of lead firms

There are many lead firms in the generics segment: this includes Aurobindo Pharma, Cipla, Dr Reddy's Laboratories, Lupin, Wockhardt, Zydus Cadila etc. R&D plays a significant role in launching of new products in this sector and this also results in profit for the firm. However, generics firms usually tend to focus more on acquisitions rather than R&D. Although companies like Sun Pharma, Reddy's Lupin, Novartis, and Pzifer are engaged in more R&D than before, a large part of the spending is on the marketing of the product (rather than R&D per se). The sector is very competitive too. Intellectual property is the bedrock for this industry and hence, to remain competitive in the future, firms will have to increase their R&D.

Barriers to integration

Overall, the industry's strengths are: low cost of production, abundant scientific and technical manpower available at low cost, strong intellectual capital, and world-class national laboratories specialized in development processes and cost-effective technologies. However, the sector has weaknesses as well, which are beginning to pose threats to growth. Some major problems are: (a) large SME base incapable of high-end manufacture, (b) insignificant share of Indian companies in R&D with a weak record for discovering new molecules, (c) poor standards and ill-defined quality checks, (d) poor packaging, © inadequate R&D infrastructure and funding,[38] and (f) lack of time-driven regulatory infrastructure for exports/imports.

In the light of these, the threats are: (a) ever-greening strategy of MNCs for denying and limiting off-patent opportunities which may impose high-entry barriers and stiff competition in the development of new drugs, (b) increasingly stringent regulatory and non-tariff barriers to the market for generic drugs in developed countries, and (c) increased competition for the production of generic and bio-generic drugs in terms of capacity and cost.[39]

Conclusion

While the Indian pharmaceutical industry has made tremendous progress over the years, it has lately started to face stiff competition from China. India is the largest exporter of formulations with a 14% market share. Indian drugs are exported to around 200 countries with about 40% of total production being exported (OPPI).[40] About 84% of APIs of all drugs manufactured in India are imported. India is dependent on China for intermediate imports such as antibiotics, vitamins, and fermentation-based products.[41] Since bulk drugs are used in the manufacture of formulations, it is important to see the correlation between exports of formulation and imports of bulk drugs. This also indicates the extent of integration in GVCs. India's strength in formulations, especially, needs to be strengthened further. Some Indian firms make APIs as well formulations, but all the APIs cannot be manufactured in-house. For other firms, APIs can be imported cheaply from China,[42] while India concentrates in formulations which can be a winning strategy. Formulations may become costlier if costlier APIs are used or if prices or volumes abroad fluctuate beyond limits. In light of this fact, the need for India now is to ensure health security and ensure the quality of imported APIs.

Drug discovery is important if India wants to move up the value chain; for this, it needs to encourage patented product development in the sector. This should be achieved by increasing public sector R&D for process innovation, improving manufacturing technologies, and increasing the supply of trained human resources. Efforts are needed to improve the regulatory environment so as to encourage discovery research, develop the diagnostic devices market, and support the bio-pharmaceuticals market. These are also measures which, it is believed, will lead the industry up the value chain.

Appendix 9.1

Table 9.1A Export and import of formulations, HS 3003 and 3004 (2006–07 to 2015–16) (USD)

Exports	2006–07	2007–08	2008–09	2009–10	2010–11	2011–12	2012–13	2013–14	2014–15	2015–16
300310	13	23	27	53	68	32	19	11	8	3
300320	63	108	146	103	117	30	10	10	20	17
300331	3	4	3	5	1	6	9	3	1	1
300339	75	254	293	228	167	161	79	93	88	58
300340	0	1	1	1	1	2	8	14	3	3
300390	152	210	243	190	276	401	452	327	252	247
3003	305	601	713	580	629	632	578	458	373	330

Imports	2006–07	2007–08	2008–09	2009–10	2010–11	2011–12	2012–13	2013–14	2014–15	2015–16
300310	2	4	8	6	7	3	1	1	2	0
300320	2	4	6	0	1	1	1	1	1	1
300331	0								0	
300339	3	4	8	5	7	8	6	3	7	1
300340			0	0		0	0	0	0	1
300390	22	25	33	32	32	33	37	34	39	28
3003	29	37	56	45	48	45	45	40	48	32

(Continued)

Table 9.1A (Continued)

Exports	2006–07	2007–08	2008–09	2009–10	2010–11	2011–12	2012–13	2013–14	2014–15	2015–16
300410	172	215	244	221	312	334	379	552	573	417
300420	378	607	763	548	653	885	857	847	924	972
300431	21	39	38	31	63	85	134	137	106	110
300432	2	1	1	2	2	6	9	9	15	18
300439	25	33	38	54	47	71	107	72	80	59
300440	23	39	47	43	37	47	73	40	45	48
300450	156	199	305	203	243	285	258	235	249	246
300490	1,851	2,176	2,594	3,201	4,282	5,570	7,005	7,912	8,256	9,650
3004	2,629	3,311	4,030	4,302	5,638	7,283	8,823	9,805	10,250	11,521

Imports	2006–07	2007–08	2008–09	2009–10	2010–11	2011–12	2012–13	2013–14	2014–15	2015–16
300410	6	8	12	215	12	321	395	64	22	20
300420	11	10	9	607	17	22	30	84	26	28
300431	27	49	42	39	74	118	138	138	194	162
300432	0	0	0	1	1	2	3	3	1	1
300439	16	30	34	33	38	52	47	64	76	80
300440	1	1	0	39	1	3	3	2	2	8
300450	5	5	9	199	9	9	7	5	4	7
300490	372	369	507	2,176	612	507	488	485	557	550
3004	437	471	612	3,311	764	1,033	1,110	846	883	856

Source: Compiled from Ministry of Commerce and Industries

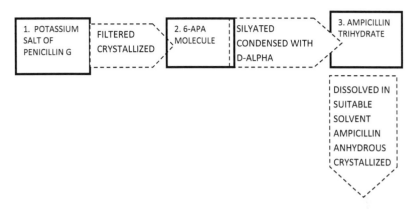

Figure 9.1A Value chain of an anti-infective drug

Notes

1 For explanation of nature of governance of GVCs, see Gereffi (1999).
2 Deloitte (2014), Competitiveness: Catching the next wave in India India's growth drivers over the next 30 years. http://www2.deloitte.com/content/dam/Deloitte/global/Documents/About-Deloitte/gx-india-competitiveness-report-infographic.pdf
3 Refers to "any pharmaceutical, chemical, biological or plant product including its salt, esters, stereo-isomers and derivatives." *Source:* Ministry of Chemicals and Fertilizers (1995).
4 Refers to a "medicine processed out of, or containing without the use of any one or more bulk drugs or drugs with or pharmaceutical aids, for internal or external use for or in the diagnosis, treatment, mitigation or prevention of diseases in human beings." *Source:* Ministry of Chemicals and Fertilizers (1995).
5 OPPI (2015). Annual Report 2014–15. Organisation of Pharmaceutical Producers of India.
6 A generic drug is a pharmaceutical drug that is equivalent to a brand name product in dosage, strength, route of administration, quality, performance, and intended use. *Source:* Center for Drug Evaluation and Research www.fda.gov/downloads/Drugs/DevelopmentApprovalProcess/SmallBusiness Assistance/ucm127615.pdf (accessed on 7 May 2017)
7 About 85% of bulk drugs are exported (OPPI 2015).
8 See Table 3: Geographical Distribution of Pharmaceutical Companies in Department of Pharmaceuticals (2012).
9 OPPI Annual Report 2014–15. This study reports that 1.1% of the global pharmaceutical market in value terms is the size of the domestic formulations market. Due to low drug prices and a relatively lower penetration of healthcare, India spends only 3.5–4% of its total gross domestic product (GDP) on healthcare and hence, ranking among the lowest globally.

In contrast, developed countries spend about 10–13% of their GDP on healthcare.

10 Frost and Sullivan (2012) report 20,000 registered units as of 2010.

11 The major therapeutic categories are 1. Anti-infectives: Penicillin, Sulphonamides, Aminoglycosides, Tetracyclines, Macrolides, Cephalosporins, Quinolones etc.), anti-parasitics (anti-protozoans, anti-malarials, anti-fungals, anti-helmintics etc.), anti-tuberculosis, and vaccines. 2. Antipyretics and analgesics: pain-killers, non-steroidal anti-inflammatory drugs (NSAIDs), and drugs for fevers. 3. Cardiovascular (CVS) drugs: cardiac therapy, anti-hypertensives, and anti-hypotensives. 4. Central nervous system (CNS) drugs: analgesics, psycholeptics, anti-epilepsy, tranquilizers and sedatives, and anti-Parkinson's disease. 5. Dermatological preparations: topical corticosteroids, antiseptics, and anti-fungals. 6. Gastrointestinals: antacids, anti-ulcerants, anti-helmintics, anti-flatulents, and anti-diarrhoeals. 7. Genitourinary and sex hormones: corticosteroids, sex hormones, and stimulants. 8. Haematologicals: anti-anaemic preparations. 9. Muscular drugs: anti-inflammatory and anti-rheumatics. 10. Respiratory drugs: cough-and-cold preparations, anti-asthmatics, antihistamines, rubs, and anti-tuberculosis. 11. Other drugs: general nutrients, minerals, and vitamins.

12 'India continues to lead China in pharma exports' *Livemint*. July 08. Kritika Singh. www.livemint.com/Politics/g0vsJg1hoVWJQ7qyBf7WmI/India-continues-to-lead-China-in-pharma-exports.html (accessed on 05 June 2017).

13 Many believe that the development of the generics sector was facilitated due to the patent regime.

14 Traditional bulk drug clusters are located primarily in Gujarat, Maharashtra, Andhra Pradesh, Tamil Nadu, Goa, Pondicherry, and Karnataka. Visakhapatnam (Vizag) in Andhra Pradesh is an upcoming bulk drug cluster that has generated significant interest among API manufacturers.

15 Vibrant Gujarat, 2017, IBEF https://vibrantgujarat.com/writereaddata/images/pdf/pharmaceutical-sector.pdf (accessed on 1 September 2017).

16 Government of India, Make in India: Pharmaceuticals, www.makeinindia.com/sector/pharmaceuticals (accessed on 15 March 2017).

17 Government of India, Make in India: Pharmaceuticals, www.makeinindia.com/sector/pharmaceuticals (accessed on 15 March 2017).

18 The exports of formulations and biologicals were USD 11214.16 million in 2015–16, and those for bulk drugs were USD 3564 million (Pharmexcil 2016).

19 3003 includes anaesthetics, eye drops, ointments etc. 3004 includes Penicillin, Ampicillin, Amoxyicillin, other antibiotics etc. *Source:* DGFT (2012). www.gov.uk/guidance/classifying-pharmaceutical-products

20 Formulation studies involve developing a preparation of the drug which is both stable and acceptable to the patient. For orally administered drugs, this usually involves incorporating the drug into a tablet or a capsule. It is important to make the distinction that a tablet contains a variety of other potentially inert substances apart from the drug itself. Pre-formulation involves the characterization of a drug's physical, chemical, and mechanical properties in order to choose what other ingredients (excipients) should be used in the preparation. Formulation studies then consider such factors as particle size, polymorphism, pH, and solubility, as

all of these can influence bioavailability and hence the activity of a drug. The drug must be combined with inactive ingredients by a method which ensures that the quantity of drug present is consistent in each dosage unit (e.g. each tablet). The dosage should have a uniform appearance, with an acceptable taste, tablet hardness, or capsule disintegration.

21 Anti-dumping process takes almost two years; by that time domestic industry is on the verge of closure. It has to be fast-tracked to protect the Indian industry (James 2014).

22 http://dipp.nic.in/sites/default/files/National_IPR_Policy_English.pdf (accessed on 1 September 2017).

23 Objective 2.10 of National Intellectual Property Rights Policy, 2016.

24 Government of India, Make in India: Pharmaceuticals, www.makeinindia. com/sector/pharmaceuticals (accessed on 15 March 2017).

25 Certain products are also subject to state pricing; these include HS Code 30041011, 30041012, 30041013, 30041019, 30041090, 30042011, 30042012, 30042013, 30042014, 30042015, 30042016, 30042017, 30042018, 30042019, 30042090, 30043100, 30043200, 30043900, 30044010, 30044090, 30045000, 30049010, 30049020, 30049053, 30049059.

26 'Natco Pharma wins cancer drug case' by R. Sivaraman (2013) *The Hindu*. March 04. www.thehindu.com/business/companies/natco-pharma-wins-cancer-drug-case/article4475762.ece

27 According to Joseph (2012), products under SITC 542 (HS 3003 and HS 3004) are formulations.

28 To market a generic drug in the US, a company has to file an Abbreviated New Drug Application (ANDA) (Joseph 2012). The number of ANDAs filed by India in the US was 3820 in 2016 (Pharmexcil 2016).

29 'PMO Push for Production of Drug APIs in India'. 2016. *The Indian Express*, October 26. The value of Chinese API imports is in the range of INR 80,000–100,000 million in the Indian formulation market. The formulation market itself is estimated at INR 10,00,000 million.

30 Neither the CDSCO nor state drug controllers have the wherewithal to ensure adequate quality control. There is need to focus on strengthening the regulatory structure. Both the procedures for licensing and inspection of drugs need to be scrutinized. A massive state-level revamp will be required. See 'PMO Push for Production of Drug APIs in India'. 2016. Indian Express. October 26. By Abantika Ghosh. http://indianexpress. com/article/india/india-news-india/pmo-push-for-production-of-drug-apis-in-india-3102758/ (accessed on 24 August 2017)

31 Quality of APIs is important but is difficult to verify especially for small firms (Bumpas and Betsch 2009).

32 Since bulk drugs are used in the manufacture of formulations, it is important to see the correlation between exports of formulation and imports of bulk drugs. This has not been attempted to the best of our knowledge. Ministry of Chemicals and Fertilizers (2016) note the correlations between total import and formulations/bulk drugs imports and total export and exports of formulations/bulk drugs export growth.

33 The Report of the Task Force, Ministry of Commerce and Industry (2008), recognizes the importance of drug research which is still emerging in the country.

34 Since 1947, the Indian economy has been premised on the concept of planning. This has been carried through the Five-Year Plans, developed, executed, and monitored by the Planning Commission.
35 Good Manufacturing Practices (GMP). See http://pharmaceuticals.gov.in/pdf/PTUAS10052013.pdf; and Planning Commission (2011).
36 There is a proposal that funding of R&D should be declared as a priority sector (Abrol 2014). The average cost of ANDAs is INR 40–200 million.
37 India boasts of over 350 drug-producing units that are endorsed by the EU as Good Manufacturing Practices (GMP) compliant and the maximum number of US FDA (US Food and Drug Authority)-approved manufacturing facilities outside the US. The domestic formulations market is worth approximately INR 750,000 million.
38 Abrol (2014) note that public sector laboratories are known to face shortage of funds and paucity in leadership. The direction of public funding of R&D is not strategic. There are four schemes specifically dedicated to R&D projects and 14 policy measures for funding pharmaceutical R&D. In the 12th five-year Plan, the Department of Pharmaceuticals has proposed to set up five to six innovation centres in identified pharmaceutical clusters.
39 With a view to encouraging the domestic production of APIs, the National Intellectual Property Rights Policy 2016 notes this in the section on commercialization of IPRs (Mani 2016).
40 The major therapeutic categories exported are anti-infectives, anti-asthmatics, and anti-hypertensives.
41 Abrol (2014) notes that fermentation plants in India had to be stopped.
42 Bumpas and Betsch (2009) note that price of APIs is the main cost driver for manufacturing.

References

Abrol, D. 2014. 'Technological Upgrading, Manufacturing and Innovation: Lessons from Indian Pharmaceuticals,' Working Paper No. 162. Institute for Studies in Industrial Development.
ASSOCHAM-YES BANK. 2015. *The Indian Pharmaceutical Industry: Changing Dynamics & The Road Ahead*. Life Sciences & IT Knowledge Banking (LSIT), YES BANK.
Bumpas, J. and E. Betsch. 2009. *Exploratory Study on Active Pharmaceutical Ingredient Manufacturing For Essential Medicines*. Washington DC: The International Bank for Reconstruction and Development/The World Bank.
Chaudhuri, S. 2005. *The WTO and India's Pharmaceuticals Industry*, New Delhi: Oxford University Press.
Deloitte. 2014. 'Competitiveness: Catching the Next Wave in India India's Growth Drivers Over the Next 30 Years,' https://www2.deloitte.com/content/dam/Deloitte/in/Documents/about-deloitte/in-about-india-competitiveness-report-2014-noexp.PDF (accessed on 16 May 2017).
Department of Pharmaceuticals. 2012. *Annual Report 2011–12*. Ministry of Chemicals and Fertilizers, Government of India.

DGFT. 2012. Chapter 30: Pharmaceutical Products. ITC (HS), Schedule 1 – Import Policy. Government of India.

Frost and Sullivan. 2012. *Indian Generic Pharmaceuticals Market – A Snapshot*. Market Insight. Frost and Sullivan.

Furtado, R. 2017. 'Top Ten Acquisitions In The Pharmaceutical Sector In India,' https://blog.ipleaders.in/top-ten-acquisitions-in-the-pharmaceutical-sector-in-india/ (accessed on 22 August 2017).

Gereffi, G. 1999. 'International Trade and Industrial Upgrading in the Apparel Commodity Chain,' *Journal of International Economics*, 48(1): 37–70.

IBEF. 2017. Pharmaceuticals, www.ibef.org/download/Pharmaceutical-January-2017-D.PDF (accessed on 18 August 2017).

James, T.C. 2014. Indian API Industry and Imports: An Industry Perspective. Presentation at Colloquium on India's Growing Dependence on Imports in the area of Bulk Drugs, organized by RIS, New Delhi, December 2014.

Joseph, R. K. 2012. 'Policy Reforms in the Indian Pharmaceutical Sector since 1994: Impact on Exports and Imports,' *Economic & Political Weekly*, XLVII(18).

Kallumal, M. and K. Bugalya. 2012. 'Trends in India's Trade in Pharmaceutical Sector: Some Insights,' Centre for WTO Studies Working Paper, CWS/WP/200/2. New Delhi: Indian Institute of Foreign Trade.

Mani. S. 2016. New IPR Policy 2016. *Economic & Political Weekly*, September 17. LI (38).

Ministry of Chemicals and Fertilizers. 1995. *Drugs (Prices Control) Order*. The Gazette of India – Extraordinary, PART II – Section 3 – Sub-Section (ii), dated the 6th January, Department of Chemicals and Petrochemicals. New Delhi.

Ministry of Chemicals & Fertilizers. 2016. *Chemicals & Petrochemicals Statistics at a Glance: 2016*. Government of India.

Ministry of Commerce and Industries. 2008. *Strategy for Increasing Exports of Pharmaceutical Products*. Report of the Task Force.

OPPI. 2015. *Annual Report 2014–15*. Organisation of Pharmaceutical Producers of India.

OPPI. 2014. *Annual Report 2013–14*. Organisation of Pharmaceutical Producers of India.

Pharmexcil. 2016. *12th Annual Report 2015–16*. Pharmaceuticals Export Promotion Council of India.

Planning Commission. 2011. 'Working Groups/Steering Committees for the Twelfth Five Year Plan (2012–2017) For Pharmaceuticals Sector,' http://planningcommission.gov.in/aboutus/committee/wrkgrp12/wg_pharma2902.pdf (accessed on 07 May 2017).

WTO. 2015. *Trade Policy Review*. Report by Secretariat, India. WT/TPR/S/313. World Trade Organization.

Others

Center for Drug Evaluation and Research, www.fda.gov/downloads/Drugs/DevelopmentApprovalProcess/SmallBusinessAssistance/ucm127615.pdf (accessed on 7 May 2017).

Government of India, Make in India: Pharmaceuticals, www.makeinindia.
com/sector/pharmaceuticals (accessed on 15 March 2017).
'India Continues to Lead China in Pharma Exports,' *Livemint*. 8 July. Kritika
Singh. www.livemint.com/Politics/g0vsJg1hoVWJQ7qyBf7WmI/India-con
tinues-to-lead-China-in-pharma-exports.html (accessed on 5 June 2017).
'Natco Pharma Wins Cancer Drug Case' by R. Sivaraman. 2013. The Hindu.
March 04. www.thehindu.com/business/companies/natco-pharma-wins-
cancer-drug-case/article4475762.ece.
'PMO Push for Production of Drug APIs in India'. 2016. Indian Express.
October 26. By Abantika Ghosh. http://indianexpress.com/article/india/
india-news-india/pmo-push-for-production-of-drug-apis-in-india-3102758/
(accessed on 24 August 2017).

10 Integration in the semiconductor microchip node in India

This chapter discusses the semiconductor microchip sector, which represents only a node in the value chain with microchips being designed in the city of Bangalore. The availability of skilled manpower at low cost has resulted in the successful integration into the value chain in this sector. However, the learning and upgrading aspects are limited since the backward and the forward nodes in the chain are absent. The future prospects for this industry will be limited unless an ecosystem for manufacturing evolves in the country.

Nature of the industry

The current consumption of electronics in India is worth about USD 64 billion; 58% of these goods are imported.[1] By 2020, the import bill for electronics is likely to exceed that for oil (currently it is at the second spot), so there is a need to set up manufacturing in the country.[2] The electronics industry can be divided into consumer electronics, electronic components,[3] industrial electronics, computer hardware, communication and broadcast equipment, and strategic equipment.[4] Communication and broadcast equipment and consumer electronics are the largest sub-sectors with 29% and 28% of revenue[5] of the USD 33 billion industry. The largest imports (in terms of percentage) are in the category telecom instruments, followed by computer hardware and peripherals.[6]

Examining the data for exports and imports (refer to Table 4.3A, Chapter 4), we note that India has a negative trade balance in the category "Machinery and mechanical appliances" (HS 84–85). The category HS 85 corresponds to "Electrical and electronic goods." According to the BEC analysis in Chapter 4, the highest imports were in HS 851770. Other items that were largely imported in the period 2009 to 2014 were "Photosensitive semiconductor devices, incl.

photovoltaic cells whether or not assembled in modules or made up into panels"; "Light emitting diodes (excl. photovoltaic generators)"; "Electronic integrated circuits as processors and controllers, whether or not combined with memories, converters, logic circuits, amplifiers, clock and timing circuits, or other circuits"; "Electronic integrated circuits (excl. such as processors, controllers, memories and amplifiers)"; etc.

It has been pointed out that India lacks hardware manufacturing capability. What is not so well known is that India contributes significantly to a particular segment in the hardware manufacturing known as the design stage. Semiconductor design is the most crucial part of chip development.[7]

The semiconductor industry in India began to flourish mainly after the 2008 financial crisis. As smaller companies could not afford costs in the West, they migrated to India. Bigger companies followed and the first company to move to India was Texas Instruments. Over the years, India has developed as a semiconductor design hub with the main cluster located in Bangalore. In this segment, only design takes place in India; some firms operate in the segment upstream of chip design, but none operate downstream. All the firms are located in Bangalore.

Semiconductor design in India started with a focus on software that involved writing the micro-code for the chip. Over time this industry evolved to include more complex designing processes. Brown and Linden (2005) look at why the Indian semiconductor industry is different from that in Taiwan and China using a framework of comparative advantage built on product, price, and market attributes. These sources of comparative advantage lead to off-shoring in order to access location-specific resources, including talent, cost-reduction, and market development. An analysis of off-shoring over time shows that the first stage to move overseas was assembly, which led to a loss of jobs in the US, but kept the firm competitive. The next step was moving of back-testing to Asia so that chips could be sold directly in Asian markets after assembly. However, outsourcing fabrication was minimal because it is an extremely capital-intensive activity with labour costs forming only a small fraction of the total cost; relatively cheap labour would therefore not result in a comparative advantage. The factors that made India an attractive destination were quite different from those in China and Taiwan: the software industry already existed in India and engineers' proficiency in English both attracted investors to India.

Value chain of the semiconductor microchip

The chip design industry in India consists of three segments: Very Large Scale Integration (VLSI), embedded software, and printed circuit boards (PCB). VLSI design is the process of designing integrated circuits by combining thousands of transistors into a single chip and involves various steps before being sent to the foundry. Embedded software, on the other hand, is any computer software which interacts with the hardware layer in the electronics in which it is supplied (India Semiconductor Association 2011). There are around 120 design companies in India as of today.

For the purpose of building a chip, several switches/transistors are put together in an array format (logic-implemented). A collection of 100 switches or so is Small Scale Integration (SSI) while 1000 switches constitute Medium Scale Integration (MSI). A collection of around 10 million switches is called Very Large Scale Integration (VLSI). Very Very Large Scale Integration (VVLSI) is also coming up now. Tools are used to embed software on the transistor. VLSI is the hardware and embedded software is the software. The total output is a combination of both hardware and software. Board design involves stitching multiple chips together. Embedded software is the most important segment within semiconductor design. Both VLSI and embedded software contribute significantly in the case of India.

From an electronics design perspective, the market can be divided into three segments:

The first segment comprises global multinational companies (MNCs) and market makers who employ around 14,000 designers. They are associated with design chain methodology and the challenges associated with shrinking process nodes (65 nano metre and below). The second segment is shared by two domains: 'pure play' design services companies and fab-less semiconductor companies. Over the last decade, multinationals have been associated with Indian service companies for complex projects in the design chain. Design services companies have moved up the value chain and bagged prestigious projects that have a worldwide impact. The third segment is the government, mainly in the areas of defence and space, with an increased focus on communication and defence products. The research and development (R&D) centres of these organizations are producing complex designs. Currently, product design involves IC design, board design, and embedded software development – all done in conjunction with each other. The traditional separation between software digital logic analog

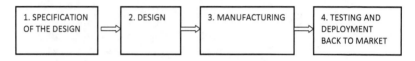

Figure 10.1 Value chain of semiconductor microchips
Source: Authors' compilation from survey

and PCBs is rapidly breaking down, resulting in design convergence. The process of semiconductor manufacturing involves multiple stages including market analysis, product definition, fund-raising, and software and hardware development. Semiconductor design is the most crucial part of the overall chip development (Figure 10.1).

1   *The process of semiconductor design involves several steps:* a block-level diagram is prepared (which takes four to six weeks), then components are gathered, schematics[8] or connecting is done, computer-aided design or CAD (all chips on a board and connect the chips), routing, Gerber,[9] chip manufacture etc. An application is developed on a board and it requires multiple chips to do an application sticking together.

In VLSI, all the transistors are integrated inside the chip, the RTL is written, and then hard silicon is added. There is another class of chips, Field-Programmable Gate Arrays (FPGAs), which contain large numbers of flip-flops; with such chips, it is possible to write custom logic (multiple times) unlike application-specific integrated chips (IC). There can be multilayer printed circuit boards (PCB).[10]

The value chain of semiconductor design is given in Figure 10.2.

2   *Process for embedding chips into a printed circuit board (PCB):* Figure 10.3 shows the process for embedding chips into a PCB.

Regulations

The Department of Telecommunications (DoT) and Department of Electronics and Information Technology (DeitY) (DeitY 2011) under the Ministry of Communication and Information Technology have been introducing policies aimed at this sector. Some of these are the National Policy on Electronics (NPE, 2012, National Policy on

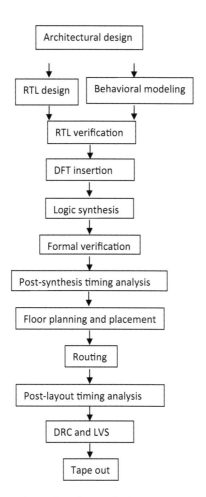

Figure 10.2 Processes in semiconductor design
Source: Based on survey findings

Information Technology, 2012), and the National Telecom Policy (NTP), 2012. The National Policy on Electronics comprises schemes outlining the vision for India's future Electronics Systems and Design Manufacturing (ESDM). The Modified Special Incentive Package Scheme (MSIPS)[11] approved by the Union Cabinet under the NPE aims to promote large-scale manufacturing in the ESDM sector. The scheme provides a subsidy for investments in capital expenditure:

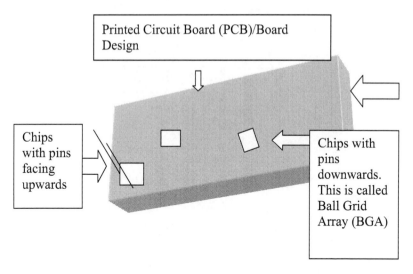

Figure 10.3 Process of embedding chips on a PCB

Source: Authors' compilation from survey

20% for investments in SEZs and 25% in non-SEZs. The National Policy on Information Technology envisions strengthening India's position as a global IT hub and using IT and cyberspace as an engine for rapid, inclusive, and substantial growth in the national economy (Meity 2012a). The NTP provides a roadmap for India to become a leader in the state-of-the-art technologies through R&D and incorporation of Indian intellectual property rights (IPR) in global standards (Meity 2012b). In 2012–13, preferential market access (PMA) was introduced and, in 2014–15, new products were added to the list.[12] Two fabrication units with an investment of INR 650,000 million have been approved. Five disability areas were identified in the Indian ESDM that were hindering its growth – taxation, high cost of finance, poor domestic availability of components, poor infrastructure, and international marketing cost. Initiatives notified by the government in 2014–15 have reduced the disability across these five areas (IESA-EY 2015). Disability has also improved across product categories.

Integration into GVCs

Although India's semiconductor design sector is a prominent one, complete product ownership is absent in India, as the basic specification of the design takes place elsewhere. There is, thus, a serious need to encourage end-to-end product ownership. Of the 90% value addition by semiconductor design, India's share is 75%.

Need for a manufacturing facility in India – India has semiconductor fabrication units but mainly for products manufactured for the defence sector. Two proposed electronic fabrication units in India include one by the JB Group in Noida and another in Ahmedabad. According to one view, absence of a fabrication unit is not a deterrent to manufacturing electronics, but another view holds that the absence of foundries is the main reason for the lack of semiconductor products. Fabrication units in India are likely to be utilized only to the extent of 10–20% while the rest of the capacity (80%) may remain unutilized. The scale or size is a problem in the case of semiconductor industry with a chip fabrication unit costing INR 180–200 million to build. In the absence of downstream electronics production and therefore adequate demand, it may not be worthwhile setting up a fabrication unit.

There are only six countries with fabrication units in the world. These are Taiwan (Taiwan Semiconductor Manufacturing Company (TSMC), which makes more than 70% of the chips available globally), the US, Singapore, China, South Korea, and Malaysia. Even if fabrication units come up in India, silicon wafers would still have to be imported, making it difficult to produce chips competitively: by the time the Indian fabrication units start production in two or three years, the costs of producing chips, already declining, will come down even further and the world would have moved to ever-smaller diameter chips. Taiwan is the main manufacturing hub for semiconductors and caters to a large proportion of the global demand including that of India. China, Italy, and Japan have several foundries also. A lot of companies have moved out of fabrication, with chip makers worldwide getting squeezed for margins and a low ratio of investment-to-returns.

Role of lead firms

The role of the lead firm in the semiconductor industry depends on whether the firm is manufacturing semiconductors or making the wafers. Since manufacturing is absent in the country, the role of the lead firms is restricted. However, Applied Materials, which is a leader in semiconductor equipment manufacturing, and Applied Materials India Private Limited, a wholly owned subsidiary of Applied Materials Inc. of the US, play a lead role. Every chip has been processed through machines manufactured by Applied Materials worldwide. Currently, engineering and R&D work is carried out from Bangalore and Mumbai from the Indian subsidiary. Engineering process in India involves diagrams and wiring, and the Indian entity is also working on tools for the future.

Barriers to integration

Product definition has still not been achieved in India because the ecosystem is absent. There is an absence of intellectual property (IP) in India. Quality of access points/roads/ports is also an issue. Semiconductor fabrication units have not been set up in India for the following reasons: high costs, inadequate infrastructure (slow turnaround in ports), and inadequate manufacturing of downstream electronic products. Customs duty is another major hurdle.[13] There are export restrictions on IP products which require regulatory clearing, especially when the services are being sold to a defence organization.

There is no appropriate regulator in the country for the industry. The government classifies the end product of an IP provider as a service, leading to the IP provider paying both service tax and a Value-Added Tax (VAT).[14]

Semiconductor designing requires skilled manpower and the skill sets are not adequate in India (India Semiconductor Association and UK Trade Investment India 2008). It is also not easy to retain employees for most startups. The semiconductor designers do not get adequate funds in India, as venture capitalists are biased towards as e-commerce projects, which are viewed as being of a relatively low risk.

India can start by moving up the value chain within the design segment. The highest value addition takes place in the Very Large Scale Integration (VLSI). Indian companies are engaged in VLSI, though the IP rests with the parent company which is outsourcing this segment to India. System design capability does not exist in the country, for which an alliance framework needs to be built. The required ecosystem has yet to fully develop, with investments directed towards building the domestic research and development (R&D) (ISA-Frost & Sullivan 2011). India can retain the fab-less model for the time being while building the IP.

Conclusion

This chapter discusses the semiconductor microchip sector, which represents only a node in the value chain with microchips being designed in the city of Bangalore. The availability of skilled manpower at low cost has resulted in the successful integration into the value chain in this sector. However, the learning and upgrading aspects are limited since the backward and forward nodes in the chain are absent. In the absence of a favourable ecosystem, the focus at this point should not be on building a manufacturing framework but on creating training facilities in universities/colleges. There is a need to build an indigenous design sector, as most semiconductor designing in India is pull (or demand) driven while only 20% is push (supply or policy) driven. There is, thus, a serious need to encourage end-to-end product ownership within the semiconductor sector in India. Investments need to be directed towards building the domestic R&D and commensurate skills need to be created. Further, as mentioned before, there are no adequate funding opportunities for semiconductor startups, as the venture capitalists do not find it attractive due to an unattractive risk-reward ratio. This is a serious gap which needs to be filled (Ministry of Communications and Information Technology 2011).

The future prospects for this industry will be limited unless an ecosystem for manufacturing evolves in the country. There could be serious repercussions for the industry if it leapfrogs to manufacturing in the absence of a sound R&D back up. We can perhaps take a cue from Taiwan, where the government worked in collaboration with the private sector to develop research institutes. Thus, the government, research organizations, and the industry helped build a network with the rest of the world, especially with the key players, the US and Japan. The role of India Electronics and Semiconductor Association (IESA) as the main representative association for semiconductor manufacturers is crucial. It must encourage IP creation within the industry by providing funding opportunities and actively voicing its concerns related to taxation, infrastructure, and other impediments to growth.

Notes

1 NITI Aayog (2016) Make in India Strategy for Electronic Products.
2 Has India's electronic manufacturing turned a corner? 2016, *Mint*, 20 February by Asit Ranjan Mishra and Moulishree Srivastava, www.livemint.com/Industry/14DELtag6kPOlM75ynD5RK/Has-Indias-electronic-manufacturing-turned-a-corner.html (accessed on 5 July 2017)
3 The component market in India is driven by microprocessor units (MPU) and memory devices, which account for nearly 50% of the total.
4 The Electronic Systems Design and Manufacturing (ESDM) sector in India comprises four divisions: electronic products, electronic components, semiconductor design services, and electronic manufacturing services (EMS).
5 In 2014–15, NITI Aayog 2016.
6 The most common components in the 25 products that are identified (and account for 82% of consumption) as high priority, include power devices

and semiconductors, processors, memory, printed circuit boards, liquid crystal displays (LCDs), and transformers (IESA-Frost & Sullivan 2014). Of these, five key components, three (power semiconductor, memory, and processor) include semiconductor chips and devices. These items are imported due to the absence of a local fabrication facility.

7 The semiconductor industry consists of integrated device manufacturers (IDM), fab-less companies, and foundries (KPMG 2009).
8 Connections linking the chips are called schematics.
9 The Gerber (GBR) format – used to describe the printed circuit board (PCB) images: copper layers, solder mask, legend etc. – is used by IC manufacturers.
10 PCB is not a part of the semiconductor design but is required to validate the design. PCB Assembly (PCBA) occurs when ICs are assembled on the PCB. Another type of surface-mount packaging (a chip carrier) used for integrated circuits is called a Ball Grid Array (BGA). BGA packages are used to permanently mount devices such as microprocessors. A BGA can provide more interconnection pins than can be put on a dual in-line or flat package. The whole bottom surface of the device can be used, instead of just the perimeter. The leads are also, on average, of shorter dimension than with a perimeter-only type, leading to better performance at high speeds. Black covering on ICs is called packaging – between the packaging is the silicon wafer. There is a chip on the PCB that contains the software for functioning of all ICs on the PCB – this is the embedded software.
11 The subsidy for investments in capital expenditure is 20% for investments in SEZs and 25% in non-SEZs for production of components in the 2014–15 budget.
12 Laptop personal computers (PCs), Light Emitting Diode (LED) products, smart cards, tablet PCs, desktop PCs, dot matrix printers, biometric access control, biometric iris sensors mandating 50% of government procurement to be from local manufacturers.
13 Inverted duty structures became a common phenomenon for IT products primarily after the implementation of the Information Technology Agreement (ITA-I), a plurilateral agreement under the WTO which recommended the lowering of tariffs for a set of IT products. Inverted duty structure is a case when import duty on raw materials is higher than that on finished products. ITA-I products are still facing disability. Refer to discussion on disability earlier in this chapter.
14 In the case of GST, while IT services are taxed at 18%, temporary transfer or permitting the use or enjoyment of any intellectual property (IP) to attract the same rate as in respect of permanent transfer of IP, which is 12%. https://community.nasscom.in/community/discuss/current-issues/gst/blog/2017/05/26/gst-rates-announced-by-the-gst-council-and-its-relevance-to-the-it-sector (accessed on 01 September 2017).

References

Brown, C. and G. Linden. 2005. 'Offshoring in the Semiconductor Industry: Historical Perspectives,' Working Paper No. 120–05. Institute for Research on Labour and Employment.

DeitY. 2011. 'Draft Project Report on "Electronics Development Fund" (EDF),' http://policy.electronicsb2b.com/wpcontent/uploads/2013/03/draft%20 DPR_version%20Nov2_11192011_AK.pdf. Government of India.

IESA-Frost & Sullivan. 2014. *Indian ESDM Market.* www.iesaonline.org/ downloads/IESA-F&S_Executive_Summary.pdf.

IESA- EY. 2015. Impact of Recent Policy Developments on Disabilities in the ESDM Sector, http://www.iesaonline.org/downloads/Impact_of_recent_ policy%20developments_on_disabilities_of_ESDM_sector.pdf

India Semiconductor Association. 2011. *Study on Semiconductor Design, Embedded Software and Services Industry.* Bangalore: India Semiconductor Association.

India Semiconductor Association and UK Trade Investment India. 2008. *Scope for Indo-UK collaboration in the Semiconductor Driven Industry.* Feedback Study – Final Report. www.iesaonline.org/downloads/ISA_UKTI_protect. pdf (accessed on 14 January 2017).

ISA-Frost & Sullivan. 2011. *ISA – Frost & Sullivan 2010–12: India Semiconductor Market Update.*

KPMG. 2009. *The Road to Recovery in the Global Semiconductor Industry: A Survey of Industry Executives – Fourth Quarter 2009.* KPMG International.

Meity. 2012a. *National Policy on Information Technology 2012.* http://meity. gov.in/writereaddata/files/National_20IT_20Policyt%20_20.pdf (accessed on 30 August 2017).

Meity. 2012b. *National Telecom Policy 2012.* http://meity.gov.in/write readdata/files/National%20Telecom%20Policy%20(2012)%20(480%20 KB).pdf (accessed on 30 August 2017).

Ministry of Communications and Information Technology. 2011. *Draft Project Report on "Electronics Development Fund" (EDF).* Department of Information Technology, Government of India. http://policy.electronicsb2b.com/ wp-content/uploads/2013/03/draft%20DPR_version%20Nov2_11192011_ AK.pdf (accessed on 30 August 2017).

NITI Aayog. 2016. *Make in India Strategy for Electronic Products.* Government of India.

Others

Has India's Electronic Manufacturing Turned a Corner? 2016. *Mint.* 20 February, by Asit Ranjan Mishra and Moulishree Srivastava, www.livemint. com/Industry/14DELtag6kPOlM75ynD5RK/Has-Indias-electronic-manu facturing-turned-a-corner.html (accessed on 05 July 2017).

11 Integration in the garments value chain
The case of India

The garments sector is an example of unsuccessful integration into GVCs. The reasons for this are many; for example, excessive use of cotton and higher costs compared to countries like Bangladesh. The sector is diverse with many clusters around the country and caters to a large domestic market, the neighbouring countries and the Middle East. The standards for these markets are quite different from those of the larger markets of the US and the EU, to which only some firms cater. Upgrading has been reported by some firms in this sector. Also, diversification into synthetic material will be important in the future.

Nature of the industry

The textile and clothing industry is a diverse and heterogeneous one covering a large number of activities, from the transformation of raw materials to fibres, yarns, and fabrics. These in turn are used to make a number of products, including garments.[1] The maximum value addition to textiles is done by the apparel sector, which is the last stage of the textile value chain. The clothing sector covers made-up products that are articles of apparel, clothing, and accessories. The apparel sector is usually the first one that developing countries enter because of low entry barriers and its labour-intensive nature. It also provides opportunities for upgrading to higher value-added activities (Staritz 2012).

The textile and the clothing sector covers approximately 1500 tariff lines; while the textile sector is covered by HS Chapters 50 to 60 and 63 of the combined nomenclature, clothing is covered by Chapters 61 and 62. Clothing products in Chapter 61 are either knitted[2] or crocheted, while apparel produced from woven textile fabrics are part of Chapter 62,[3] indicating that the basis for classification is thus the underlying manufacturing process.[4,5]

India is among the world's top 15 exporters of textiles and clothing.[6] In 2013, exports from India were USD 19 billion and its share in the world was 6.2%.[7] India also imported USD 4 billion worth of textiles in 2013.[8] By contrast, India's clothing exports were worth USD 17 billion and its share was 3.7% of the world's exports of clothing. While the exports of textiles by India increased from USD 2.1 billion in 1990 to 19 billion in 2013, exports of clothing (garments) increased from USD 2.3 billion in 2000 to 18 billion in 2014. The top items exported by India are "T-shirts, Singlets, vests, etc." (HS 6109), and "Women's or Girls Suits, Ensembles, Jackets, Blazers, etc." (HS 6204) in 2015–16.[9] The readymade garment segment contributes to 43% of the Indian textile exports, which includes cotton garments and accessories, man-made fibre garments, and other textile clothing (Ministry of Textiles 2016).

The garment industry was one of the most protected industries (Gereffi and Frederick 2010). However, with the removal of quotas in 2005, the international restrictions on apparel trade is now limited. However, disruptions due to trade agreements such as Trans-Pacific Partnership (TPP) cannot be ruled out.[10]

The structure of the garment industry is rather complex, with the bulk of units being small and medium firms.[11] The Annual Survey of Industries reports that there were 3760 garment manufacturing units in 2009–10 (using the definition of "Factory" in the Factories Act, 1948). In 2001–02, the same figure was 3273, and in 2006–07 it was 3627. The Annual Survey of Industries collects data only for registered manufactures. The small and medium sector is surveyed by the Micro, Small, and Medium Sector (MSME) survey (Government of India 2009). The Fourth MSME Census reported 214,557 registered MSMEs in 2006–07.[12] This covers only registered units and unregistered small and medium units are not counted.[13]

The textile sector in India employs 12.3 million people and produces 3.6 million tonnes of apparel and garments (Ministry of Textiles 2016). The garment industry in India caters to both the domestic market and exports.[14] In 2008, it was estimated that while the size of the domestic apparel market was worth USD 15 billion, apparel exports were USD 9.7 billion (Confederation of Indian Textile Industry or CITI). In 2008, a study by the Apparel Export Promotion Council (AEPC) pointed out that India produced 8900 million pieces, of which 2100 million pieces were exported. Based on data provided by the textile commissioner[15] (Technopak 2012), estimates suggest that the contribution of the textiles and garments sector to employment is significant. It is the second largest employer in the country, providing

19% of the industrial workforce in 2013. The garments industry provides a quarter of the jobs in this sector.[16]

Garment production is organized into clusters with units scattered all over the country. The clusters are categorized into two: (a) type of garment (i.e. knitted or woven) and (b) variety of product (men's, women's, kids' wear). For the domestic market in 2009, men's wear comprised 43% of the total production amounting to INR 663,000 million, and women's wear stood at INR 577,450 million, 37% of the total. Boy's and girl's wear stood at INR 15765 (10% of the total) and INR 141,900 (9% of the total) million, respectively (Indian Textile and Apparel Compendium, 2010 Technopak).

The major clusters are located in Delhi-NCR, Mumbai, Ludhiana, Kolkata, Tirupur, and Bangalore.[17] AEPC (2009) estimated that 95% of the production is in the top 19 clusters, whose annual production is 8900 million pieces. Of this, 6800 million pieces fulfil domestic demand and 2100 million pieces are exported. The total number of garment units in these 19 clusters is 33,371. The clusters are specialized in terms of type of garments (either woven or knitted) and the variety of the products (men's, women's, or children's). Details of the 19 major manufacturing clusters are presented in Table 11.1. The table shows the products made in the various clusters, along with the raw material used and the principal market for the products.

Table 11.1 shows that the Indian garment industry is diverse in terms of the product, location of clusters, the number of units etc. The striking feature of Table 11.1 is the dominant use of cotton. While some clusters specialize in products for the export market, others produce primarily for the domestic market: the two kinds of products differ significantly. To illustrate this, two examples are taken: women's blouses and T-shirts. The T-shirt is a mass-produced item usually made in the clusters of Tirupur, Ludhiana, or Mumbai. Women's blouses are usually produced in the Delhi-NCR and there is more value addition and gain for the firm than in the case of T-shirts. The domestic market is another category, with products of a lower quality than those exported, and mass-produced items. The segment can be subdivided into items that are branded and sold through organized retail and those that are not branded. The prices of the unbranded segment are significantly lower than those in the branded segment (for a comparable product). The branded segment faces competition from imports while in the latter there is competition from Bangladesh. However, India is not among the world's top 15 importers. The unstitched segment produces saris, dhotis, and dress material mainly for the domestic segment (with some export to countries like Bangladesh and the Middle East).

Table 11.1 Major garment clusters in India

Cluster	Product	Total units	Woven/ knitted	Nature of product (raw material base)	Principal market
Bangalore	Shirts, trousers, denim for men	850	Woven	Cotton based (70%)	Export + domestic
Bellary	Bottom wear for men	1305	Woven	Cotton based and blends of viscose	Domestic
Chennai	Men's shirts	650	Woven	Cotton	Export
Delhi-NCR (Okhla)	Women's wear	250	Knit	Cotton	Export
Delhi-NCR (Noida)	Fashion wear	750	Woven		Export
Delhi-NCR (Gurgaon)	Fashion wear	675	Woven		Export
Delhi-NCR (Faridabad)			Woven		
Indore	Kids' wear	2000	Woven	Cotton	Domestic
Ludhiana	Winter wear and t-shirts	2500	Knit	Woolen/acrylic	Domestic
Kolkata	Kids' wear, inner wear, work wear	12291 (7291 knit) + (5000 woven)	Knit and woven	80–85% cotton	Domestic
Jaipur	Women's wear	950	Woven	Cotton	Export
	Men's and kids'			PC and cotton	Domestic
Mumbai	Men's shirts	6000	Knit and woven	84% cotton	Domestic + export
Tirupur		2500	Knit		Export
Kanpur		500	Knit		
Madurai		150	Woven		
Salem		100	Woven		
Ahmedabad		500	Woven		
Nagpur		500	Woven		
Jabalpur		400	Woven		
Smaller centres					
Chitradurga		NA	Woven		
Rayadurg		NA	Woven		
Pune		NA	Woven		

Source: Authors' compilation based on AEPC (2009)

The highest import duty (30%) is on cotton, carded and combed, among the items used in the garment/textile industry. The import tariffs on man-made fibres, filaments, and yarn is 10% and the items imported most in the period 2009 to 2013 were fabric dipped in rubber or plastic (among the items in the HS Category 54 to 60).

Value chain in the garments industry[18]

Steps in the transformation of the fabric to garments include cutting, stitching, sewing, fastening of trims,[19] embellishments, packing, marketing etc.[20,21] Figure 11.1 shows the value chain for the production of a basic garment such as a T-shirt or top. Depending on the nature of the product, a step for dealing with embellishments and embroidery may be added. About 55–60% of the cost of production of a garment is on the raw material, which includes fabric, accessories, sewing thread etc.[22]

Integration into GVCs

In the context of garments, trade in tasks includes the Cut-Make-Trim (CMT), which is the basic assembly approach. This means that one firm could design the item, another could produce it, while assembly and final production could be carried out by a third firm.

Integration into GVCs would imply India's involvement in certain parts of the value chain with other parts being carried out in other countries. Also, as noted previously, products specifically catering to the domestic segment, such as unbranded garments, and those in the unstitched category, are not likely to be integrated into GVCs. This leaves the branded segment and products that are exported. We discuss the scope of learning and upgrading in these two categories.[23]

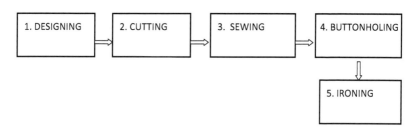

Figure 11.1 Value chain for production of garments

Source: Authors' drawing based on Applebaum and Gereffi (1994)

In India, apart from the domestic market, integration with regional chains is important in the context of the garments industry. India exports items like Bangladesh (Ray et al. 2016). Some Indian firms have production arrangements with firms in Bangladesh since production costs are lower there; however, this is rather limited.

A report by the World Bank, Lopez-Acevedo and Raymond (2016), explores the gains in employment that countries in South Asia, including India, can expect due to the rise in wages in China. The South Asian countries were outperformed by Vietnam, Indonesia, and Cambodia in terms of exports, product diversity, and non-cost related factors. The key factors for global buyers are firm capability,[24] cost, quality, lead time, and reliability. Access to inputs, full-package services, and social and environmental compliance are also important. According to Roy (2009), the garments industry is delinked from GVCs even though exports are significant. According to Tewari (2008), India's export strategy consists of shipping smaller volumes and shorter runs of relatively high-value products.

Learning

The scope for learning and upgrading depends on the product in question. As has been pointed out by Pietrobelli and Rabellotti (2011) in the context of Latin America, economic sectors may be grouped into four large categories, depending on the way that learning, innovation, and upgrading occurs. The categories are: Traditional manufacturing (mainly labour-intensive where "traditional" technology is used in industries such as textiles, footwear, tiles, and furniture); resource-based industries (involves the direct exploitation of natural resources and examples include copper, marble, fruit); complex product systems' industries (which include automobiles, auto parts and aeronautics industries, ICT, and consumer electronics); and specialized suppliers (refers to software).

The garment industry is a diverse industry ranging from very basic products such as bottoms, T-shirts etc. to fashion products for women. The production technology is very standardized (as also suggested by Pietrobelli and Rabellotti 2011) for certain products and the margins for such products are very low.[25] For simple products such as T-shirts, the scale and the lead time can contribute to differences in the competitiveness of countries. Other differences arise on account of fabric quality and the thread used in stitching. India's strength in garments lies in these higher value-added products and its unit value is higher than Bangladesh but lower than Pakistan.

According to the Lopez-Acevedo and Raymond (2016), unit values are medium in India while wages are lower compared to Pakistan and China.[26] End markets are influenced by tariff rates and market access preferences. Interestingly, India specializes in a different part of the chain compared to countries such as Pakistan.[27] In the garments segment, Bangladesh and Pakistan specialize in three product categories: trousers, knit shirts, and sweaters/sweatshirts, while Sri Lanka specializes in intimate wear and swim wear.

In the context of the garments industry in India, the scope for learning exists when the buyer provides specifications (these items are usually exported), but the scope for upgrading may be limited, as has been pointed out by Giuliani et al. (2005) in the case of captive chains. High value addition occurs in design, which requires conceptualization at the design stage and skills at the cutting stage. Unless a garment is cut properly, it cannot be stitched well. There is scope for learning in fashion garments where the embellishments and the trim can change the "look" of the product. Scale is less of a problem and, in fact, handcrafted products often fetch a premium. The storage and packing of such products when they are shipped is also likely to be different from those of standard products with formats such as "on hanger" used to prevent the items from becoming crumpled during transport.[28] Such products have high margins but the "rent" is usually captured by the buyer specifying the design.[29] Some firms (in the Delhi-NCR) are setting up design studios either abroad (e.g. Italy) or in India to overcome this problem.

In summary, the question of learning relates to the product in question and cannot be generalized to the entire industry; however, the scope for upgrading may be higher in branded products that are being supplied to the domestic market. This is further discussed in the following sections.

Upgrading

The most value addition occurs in the design, branding, and marketing stage (Gereffi and Memedovic 2003). According to Navas-Aleman (2011), it is rare for developing country manufacturers to design their own exports even when operating in GVCs and even rarer for them to own exports brands. As Keesing and Lall (1992) note, lack of design and marketing skills leaves firms from developing countries in a vulnerable situation with respect to global buyers. This industry is an example of a buyer-driven chain with power asymmetrically held by global buyers of the final product over producers (Gereffi and Frederick 2010).

In the context of the Indian garment industry, there are several points to be noted. First, while designs are not very important for the non-branded segment, they are so for the branded segment.[30] Second, the market matters. As shown in Ray et al. (2016), in many instances, especially when supplying to the export markets of the US/EU, the design and the specification are both provided by the buyer and, as a consequence, value cannot be captured by Indian firms. This is not the case when firms are supplying products to the Middle East market or the Indian domestic market. Hence, value cannot be captured by the Indian firms when supplying to US/EU markets, when designs and specifications are supplied by the buyer. While there is some upgrading, especially when the products are being sold by Indian lead firms in the Middle East, lower upgrading occurs when firms supply to the US/ EU.[31] In the latter case, the scope for learning is greater in case when products are supplied to the EU/US.

Role of lead firms

There are three main types of lead firms: retailers, brand marketers, and brand manufacturers in the garments industry. Lead firms are usually engaged in high-value activities such as design, marketing, consumer services, and logistics. Gereffi and Frederick (2010) provide examples of each type of lead firm – within retailers, there are mass merchants (e.g. Walmart, Target, Tesco etc.), and specialty retailers (e.g. Gap, H&M etc.). Brand manufacturers (e.g. VF, Inditex (Zara)) are involved in the production process through ownership or supply of inputs. Brand marketers (e.g. Nike, Hugo Boss, Levi's etc.) and retailers source from OEMs or full-package producers. The buyer, in this case, provides detailed garment specification while the supplier is responsible for acquiring the inputs and coordinating all parts of the production process (Bair and Gereffi 2001; Bair 2006). Gereffi and Frederick (2010) feel that post the WTO's Multifibre Arrangement (MFA) phase, the emergence of private label sourcing, East Asian transnational manufacturers, and agents who act as intermediaries between buyers and sellers (like Li & Fung) have changed the landscape of the industry. The traditional agent-sourcing model is popular with buyers that require smaller volumes, or larger buyers that require small quantities of certain items. Many buyers have established overseas sourcing offices in their main producing countries. Buyers tend to source fashion intensive products from suppliers that can deliver speedily and are flexible. Basic products are sourced from the lowest cost producers (Gereffi and Frederick 2010).

Producers now need to establish long-term relationships with buyers and production networks. Such relationships are beneficial for both buyers and suppliers – they lead to reduced lead times, standardization of the production process, and preferential transportation and logistics. Suppliers benefit from guaranteed demand. Some of the global majors such as Gap are directly sourcing from India. VF Corporation is direct sourcing manufacturer in India. For a full-package supplier, the next step is to enter new emerging market as a lead firm (Gereffi and Frederick 2010). For most Indian firms, this next step is yet to happen.

Barriers to integration

The reasons for the low integration of India's garment industry can be found in the costs associated with production, logistics costs, and time involved in exporting/importing. Tewari and Singh (2010) find that costs of power, transportation, labour, and taxes are higher in India compared to other competitor countries such as China and Bangladesh. Also adding to the costs are the high rentals[32] in cities such as Delhi and Mumbai on account of which many firms relocate to the outskirts of cities such as Manesar (for Delhi) and Bhiwandi (for Mumbai). However, there are other logistical issues involved in these locations which can add to the costs (such as transportation of labour) (AEPC 2009; Roy 2009).

The other possible reasons for the low integration are the large size of the domestic market and the fact that cotton is the dominant fabric in use. Since the ease of supplying to the domestic market is greater (owing to high export standards and strict delivery schedules), certain firms prefer to cater to the domestic market. However, firms which start exporting also find that it has benefits such as timely payments if paperwork is in order. Domination of cotton as the fibre base means that firms can cater only to the summer demand and remain out of the winter wear market. Some firms are trying to overcome this problem by supplying to the South American countries (such as Brazil or Peru), where it is summer in the Northern Hemisphere's winter, allowing production all year round.

According to Lopez-Acevedo and Raymond (2016), firms in South Asia need to move up in the apparel GVC by expanding to multiple high-end product categories and increasing the size of its export markets. For India, although it is a more diversified market compared to the other South Asian countries, the main problem areas are its low productivity, over-reliance on cotton, and low quality due to inefficiencies in the textile supply base.[33] The local textile mills provide grey fabric which needs to be dyed, leading to delays. About 65% of the fabric production occurs in power looms.[34] India's focus in on the domestic market and FDI is lacking in this sector, as South Asia is not aligned with East Asia. To be part of the GVC, India needs to be more competitive.[35]

Conclusion

The importance of the garment sector in a developing country is paramount. This is due to its employment potential and to it often being the stepping stone to deeper industrialization. Countries such as Japan and South Korea started their industrialization process with garments. In the context of GVCs, a country is part of the chain if it is cost competitive. Cost competitiveness is ever-changing in this world: other countries like Vietnam are presently competitive but may soon become uncompetitive due to rise in wages elsewhere. Hence, in order to benefit from the process of integration, countries need to develop an institutional framework, allowing workers to shift to other industries if a certain industry becomes uncompetitive. Without these safeguards, the costs of integration may be higher than the benefits.

Notes

1 The garment sector is an important one for developing countries to enter the global market as well as an opportunity for industrialization (UNCTAD 2005). We focus on garments only in this chapter.
2 Knitting is a technique to weave a fabric wherein no intersection takes place, but yarns are interlaced in loop form. Most commonly hosiery knitted apparels are T-shirts, sweaters, lower, night suits etc. Hosiery products are made from knitted fabrics.
3 Woven fabrics are made through intersection of yarns in vertical direction (called warp) and horizontal direction (called weft). The most commonly used woven apparels are trousers, shirts, suits, ladies' suits, and saris.
4 In this chapter, apparel, clothing, and garments are used interchangeably.
5 Textile production is more capital intensive than garments. Usually developing countries account for a larger share in garments than textiles. The textile and garment industries are completely different: the textile industry is concerned with the production of cloth while the garment industry is concerned with articles made from the cloth that the textile industry produces. The processes in the textile value chain include yarn production, spinning, weaving, pre-treatment, dyeing and printing, and finishing.

 6 The top exporters include China, EU 27, Bangladesh, and Turkey (Gereffi and Frederick 2010)
 7 WTO, www.wto.org/english/res_e/statis_e/its2014_e/its14_merch_trade_product_e.htm (accessed on 13 July 2017).
 8 The major consumption of garments is in the US, the EU, and Japan.
 9 Based on information from the Export Import data from the Ministry of Commerce and Industries, Government of India.
10 This will not be discussed in this chapter. However, with the withdrawal of the US from the agreement, the supplies to the US market may not be affected. Recently, other members agreed to go ahead with the agreement without the US (www.cnbc.com/2017/07/18/trans-pacific-partnership-members-look-to-move-on-without-us.html) (accessed on 02 February 2017).
11 According to Roy 2009, the gross value-added of the Annual Survey of Industries (ASI) sector is 80% for the garment industry while the Directory Manufacturing Establishment (DME) accounts for 20% (based on data from National Sample Survey Organization (NSSO), data for (ASI) for 2004–05 while for DME for 2005–06. The employment of the ASI sector is 64% while that of the DME sector is 36%. This is based on information from eight major garment-producing states. West Bengal is the only exception which has a larger share of the DME sector.
12 The employment provided was 0.901 million in 2006–07. *Source:* Ministry of Micro, Small, Medium and Enterprises (2016).
13 The number of unregistered units was 2.952 million, which provided employment to 5.105 million in 2006–07.
14 India is a full-package provider, which means that it can carry out all the steps involved in the production of a garment. This includes design, fabric purchasing, cutting, sewing, trimming, packaging, and distribution (Gereffi and Frederick 2010).
15 Ministry of Textiles, Textile Committee. 2011. *National Household Survey 2010: Market for Textile and Clothing.*
16 It is unclear whether the employment provided in the micro, small, and medium enterprises (MSME) sector is covered in this estimate.
17 A description of these clusters is provided in the AEPC report 2009; also see Roy (2009) for a discussion on the Tirupur and the Delhi-NCR cluster.
18 Apparel chains are buyer-driven chains (Kaplinsky and Morris 2001) where production is organized in globally dispersed production networks, coordinated by lead firms. Activities that add value to the product (such as design and branding) are often coordinated by lead firms. The smile curve of value addition in the apparel industry has production at its lowest point (Gereffi and Frederick 2010).
19 Trim supplier is not present in India, which adds to costs and leads to delays (Lopez-Acevedo and Raymond 2016).
20 The steps such as spinning, dyeing, printing etc. are part of the textile value chain. The garments value chain starts from the fabric, which is the end product of the textile value chain.
21 The apparel value chain is organized around five main segments: (1) raw material supply, including: natural and synthetic fibres; (2) provision of components, such as the yarns and fabrics manufactured by textile companies; (3) production networks made up of garment factories, including their domestic and overseas subcontractors; (4) export channels

established by trade intermediaries; and (5) marketing networks at the retail level (Fernandez-Stark et al. 2011)

22 Our survey conducted in 2013–15. This is corroborated by Lopez-Acevedo and Raymond (2016).

23 This is not to imply that there is no scope for learning and upgrading in the case of the non-branded and the unstitched category. However, given the linkages of these categories with GVCs, it is likely to be even less; we restrict our arguments to the other categories for which there is potential to integrate with GVCs.

24 This is especially true in the case of the captive chains.

25 The bargaining power of the supplier depends on the complexity of the capability required to perform a task – and as pointed out by Nathan et al. (2016), garment manufacturing firms have low bargaining power and the prices they get are likely to be the prevailing price of the CMT.

26 Labour costs are about one-fifth of the total costs while rent and utilities constitute about one-fifth of the total costs.

27 Taneja et al. (2017) observe that Pakistan does not have the finer quality of cotton and specializes in production of yarn with under 20 counts. India, on the other hand, produces a variety of yarn ranging from 20 to 150 counts.

28 Our survey, 2013–2015.

29 Mahutga (2014) suggest that although value is produced all along a value chain, the rent is captured by certain segments due to capability and bargaining power.

30 Lopez-Acevedo and Raymond (2016) note that brand development is the highest in India (among the South Asian countries).

31 This reiterates the point made earlier regarding the role of the governance of the value chain in upgrading.

32 Our survey, 2013–2015.

33 Raw materials constitute about two-thirds of the total cost according to Lopez-Acevedo and Raymond (2016).

34 Yarn can be spun in the form of a coon or in the form of hank yarn. The coon is the standard spun yarn which is used by the mills and power looms for the process of fabrication both in the domestic and export market (Taneja et al. 2017). The Hank Yarn Obligation is a mechanism to ensure adequate availability of hank yarn to handloom weavers at reasonable prices. The existing hank Yarn Packing Notification dated 17.04.2003 promulgated under Essential Commodities Act, 1955 prescribes that every producer of yarn who packs yarn for civil consumption shall pack at least 40% of yarn packed for civil consumption in hank form on a quarterly basis and not less than 80% of the hank yarn packed shall be of counts 80s and below. *Source:* Press Information Bureau (2012).

35 In terms of cost of production, the logistics and the time cost.

References

Apparel Export Promotion Council. 2009. *Indian Apparel Clusters – An Assessment.* New Delhi: Apparel Export Promotion Council.

Appelbaum, R. P. and G. Gereffi. 1994. 'Power and Profits in the Apparel Commodity Chain' in E. Bonacich et al. (eds.), *Ial Production: The Apparel*

Industry in the Pacific Rim, pp. 42–64. Philadelphia, PA: Temple University Press.

Bair, J. 2006. 'Regional Trade and Production Blocs in a Global Industry: Towards a Comparative Framework for Research,' *Environment and Planning A*, 38(12): 2233–2252.

Bair, J. and G. Gereffi. 2001. 'Local Clusters in Global Value Chains: The causes and Consequences of Export Dynamism in Torreon's Blue Jeans industry,' *World Development*, 29(9110): 1885–1903.

Fernandez-Stark, K., Frederick, S. and G. Gereffi. 2011. *The Apparel Global Value Chain: Economic Upgrading and Workforce Development*, Center on Globalization, Governance & Competitiveness, Duke University.

Gereffi, G. and S. Frederick. 2010. 'The Global Apparel Value Chain, Trade, and the Crisis: Challenges and Opportunities for Developing Countries,' Policy Research Working Paper 5281, Washington, DC: World Bank.

Gereffi, G. and O. Memedovic. 2003. *The Global Apparel Value Chain: What Prospects for Upgrading by Developing Countries?* United Nations Industrial Development Organization (UNIDO).

Giuliani, E. Pietrobelli, C. and R. Rabellotti. 2005. 'Upgrading in Global Value Chains: Lessons from Latin America Clusters,' *World Development*, 33(4): 549–573.

Government of India. 2009. *Quick Results Fourth All India Census of, Micro, Small & Medium Enterprises 2006–2007*. MSME Policies.

Kaplinsky, R. and M. Morris. 2001. *A Handbook for Value Chain Research*. Prepared for the International Development Research Centre (IDRC), pp. 4–6 (emphasis added) (accessed 19 January 2015) SustainAbility, UNEP and UN Global Compact.

Keesing, D. B. and S. Lall. 1992. 'Marketing Manufactured Exports from Developing Countries: Learning Sequences and Public Support,' in G. Helleiner (ed.) *Trade Policy, Industrialization, and Development: New Perspectives*. Oxford: Clarendon Press.

Lopez-Acevedo, G. and R. Raymond. 2016. *Stitches to Riches? Apparel Employment, Trade, and Economic Development in South Asia*. Directions in Development – Poverty; Washington, DC: World Bank.

Mahutga, M. 2014. 'Global Models of Networked Organization, the Positional Power of Nations and Economic Development,' *Review of International Political Economy*, 21(1): 157–194.

Ministry of Micro, Small and Medium Enterprises. 2016. *Annual Report 2015–16*. Government of India.

Ministry of Textiles. 2016. *Annual Report 2015–16*. Government of India.

Nathan, D., Tewari, M. and S. Sarkar (eds.). 2016. *Labour Conditions in Asian Value Chains*. Cambridge: Cambridge University Press.

Navas Aleman, L. 2011. 'The Impact of Operating in Multiple Value Chains for Upgrading: The Case of Brazilian Furniture and Footwear Industries,' *World Development*, 39(8): 1386–1397.

Pietrobelli, C. and R. Rabellotti. 2011. 'Global Value Chains meet Innovation Systems: Are there Learning Opportunities for Developing Countries?' *World Development*, 39(7): 1261–1269.

Press Information Bureau. 2012. *Hank Yarn Obligation.* Government of India.

Ray, S., Mukherjee, P. and M. Mehra. 2016. 'Upgrading in the Indian Garment Industry: A Study of Three Clusters,' ADB South Asia Working Paper Series, No. 43. Asian Development Bank.

Roy, S. 2009. 'Garment Industry in India: Lessons from Two Clusters,' Working Paper 2009/01. Institute for Studies in Industrial Development.

Staritz, C. 2012. 'Apparel Exports – Still a Path for Industrial Development? Dynamics in Apparel Global Value Chains and Implications for Low-income Countries,' Working Paper 34. Austrian Foundation for Development Research (ÖFSE).

Taneja, N., Ray, S. and D. Pande. 2017. 'Exploring the Trade in Textiles and Clothing between India and Pakistan,' in N. Taneja and I. Dayal (eds.), *India-Pakistan Trade Normalisation: The Unfinished Agenda.* Singapore: Springer.

Technopak. 2010. *Indian Textile and Apparel Compendium 2010.* New Delhi: Technopak.

Technopak. 2012. *Textile & Apparel 2012 Compendium.* New Delhi: Technopak.

Tewari, M. 2008. 'Deepening Intraregional Trade and Investment in South Asia The Case of the Textiles and Clothing Industry,' Working Paper 213. New Delhi: Indian Council for Research on International Economic Relations (ICRIER).

Tewari, M. and M. Singh. 2010. *Benchmarking the International Competitiveness of the Indian Garment and Textile Industry.* New Delhi: ICRIER.

UNCTAD. 2005. *TNCs and the Removal of Textiles and Clothing Quotas.* New York and Geneva: United Nations.

12 Integration in the specialty chemicals value chain

The case of India

This chapter covers the case of India's participation in the specialty chemicals value chain. Specialty chemicals manufacturing is moving eastward on the global map and India's share is increasing every year. It is a highly knowledge-intensive sector and the value chain is partly network type (relational) and partly modular in nature.[1] However, the industry is currently fragmented and systematic efforts are needed to align production processes with global best standards for significant integration into GVCs and upgrading thereafter. The current level of knowledge-sharing remains limited.

Nature of the industry

Specialty chemicals lie at the bottom of the supply chain of chemicals.[2] They are produced in the later stages,[3] incorporate a larger degree of complexity, and are produced in low volumes. Specialty chemicals are high-value and low-volume products sold on the basis of performance, rather than specifications. The specialty chemicals segment is a part of the chemicals industry, which provides key inputs for industries such as paints and inks, crop protection, dyes and pigments, construction, electronic chemicals, agrochemicals, water treatment chemicals, pharmaceuticals, and specialty polymers. These products are sold directly for use in the end markets, including the automotive, construction, pulp, paper and printing, and textiles sectors. Specialty chemicals accounted for 21% of the global chemicals market (Bamber et al. 2016). Some of the world's leaders[4] in specialty chemicals are Germany, France, the UK, Italy, South Korea (electronic chemicals), China (agrochemicals), and India (pharmaceuticals).

Globally, the fine and specialty chemicals[5] manufacturing is moving eastwards.[6] As Elsevier (2014) puts it, the 2008 financial meltdown contributed to a worldwide strategic shift in chemicals manufacturing and related research and development (R&D).[7] The European chemical industry has been declining for a long time with manufacturing picking up in the Middle East and Asia (Cefic 2014). The Asian commodity chemical manufacturing is moving to (and is dominated by) India and China (EXIM 2012). Countries such as Singapore, South Korea, Thailand, and Malaysia have also taken big strides in establishing themselves as low-cost sourcing options.

Since a large number of products are produced in the specialty chemicals segment, many different feedstocks are used. Feedstock or raw materials do not account for the major costs in the industry, but product development and marketing activities do. Companies can use specialty chemicals to develop new products that give them a competitive edge in the marketplace. Specialty chemicals play a key role in the development of new products, as these help in creating product differentiation, enabling manufacturers to compete in the marketplace with unique features and benefits. The specialty chemicals industry is not so much about economies of scale (as with commodity chemicals), but about economies of scope, because the same product (specialty chemical) can be used for multiple applications.

Value chain in the specialty chemicals segment

There are several specialty chemicals,[8] each with a different value chain depending on the feedstock or basic raw material used. It is a highly knowledge-intensive sector and the value chain is partly network type (relational) and partly modular in nature. In general, the basic processes involved include granulation through which the chemical compound is formed, stabilization, testing, and packaging the product.[9] Table 12.1 illustrates the different feedstocks and end products in the segment.

Indian specialty chemicals sector

The Indian specialty chemicals market was worth about USD 21 billion in the year 2015.[10] It has grown at the rate of 12% per annum (between 2006 and 2011).[11] The specialty chemicals market in India is expected to grow at about 14% per annum to reach USD 90 billion by 2023 (FICCI-TSMG 2014a). India is among the top 10 specialty and final products exporters in 2014 (as well as top 10 commodity chemicals exporter in 2014), with a world share of 1.5% (Bamber et al. 2016). India's strengths lie in agrochemicals,[12,13] textile chemicals,[14] and construction chemicals.[15] Table 12.1A in Appendix 12.1 shows the share of the various sub-segments in 2011.[16]

Table 12.1 Value chain of specialty chemicals

Feedstock	Basic chemicals		Building blocks for specialty chemicals	Specialty chemical	End use
Naptha	Olefins/Diolefins	Ethylene	Ethylene Oxide		Textiles, agrochemicals, coatings, automotive, pharmaceuticals, leather, animal feed, colorants, petroleum
		Propylene	Phenol and Alkylphenols		Resins, polymers, adhesives, fibres, surfactant raw materials
			Acrylate Monomers		Emulsion paints, pressure-sensitive adhesives, coatings, textile binders, paper chemicals, leather chemicals, water treatment chemicals, plastics
			Propylene Oxide	Polyether Polyols, Propylene Glycols, and Glycol Ethers	Polyurethanes, unsaturated polyester resins, and surfactants (used in paints, textiles, leather, and agrochemicals)
	Aromatics	Benzene	Aniline		Polyurethane (PU) raw material, Methylene Diphenyl Di-isocyanate (MDI)
			Phenol	Epoxy resins, Polycarbonate	Resins, polymers, adhesives, fibres, surfactant raw materials
		Toluene			Solvent in surface coatings, Benzene, Toluene Di-isocyanate
Coal tar	Naphthalene			Polycarboxylic Ether (PCE)	Construction chemicals (concrete admixtures), dyes, and intermediates
Vegetable/animal oils and fats	Fatty acids		Fatty alcohols		Surfactants used in textiles, soaps and detergents, personal care products, paints and coatings, agrochemicals
Carbon monoxide + hydrogen			Oxo-Alcohols		Plasticizers
Mineral sands (Ilmenite, Rutile, Leucoxene, Zircon)			Titanium Dioxide		Plastics and paper industry, textiles, leather, ceramic, cosmetic industries

Source: Authors' compilation from survey

Manufacturing specialty chemicals require highly skilled manpower (scientists with advanced degrees such as PhDs in R&D facilities, available in India) since the products are largely customized and a knowledge of chemistry is at the core of processes. Cheap manpower is available for the labour-intensive, batch-type processes used to make specialty chemicals. Capital costs in India are 40–60% lower than those in Europe while operating costs are about 60–70% lower than those in the EU and the US. Production in this segment is mostly done in batches, which is another advantage for India since it cannot match China in scale.

India's consumption share in the global specialty chemical industry is estimated to grow from about 2.8% in 2013 to 6–7% in 2023, with a market size in the range of USD 80–100 billion.[17] India's specialty chemicals sector is driven by high growth in the end-user and urban sectors. The consumption of specialty chemicals in India is expected to be worth USD 45 billion by 2017 and USD 80–100 billion by 2021. The drivers of growth are likely to be the expanding market size of the Indian economy, increasing urbanization, and awareness of specialty chemicals, resulting in greater end-use demand, improvements in infrastructure development, and consumption standards.

Some companies cater to the domestic market while most cater to both domestic and international customers. Again, while some of them are confined to manufacturing in some limited sectors, others produce chemicals that have applications across a variety of sectors. A handful of companies are now also involved in what is known as Contract Research and Manufacturing Services (CRAMs). This involves provision of services on a contract basis in the form of either pre-clinical or clinical research services or services, ranging from drug development to manufacture, to other industries.

Companies with a strong focus on R&D and a diversified product profile are doing well in the market and these are mostly the MNCs.[18] As India moves towards greater production of specialty chemicals because of rising demand, more advanced technologies will be required by specialty chemical companies.[19] This could lead to increased collaborations with global MNCs, together with increased M&A activity.[20]

Integration into GVCs

Indian companies have now started manufacturing in upscale plants, are exporting a significant proportion of the output to the US, Europe, Africa, and other Asian countries, and are meeting stringent quality assurance norms such as ISO 9001–2008. India exports specialty chemicals to nearby Asia Pacific countries which do not have competitive scales of production and to developed countries in Europe and the US. Compliance with global regulations and India's manufacturing competitiveness in the segment are slowly helping its export market to grow. India is strong in bio-based products and there is great potential for export of these value-added products.

Upgrading

Competitiveness and product quality upgradation in the sector are improving. A company's strength in this sector is based on R&D capabilities and intellectual property (Bamber et al. 2016). The critical success factor for the industry is its capability to provide product/application development at a favourable price-performance ratio.[21]

In the specialty stages, a clear trend towards commoditization is observed as new competitors try to gain market share in this highly profitable market. However, the industry is currently fragmented and systematic efforts are needed to align production processes with global best standards for significant integration into GVCs and upgrading[22] thereafter. India needs to move towards process development and focus on customization of products to exploit the value chain. The current level of knowledge-sharing remains limited. Advanced intermediates, state-of-art R&D, and knowledge of the analytical sciences, together with high safety standards, are required to move up the value chain. With the right technology and support from government, the challenge of feedstock can be mitigated.[23] Commodity chemicals companies can improve their product portfolio by adding specialty chemicals which would help improve their margins; however, this will need significant investments in research and development, even for small-scale firms – given that most of such products meet specific requirements.[24] Such a move would move ahead the "Make in India" initiative.[25]

Certain developments and features of China's chemicals industry are leading to new opportunities in India:[26] first, China's artificial subsidies are tapering off; second, its currency is now appreciating, which can affect its export performance; third, China has major advantages in basic commodity chemicals which it can produce in bulk (and not so much in specialty) and which do not require application of complex chemistry; fourth, as global best standards and norms for production become more stringent, there will be an increasing pressure on China to comply, which might result in some consolidation and lead to increase in scale of plants.

Role of lead firms

The Indian textile chemicals segment is dominated by global majors such as BASF, Huntsman, and Archroma. While there are more than 500 textile chemical manufacturers, they cater to the unbranded fabric market. The global majors are focusing on eco-friendly products and high-end production that add value to the fabric. Environmentally friendly chemicals such as bio-auxiliaries are being used by them. For Indian firms to follow suit, innovations are required that enhance anti-microbial, anti-fungal, or flame retardant properties.

In the construction chemicals segment, the leaders are BASF, Pidilite, Fosroc, Sika, SWC-Chryso etc. There are 300 firms in the construction chemicals segment. Firms like Pidilite have been able to develop brands such as Fevicol in India.

Barriers to integration

The Indian specialty chemicals sector is still evolving. Consolidated and credible statistics about industry size and other details are unavailable. Small-sized firms particularly lack in infrastructure, funds, and know-how of processes.[27] Therefore, consolidation needs to be encouraged in the industry.

Several other issues need attention: manufacturing processes are not well planned in the industry; standards such as the BIS exist but are not mandatory. At each stage of the manufacturing process, a 2% Central Sales Tax (CST) is applied, which is not recoverable and adds to costs.[28] Local taxes levied on electricity are also a problem, as are power shortages. Infrastructure and labour costs are important factors for business and high costs of these factors drive down margins of firms. The industry is of the view that even the Dahej PCPIR is far behind the best in the world and still has to contend with problems such as water shortage.[29]

Investments by international companies have been small, at best. Overall, the sector is still nascent in India and the challenge is to tap the opportunity. Indian companies spend about 5% sales turnover on R&D, which should be increased. To solve feedstock problems, industry leaders have been lobbying for 10–15% of Polypropylene and other key feedstock to be reserved for the downstream sector.

Conclusion

This chapter covers the case of India's participation in the specialty chemicals value chain. Specialty chemicals manufacturing is moving eastward on the global map and India's share is increasing every year. Global companies are looking to invest in India, as the market for specialty chemicals is driven by India's GDP growth. Approval processes have taken two to five years in the past. Conditions for international players to enter the market have been challenging, given India's limited production of petrochemicals and modest infrastructure.

There is an urgent need to develop India's Petroleum, Chemicals, and Petrochemicals Investment Regions (PCPIRs): until now only one of the five at Dahej (Gujarat) has made progress. Experts feel that specialty chemical manufacturers should be holistically integrated into the PCPIRs to ensure their strong development and better utilization of resources.[30] This would also provide them with backward linkage support in production. Formation of clusters of companies should be encouraged in which the utilities should include common Effluent Treatment Plants (ETP), compressed air sections, steam boilers, refrigeration sections, and cooling towers. Operation of effluent treatment and steam treatment units can then be outsourced since these are not the main activities of chemical units. The government can also encourage establishment of specialty parks separately or within PCPIRs, as well as the establishment of centralizing zones/SEZs.

The industry is currently fragmented and systematic efforts are needed to align production processes with global best standards for significant integration into GVCs and upgrading thereafter. Indian companies can collaborate with global firms to jointly manufacture specialty chemicals in the country. Other problems are related to infrastructure; for example, transport from PCPIRs also needs to be resolved. The current level of knowledge-sharing remains limited.

Appendix 12.1

Table 12.1A Segment-wise size of specialty chemicals (2014)

Segment	Indian market size (USD billion)	Global market size (USD billion)
Dyes and pigments	4.9	27.8
Construction chemicals	0.6	17.5
Textile chemicals	1.1	20.3
Flavours and fragrances	0.7	25.6
Water chemicals	0.4	25.1
Surfactants	2.6	30.4
Polymer additives	0.4	43.4
Personal care ingredients	0.3	2.7
Agrochemicals	5.7	54.5

Source: Avendus (2016)

Notes

1 For explanation of nature of governance in GVCs, see Gereffi (1999).
2 Various classifications are followed in this segment – some specify that pharmaceuticals are part of the specialty chemicals sector while others do not. In this chapter, we discuss only the specialty chemicals related to construction, textiles etc. Pharmaceuticals have been discussed separately in Chapter 9.
3 Refer to Chapter 7 of this book.
4 The prominent global firms are AkzoNobel, Degussa, Ecolab Ciba, Rohm & Haas and Clariant. Diversified companies such as BASF, Dow, Dupont, Mitsui, and Bayer are engaged in all aspects of the chain (Bamber et al. 2016)
5 See Table 7.1 of this book.
6 Due to the close link between chemical consumption, manufacturing, and economic growth, there has been a shift to the Asia Pacific region or growth centres of "Factory Asia." Bamber et al. (2016).
7 Due to differentiated nature of products in the specialty chemicals segment, research and development (R&D) and intellectual property protection are more important (Bamber et al. 2016).
8 Specialty chemicals include textiles chemicals, water chemicals, construction chemicals, surfactants etc.
9 Processes include chlorination, sulphonation, nitration, ethoxylation, hydrogenation, condensation etc.
10 Avendus (2017). Estimates based on nine key segments: "Agrochemicals," "Flavours and fragrances," "Dyes and pigments," "Surfactants," "Polymer additives," "Personal care ingredients," "Construction chemicals," "Water chemicals," and "Textile chemicals."
11 Tata Strategic Management Group 2012. Knowledge and Strategy paper on Specialty Chemicals. FICCI-TSMG 2014a.
12 Agrochemicals are insecticides, pesticides, fungicides, and other pesticides.
13 India is a major exporter of generic agrochemicals and is among the top 10 exporters globally. Agrochemicals is a success story and should not be discussed in this chapter. It has been discussed in Avendus (2016) and FICCI (2015).
14 i) **Textile auxiliaries** cover a wide range of functions, from cleaning natural fibres and smoothing agents to improving easy-care properties. It includes complexing agents (which form stable water-soluble complexes), surfactants (which lower the surface tension of water so grease and oil are removed more easily), wetting agents (which accelerate the penetration of finishing liquors), sequestering agents, dispersing agents, and emulsifiers. ii) **Textile chemicals** (basic chemicals such as acids, bases, and salts). iii) **Colorants**, such as dyes, dye-protective agents, fixing agents, levelling agents, pH regulators, carriers, and ultraviolet (UV)–absorbers. And iv) **Finishes** (https://oecotextiles.wordpress.com/2013/01/10/chemicals-used-in-textile-processing/) (accessed on 14 March 2017). In India, companies such as Welspun produce several of these items; www.welsum.com.tw/WELSUM/EN/EN_Products_020_Textile_Auxiliaries.html (accessed on 01 September 2017).

15 The construction chemicals segment can be divided into concrete admixtures, flooring and waterproofing materials (epoxy- and Polyurethane-based), waterproofing agents (based on bitumen, PU and polymers like SBR and acrylic, available either in liquid, solid, or slurry form), repair and rehabilitation (cementation repair mortars, epoxy-based mortars, and other products like rust removers and anti-corrosion products). Other products include sealants, grouts, and tile adhesives. The construction chemicals industry was estimated to be worth INR 35,000 million in 2014–15 with admixtures constituting of 42% of the market share, flooring and waterproofing agents accounting for 14% each, chemicals for repair and rehabilitation accounting for 12%, and adhesives and sealants accounting for 18%. The major players in this segment are Pidilite, BASF Construction Chemicals, Sika India, Fosroc India, Structural Waterproofing Company (SWC) Private Limited etc. (FICCI and TSMC (2014b), Indian Construction Chemicals Industry Imperatives Of Growth).

16 Reactive dyes have been discussed in Chapter 3. Agrochemicals is another important sub-segment that has not been covered in this book. See Avendus (2016) and FICCI-TSMG (2014b).

17 www.business-standard.com/content/b2b-chemicals/specialty-chemicals-industry-making-india-a-global-manufacturing-powerhouse-115100 700405_1.html (accessed on 04 September 2017).

18 Companies such as Asian Paints and United Phosphorus have seen good growth and returns over the past decade. Asian Paints figures in the list of 100 most innovative companies of Forbes. www.forbes.com/companies/asian-paints/ (accessed on 04 September 2017). The international companies in this segment include Syngenta and Bayer in the crop protection chemicals market, Kansai Nerolac (which is a subsidiary of Kansai Paints) in the paints segment, BASF (which took over Ciba in 2009), and DuPont (McKinsey 2012).

19 In certain segments, India's capability is restricted to a few firms. There are only three companies with high fluorine-based capacities. These are SRF Limited, Navin Fluorine International Limited, and Gujarat Fluorochemicals (Emkay Research 2016).

20 www.pwc.in/assets/pdfs/publications/2016/winning-together-investment-opportunities-and-synergies-for-the-us-and-india.pdf (accessed on 24 July 2017). Collaborations in this segment include Huntsman (USA) acquiring Baroda division of Metrochem Industries in the textiles chemicals segment. Chryso (France) acquired Structural Waterproofing Company in the construction chemicals segment (Avendus 2016).

21 Branding and engaging with customers is very important and a key driver of profit in this industry (Bamber et al. 2016). Branding is especially relevant for the agrochemicals and the polymer additives segment (Avendus 2016).

22 In the commodity segment, given the lack of product differentiation, firms improve their competitiveness by introducing process improvements. The upgrading into production of specialty chemicals characterized by higher mix and low volume (and product differentiation) depends on intellectual property protection. Product upgrading trends in recent years have been towards more efficient, less wasteful, and non-toxic products. Functional

upgrading involves development and formulation of new specialty chemicals (Bamber et al. 2016).

23 A wide range of building blocks for specialties production, such as Oxo-Alcohols, Vinyl Acetate Monomers, Phenol, Propylene Oxide, and H-acid are produced in limited volumes in India. India's capacity for ethylene is only 4 million tonnes per year of the 147 million tonnes per year produced by the world. Moreover, most Ethylene Oxide (EO) output in India is used to make Monoethylene Glycol (MEG). By contrast, the US has 27 million tonnes of capacity per year and China has 16 million tonnes per year of the same.

24 There is a need for Indian companies to enhance basic R&D by consistent allocation of funds. Specialty chemicals can become obsolete very fast due to high competition from other competing products. Companies must invest heavily in R&D to meet consumer needs and have to adopt interdisciplinary approach to research.

25 The reference is to the "The Make in India" initiative launched by the prime minister of India in September 2014 as part of a wider set of nation-building initiatives. It is a policy move devised to transform India into a global design and manufacturing hub. For details, see www.makeinindia.com/home (accessed on 04 September 2017).

26 China is India's biggest competitor in the sector currently.

27 SMEs face problems related to infrastructure, governance etc., sometimes being forced to shut down when these problems become insurmountable. This is important especially since specialty chemical manufacturing is a time-consuming process and obtaining results from R&D can take too long.

28 Under GST, Central Excise Duty, additional Excise Duties, Additional Customs Duty (CVD), Special Additional Duty at Customs (SAD) have been subsumed under the Central Indirect taxes and Levies. http://empcom.gov.in/content/20_1_FAQ.aspx (accessed on 04 September 2017).

29 Water is sold at INR 150/cubic metre there even when INR 10/cubic metre is also considered expensive by companies.

30 For details, see Confederation of Indian Industry. 2013.

References

Avendus. 2016. *Specialty Chemicals in India*. Avendus Capital Private Limited.

Avendus. 2017. *Specialty Chemicals: From Opportunity to Reality*. Avendus Capital Private Limited.

Bamber, P., Frederick, S., and G. Gereffi. 2016. *The Philippines in the Chemical Global Value Chain*, Report, Duke Center on Globalization, Governance and Competitiveness at the Social Science Research Institute.

Cefic. 2014. *Competitiveness of the European Chemical Industry: How to Regain Ground in the Global Market*. The European Chemical Industry Council. Report on Key Feedstock for Specialty Chemicals. Confederation of Indian Industry.

Confederation of Indian Industry. 2013. CII Report on Key feedstock for Specialty Chemicals, CII.

Elsevier. 2014. *Going East: Fine and Specialty Chemicals Drive Chinese R&D*. Amsterdam: Elsevier.

Emkay Research. 2016. *Specialty Chemicals: Opportunities are Shifting to India*, Specialty Chemicals: Sector Update.

EXIM. 2012. 'Indian Chemical Industry: Exploring Global Demand,' Occasional Paper No. 154. Export-Import Bank of India.

FICCI. 2015. *Ushering in the 2nd Green Revolution – Role of Crop Protection chemicals*. New Delhi: Federation of Indian Chambers of Commerce and Industry.

FICCI-TSMG. 2014a. *Spurting the Growth of Indian Chemical Industry – Handbook on Indian Chemicals and Petrochemicals Sector*. Federation of Indian Chambers of Commerce and Industry; and Tata Strategic Management Group.

FICCI and TSMG. 2014b. *Indian Construction Chemicals Industry Imperatives of Growth*. Federation of Indian Chambers of Commerce and Industry; and Tata Strategic Management Group.

Gereffi, G. 1999. 'International Trade and Industrial Upgrading in the Apparel Commodity Chain,' *Journal of International Economics*, 48(1): 37–70.

Mckinsey. 2012. *Winning in India: The Specialty-chemicals Opportunity*. Mckinsey.

Ministry of Chemicals and Fertilizers. 2013. *Chemicals and Petrochemical Statistics at a Glance: 2013*. Government of India.

Tata Strategic Management Group 2012. Knowledge and Strategy paper on Specialty Chemicals.

Part IV

Conclusion and policy implications

Introduction to Part IV

This section presents two chapters: Chapter 13 on the sectors that have the potential to help integrate India in GVCs in future and Chapter 14 which summarizes and concludes the book.

13 Sectors that hold promise

The case of India's diamond sector

Diamond cutting and polishing industry

One of the sectors that contributes significantly to exports is the gems
and jewellery sector. In this sector, the diamond cutting and polishing
is an important one and accounted for 54% of the total gems and
jewellery export basket (Ministry of Commerce and Industry 2013).
The sector is interesting from the point of view of the GVCs since
the rough diamonds are not produced in India but are imported from
countries like Belgium and the United Arab Emirates (UAE). Also
85% in terms of volume and 60% in terms of the value of the world's
supply of diamonds is catered to by India. India has created a niche
in the small diamonds category. The larger the stone, the greater the
profit from value addition. The maximum value addition comes from
the activity of "perform."[1] The value addition of the diamond polishing has reduced somewhat in the last decade. The main competition in
this sector is coming from China.

India is a leading exporter of cut and polished diamonds in the
world. The country is a global diamond polishing hub, contributing
60% of the world's supply in terms of value, 85% in terms of volume, and 92% in terms of pieces. More than 90% of the world's diamond setting in jewellery is undertaken in India. Diamonds account
for about 55% of the gems and jewellery export basket of the Indian
industry, which specializes in cutting and polishing the end product
and employs around one million people throughout the country.

The industry is considered to play a vital role in the Indian economy,
as it contributes a major chunk to the total foreign reserves as well
as the gross domestic product (GDP). The Government of India has
viewed the sector as a thrust area for export promotion. The Indian

government presently allows 100% FDI in the sector through the automatic route (Department of Industrial Policy and Promotion 2017). According to some estimates, the gems and jewellery market in India is expected to grow at a compound annual growth rate of 16% over the period 2014–19, driven mainly by a rise in per capita income of the population.

The industry is dependent on revenues generated through exports and hence the global business climate to a great extent. Learning and diffusion of the latest technologies have occurred, but due to the absence of the full chain in India, upgrading has not occurred. In the future, the industry needs to move up the value chain in order to compete with rising competitors in the segment such as China (manufacturing) and Dubai (trading). The industry is also mainly concentrated in few geographical pockets of the country and needs to be scaled up. Skill development is the industry is fragmented and not standardized or systematic. Development programmes in this area are needed for continued growth of the sector.

The aerospace industry[2]

India's aerospace market is one of the fastest growing in the world, with all segments, including civil and military aviation and space, witnessing high rates of growth. India has the world's third-largest armed force and is the ninth-highest defence spender globally. The allocation of defence in its union budget is approximately USD 34.53 billion (fiscal year 2016–17), around one-third of which is spent on capital acquisitions. Nearly half of the country's defence equipment is approaching obsolescence and the import dependence is very high.

India is also the ninth-largest civil aviation market globally. A compound annual growth rate of around 10% was recorded in domestic passenger traffic and 8.8% in international passenger traffic during fiscal year 2006–16. The total passenger traffic stood at 224 million during 2016. Rapid growth in traffic volumes has put extreme pressure on the existing infrastructure. As a result, the thrust is now on modernization of airports, communications, navigation, and surveillance systems for air traffic management, radars, and facilities for maintenance, repair, and overhaul of aircraft and sub-systems.

In the space sector, India's manufacturing programme stands out as one of the most cost-effective in the world. In the last four decades, India's space programme has attracted global attention for its accelerated rate of development. It has launched 51 satellites for 20 countries to date and has the potential to serve as the world's launchpad.

The factors driving growth in manufacturing in the aerospace industry include strong gross domestic product (GDP) growth resulting in rapidly growing domestic aircraft demand, a favourable policy environment including liberalization of FDI policies, offset requirements, a strong domestic manufacturing base and its cost advantages, a well-educated talent pool, IT competitiveness of the country, and a liberal special economic zones (SEZs) law providing for attractive fiscal benefits for developers and manufacturers. These factors and presence of favourable government incentives have attracted the attention of major global aerospace companies which have set up bases for manufacturing and supply chain sourcing in the country. This trend is likely is likely to continue and the sector is expected to record a high rate of growth in the future. However, challenges exist and could include constraints in access to modern technologies, funding, availability and high cost of raw material, and problems in obtaining approvals and certifications.

The Government of India has made the development of the indigenous aerospace and defence sector a high priority. In the past few years, it has laid out favourable policies to ease the business environment for private and foreign players and to promote self-reliance, indigenization, technology upgradation, and achieving economies of scale, including developing capabilities for exports. Up to 100% FDI is allowed in the sector, wherein up to 49% is permissible under automatic route while FDI beyond 49% is permissible after obtaining prior approval of the government, where it is likely to result in access to modern technology. Foreign institutional investors, foreign portfolio investors, and venture capital firms have been allowed to invest up to 24% in companies. Other policy initiatives have included relaxing norms of industrial licensing and defence exports, bringing flexibility in discharging offset obligations,[3] and providing a more level-playing field for private players. The Defense Procurement Procedure 2016 (DPP), made effective in April 2016, has introduced a key new acquisition category called Indigenous Design Development and Manufacturing (IDDM), which has been given the highest priority. Incentives for promotion of exports have also been introduced including for units in special economic zones (SEZs)/national investment and manufacturing zones. Apart from these, each Indian state offers incentives for setting up industrial projects.

Globalization of maintenance, repair and overhaul services, manpower cost competitiveness, availability of talent, locational advantages, and presence of specialist capabilities could contribute towards making India a potential global/regional hub in coming years. Factors leading to civil aviation growth include international trade, globalization, declining airfares, additional travel routes, and increased flight availability.

The electronics hardware industry[4]

The demand for electronics hardware in the country is projected to increase from USD 45 billion in 2009 to USD 400 billion by 2020. This provides a huge opportunity for India to become an electronics system design and manufacturing (ESDM) hub to meet its domestic requirements and global requirements. Most of this demand is presently being met through imports, which provide a huge opportunity for import substitution.

Mobile phone manufacturing is one of the prominent segments of the industry. India has the world's second largest smartphone user base with approximately 220 million smartphone users and above 1 billion mobile phone users. Mobile phone manufacturing in India increased by 185% from USD 2.92 billion in 2014–15 to USD 8.30 billion in 2015–16.[5] The government has identified growth of mobile phone manufacturing and assembly as a thrust area within the electronics hardware manufacturing sector to stimulate the growth of the information technology/information technology enabled services (IT/ITeS) industry and employment in the country under its "Make in India" programme. Focus is also on indigenous manufacturing of semiconductor wafer fabrication (fabs), fab-less design, set-top boxes, Very Small Aperture Terminals (VSATs), consumer and medical electronics, smart energy meters, smart cards, and micro-ATMs (automatic teller machines). Government schemes like "Digital India," "Design in India," "Startup India," and many other incentives along with a liberalized FDI policy have boosted manufacturing in this segment in India's electronics system design and product development space.[6]

Overall, the demand for electronics hardware is fuelled by a variety of drivers: these include high growth rate of the economy and the emergence of a vast domestic market catering to the gen-next and thriving middle-class with increasing disposable incomes. The electronics market is anticipated to reach USD 400 billion in 2022 from USD 69.6 billion in 2012, growing at a compound annual growth rate (CAGR) of 24.4% during 2012–20. As against this, according to government estimates, the Indian electronics and hardware industry is expected to grow at a CAGR of 13–16% during 2013–18 to reach USD 112–130 billion by 2018.

India's paper industry[7]

India's paper sector is domestically oriented but showing signs of increased connectedness with the world. India is the fastest growing market for paper globally and its paper consumption is projected to grow in sync with its increasing economic growth in the future. The industry accounts for about 3% of the world's production of paper and its estimated turnover is approximately INR 5,00,000 million (USD 8 billion). The industry provides employment to more than 0.5 million people directly and 1.5 million people indirectly (Indian Paper Manufacturers Association).

The industry is dispersed throughout the country and is dominated by about 750–800 small integrated paper mills. Manufacturing consists of writing and printing paper; paperboard/packaging, newsprint and specialty paper, and others. The industry has strong backward linkages with the farming community and has agro-forestry roots. Approximately 31% of these are based on wood, 47% on recycled fibre, and 22% on agro-residues. The operating capacity of the industry is around 13 million tonnes. During 2015–16, domestic production was estimated at 12.2 million tonnes. Paper consumption is around 13.9 million tonnes and demand of paper has been growing around 8% per annum. However, per capita consumption is low, at 10 kg against the global average of around 55 kg.

So far, growth in paper industry has mirrored growth in GDP. Foreign participation has remained almost negligible. However, with increasing population and quality of life, the sector is expected to grow.[8] With entry of new players and consolidation in the sector, the industry landscape is likely to be significantly altered by 2020 with the domestic capacity reaching 20 MT by then.[9] Economic and income growth, population growth (changing demographics – urbanization, young population), rapidly changing lifestyles, improving living standards etc. are key growth drivers of this industry.[10] On the global front, while developed countries still capture much of the value in paper GVCs, Asia is now emerging as an export base for industries that use paper-based shipping materials and is driving much of the global industry's growth. Large countries like China and India have become important markets and large importers of inputs (woodchips, pulp, and recovered paper) in the last decade.

India's overall participation in the paper GVCs is limited. The industry is facing several challenges in enhancing export volumes including non-availability of raw materials and difficulties in accessing cheaper capital. The sector is comparatively small compared to the size of the country and forest resources available (Invest in India, Forest Industry). Development challenges include consolidation of the fragmented industry, achieving economies of scale, modernization of mills, productivity improvement and building new capacities, quality benchmarking, creation of a robust raw material base, enhancement of the industry's competitiveness to face global competition, and establishment of environmental standards. The country has had no significant capacity additions in the last 15 years due to unattractiveness of the industry and reluctance to accept new technologies. In the near future, the market environment is likely to change for Indian companies as new and differentiated products are introduced. The demand for paper products is likely to go up but the challenge is to remain cost competitive.

Notes

1 Preliminary shaping of gem substance for lapidary faceting. Other steps in the value chain are marking and trimming, sawing, marking (perform), calibrating, sanding/lapping, doping, faceting/polishing.
2 For details, see Make in India, www.makeinindia.com (accessed on 22 July 2017) and CII-PWC (2009).
3 The offset policy stipulates the mandatory offset requirement of a minimum 30% for procurement of defence equipment in excess of USD 306.69 million. It was introduced in the capital purchase agreements with foreign defence players to ensure that an ecosystem of suppliers is built domestically. For details, see http://pib.nic.in/newsite/PrintRelease.aspx?relid=107868.
4 http://digitalindia.gov.in/content/electronics-manufacturing (accessed on 01 September 2017) http://electropreneurpark.res.in/ (accessed on 25 July 2017). http://indiainbusiness.nic.in/newdesign/index.php?param=newsdetail/10473 (accessed on 30 August 2017) and Make in India (2016).
5 For recent figures on surge in mobile phone manufacturing, see http://pib.nic.in/newsite/PrintRelease.aspx?relid=174994 .
6 The finance minister in his budget speech in February 2017 made the remark, "creating an eco-system to make India a global hub for electronics manufacturing. Over 250 investment proposals for electronics manufacturing have been received in the last two years, totaling an investment of INR 1.26 lakh crores. A number of global leaders and mobile manufacturers have set up production facilities in India." The allocation for incentive schemes like MSIPS and EDF to INR 745 crores in 2017–18. For details, see http://indiabudget.nic.in/budget.asp (accessed on 01 September 2017).
7 www.business-standard.com/article/companies/paper-mills-profits-improve-in-apr-jun-quarter-116083000782_1.html (accessed on 30 August 2017), HICT (2016) and IPMA (2015) www.business-standard.com/article/markets/indias-paper-demand-to-rise-53-by2020-114041800784_1.html (accessed on 8 July 2017), www.investinindia.com/industry/forest/forest-industry (accessed

on 01 August 2017). Duke CGGC (2016), and http://ipma.co.in/ (accessed on 8 July 2017).

8 'India's Paper Demand to Rise 53% by 2020'. 2014. Business Standard. April 19. By Dilip Kumar Jha. www.business-standard.com/article/markets/indias-paper-demand-to-rise-53-by2020-114041800784_1.html (accessed on 8 July 2017).

9 'Paper Industry Will Face More Competition, Shakeout: BILT,' 2012. *Business Line*. 11 December. By V. Rishi Kumar. www.thehindubusinessline.com/companies/paper-industry-will-face-more-competition-shakeout-bilt/article4188657.ece (accessed on June 15, 2017).

10 'Paper Mills' Profit Improves in June Quarter,' 2016. *Business Standard*. 31 August. www.business-standard.com/article/companies/paper-mills-profits-improve-in-apr-jun-quarter-116083000782_1.html (accessed on 30 August 2017).

References

CII-PWC. 2009. *Changing Dynamics: India's Aerospace Industry*. PricewaterhouseCoopers, www.pwc.in/assets/pdfs/industries/changing-dynamics-india-aerospace-industry-091211.pdf (accessed on 21 March 2017).

Department of Industrial Policy and Promotion. 2017. *Gems & Jewellery Sector: Achievement Report*, www.makeinindia.com/article/-/v/gems-amp-jewellery-sector-achievement-report (accessed on 21 August 2017). Ministry of Commerce, Government of India.

Duke CGGC. 2016. *The Philippines in the Paper Global Value Chain*. Center on Globalization, Governance & Competitiveness, Duke University www.cggc.duke.edu/pdfs/2016_Philippines_Paper_Global_Value_Chain.pdf (accessed on 19 March 2017).

IPMA. 2015. *Paper Industry: Myths Versus Realities*. Indian Paper Manufacturers Association. http://ipma.co.in/wp-content/uploads/2015/09/Myths-versus-Realities.pdf (accessed on 06 April, 2017).

Ministry of Commerce and Industry. 2013. *Report of the Task Group for Diamond Sector to Make India an 'International Trading Hub For Rough Diamonds'*. Government of India.

Ministry of Defence, 2014. 'Defence Offset Policy' Press Information Bureau, August 1, 2014. Government of India.

Ministry of Electronics & IT, 2017. 'Key Achievements.' Press Information Bureau, December 29, 2017. Government of India.

Others

'As Margins Pinch, Paper Industry Seeks Anti-dumping Duty on Imports,' 2015. *Business Line*. March 11. By V. Rishi Kumar. www.thehindubusinessline.com/economy/paper-industry-wants-dumping-duty-imposed-on-cheaper-imports-expresses-concern/article6982725.ece (accessed on 10 February 2017).

HICT. 2016. *Newsletter, Haldia International Container Terminal*. Issue III. www.ict.in/hict/pdf/HICT_NEWSLETTER_III.pdf (accessed on 25 August 2017).

Indian Paper Manufacturers Association (IPMA), http://ipma.co.in/ (accessed on 1 February 2017).

Invest in India, Forest Industry, www.investinindia.com/industry/forest/forest-industry (accessed on 1 August 2017).

Make in India. 2016. Electronic Systems – Highlights 2O16, www.makein india.com/article/-/v/electronic-syste-1 (accessed on 16 January 2017). Government of India.

14 Conclusion

The global value chain (GVC) literature has examined the phenomenon of fragmentation of production which has led to dispersion of production across the globe. This approach has been used to study why participation into GVCs is beneficial for firms through income generation, value capture etc. In the context of developing countries, GVCs are particularly important for learning and upgrading of production processes.

India has been growing at a phenomenal rate in the last decade or so. According to different estimates, the country has a good chance of continuing as the world's fastest growing large economy and being counted among the top three world economies by 2050. However, India's overall participation rate in GVCs is low, although it has done well in quite a number of niche segments. This book examines why India lags behind in GVC participation and what can be done to enhance India's participation.

While there are numerous examples of successful integration of firms and countries in GVCs, there are fewer studies of the difficulties faced by firms in inserting into GVCs. India presents a unique example of manufacturing capability in most sectors, but low integration in GVCs. This provides a rationale to examine cases from India to understand why and how integration may have been impeded.

Participation in GVCs is determined by three factors: capacity of a country to join a GVC, capacity to remain part of the GVC, and capacity to move up the value chain. The capacity of a country (or its firms) to join a GVC depends on the tasks that the firm can perform in the GVC. It also depends on the governance structure in the GVCs. There are five types of governance structure (i.e. modular, hierarchical, captive, relational, and market) that can evolve in chain, each with its own governance structure. Governance type captures the ability to exert control over the chain. The governance of the GVC influences how learning takes place, and hence different mechanisms emerge in different chains (Pietrobelli and Rabellotti 2011). The framework used in this book draws on the role of the governance types in fostering learning (and innovation depending on the institutional setup) in a developing country with a large domestic market. The benefits from integrating into GVCs will accrue and be enhanced if the GVC sector is integrated into the rest of the economy; hence, it is vital to examine these linkages as well.

Two factors govern upgrading or the moving up of a value chain by a firm. These are the role of the lead firm in the governance of the chain and the nature of technology in the sector. Lead firms put pressure on suppliers to innovate but do not become involved directly in the learning process. Upgrading is neither automatic nor does it provide a country the capability to carry out the entire range of activities to compete in the global economy (Navas-Aleman 2011). Upgrading is likely to be lowest in quasi-hierarchical and captive chains compared to a situation where the chain is modular or relational. Thus, the process of upgrading is sector specific and efforts to achieve upgrading have to be seen in the context of the sector that is being targeted.

Findings of the book: messages for laggards

The questions that motivate this book are: First, what is the evidence of India's lagging in GVC trade? We present evidence from the literature and data using the Broad Economic Categories (BEC). As noted in Chapter 4, the following sectors are important for value chain activity of India: "Mineral fuels and oils, and products thereof," "Organic chemicals," "Pharmaceutical products," "Natural or cultured pearls," "Aircraft, spacecraft and articles thereof," and "Ships, boats and floating structures." Case studies covering automobiles (Chapter 6), pharmaceuticals (Chapter 7), petrochemicals (Chapter 8), reactive dyes (Chapter 9), and semiconductor microchips (Chapter 10), which form the main thrust of this book, are presented. These are cases where there is successful integration by Indian firms and, for greater value addition, upgrading is critical. The lagging sectors, where India has limited integration or has failed to integrate into GVCs, are discussed in Chapter 12, which focuses on specialty chemicals; the case of garments is covered in Chapter 11.

For India, we have examined the tasks that the firms are excelling in in the context of the several GVCs that have been examined in this book. We have noted value-added exports are occurring in most of the segments examined. The case studies provide the reader with a wide variety of experiences, throwing light on the process of knowledge dissemination and manufacturing practices in various sectors. The bargaining powers of the suppliers play an important role in the entire process. The case studies illustrate how the governance structure affects dissemination of knowledge in various sectors.

The second question is: What explains India's lagging position in GVC trade? This question is answered through an examination of the role of lead firms, governance structures in value chains, and diffusion of technology in each chain examined. This book provides examples of why India has failed to integrate in GVCs. In the context of India, we have observed that, in the chemicals industry, the knowledge and production processes are proprietary and upgrading requires investment in research and development (R&D), while, in garments, production processes are more standardized and upgrading can come from use of newer raw materials.

Role of lead firms

GVCs are networked through lead firms. Usually lead firms are multinational corporations (MNCs), and these firms create networks by breaking down the value chain into a variety of discreet functions and locating them wherever they can be carried out most effectively, where they can improve the firm's access to resources and capabilities, and where they are needed to facilitate the penetration of important growth markets (Ernst and Kim 2002). In GVCs, MNCs transfer technology by training engineers in local firms, providing detailed blueprints and setting strict quality control criteria (Westphal et al. 1985; Enos and Park 1988). From a policy perspective, how GVCs integrate into the economy is critical and the role of the lead firm is very important in this context. Lead firms focus on trade facilitation and better public-private sector coordination in certain sectors.

In the Indian context, although lead firms have been few, they have performed important roles in each of the sectors discussed in this book. This is discussed below in the context of each of sector in the book.

Automobiles: The automotive industry is one of the most successful examples of India's participation in GVCs. The value chain is modular in nature and lead firms have significantly contributed to the development of supplier firms through transfer of technology and imports. However, the absorption of global best practices and learning has been slow. India still needs to mature and take steps for upgrading, especially in the components segment.

Reactive dyes: India holds about 40% share of world production in this segment and has recorded a double-digit growth rate in the past few years. Firms like Atul, Sudarshan, and Clariant are integrated into GVCs through exports. Firms are trying to cater to their feedstock requirement by backward integration. With a number of strengths over its competitors, the industry can capitalize its position on the global map, leading the way for the entire dyes and pigments sector to take off. However, the efforts of private players have to be aligned with adequate government support if the sector is to integrate further in GVCs.

Pharmaceuticals: The Indian pharmaceutical industry has made phenomenal progress over the years and is considered as a reliable source for supplies globally. The firms have certain unique strengths and growth models that keep them ahead of international competitors. The sector has been one of the topmost recipients of foreign investment domestically. R&D is critical for this sector, and while Indian firms are doing more R&D than before, there has been no drug discovery in the country. Moreover, knowledge transfer has been limited and the industry is facing serious obstacles to upgrading. Improved regulations and a favourable policy environment are needed along with concerted research efforts by firms themselves if the industry is to enhance integration and go up the value chain.

Semiconductor microchips: The availability of skilled manpower at low cost has resulted in the successful integration into the value chain in this sector. However, the learning and upgrading aspects are limited since the backward and the forward nodes in the chain are absent. There is a need to develop an indigenous design sector, as most semiconductor designing in India is pull driven while only 20% is push driven. There is need to encourage end-to-end product ownership within the semiconductor sector in India.

Garments: The Indian garments sector is an example of unsuccessful integration into GVCs. The reasons for this are, for example, excessive use of cotton and higher costs compared to countries like Bangladesh. The sector is diverse with many clusters around the country and caters to a large domestic market, the neighbouring countries, and the Middle East. The standards for these markets are quite different from that of the larger markets of the US and the EU, to which only some firms cater. Lead time is very important for this sector, as is turnaround time in ports. Upgrading has been reported by some firms in this sector. Also, diversification into synthetic material will be important in the future.

Specialty chemicals: Specialty chemical manufacturing is moving eastward on the global map and India's share is increasing every year. It is a highly knowledge-intensive sector and the value chain is partly network type (relational) and partly modular in nature. However, the industry is currently fragmented and systematic efforts are needed to align production processes with global best standards for significant integration in GVCs and upgradation thereafter. The segments of textile chemicals and construction chemicals examined in Chapter 12 exhibit different levels of integration. While the current level of knowledge-sharing remains limited in the textile chemicals segment, which is dominated by global majors, in the construction chemicals segment, the story is different. Indian firms like Pidilite have also been able to develop brands.

Learning and upgrading

As indicated in Table 5.3, the learning outcomes vary by sector. The tacitness of knowledge determines the learning outcomes and transfer of manufacturing practices. Upgrading also differs across sectors, since the role of the lead firm varies from sector to sector due to the type of governance within the chain. Over the years, even highly value-added technology, capital-intensive, and knowledge-intensive processes are being relocated to developing countries. Thus GVCs have provided new opportunities for local capability formation in developing countries and have emerged as a key catalyst for international knowledge diffusion (Ernst and Kim 2002).

For the host country to benefit from technology transfer, knowledge spillovers and increase in value addition can translate into better jobs, and so on, only if links with the rest of the economy are strong. This latter factor is crucial in adjudging the role of GVCs in a country's development. The role of the government in promoting upgrading may be limited if the lead firms make most of the decisions in a sector, and linkages with the rest of the economy remain weak (Taglioni and Winkler 2016).

Implications for policy

The question of the impediments to India's engagement in GVCs leads on to the policy implications of how to overcome these barriers. Many barriers or incentives to trade are common to trade in general, but some can be specific to GVC trade. For instance, participation in

GVCs requires further opening to imports and an integrated framework of analysis encompassing goods, services, and foreign direct investment (FDI); or imposing of private standards by a lead firm. Based on the cases presented, the barriers in each sector are discussed. There are regulatory barriers, administrative barriers, and issues related to standards. Also, logistics and infrastructural barriers are common to all sectors, though they may be more critical in certain sectors.

Policy for firms and associations

While India has done well in certain segments, several challenges remain. A thrust on knowledge creation is needed. Access to technology and the need for R&D has also been highlighted. India has low investment in R&D: in certain sectors like the pharmaceuticals, specialty chemicals, and automobiles, R&D is critical. India does not gain any advantage from chip design since the intellectual property rights (IPR) rest with other countries.

Regulatory changes

The logistical and infrastructural barriers in India have been discussed in several of the chapters. For integration into value chains, time is of the essence and turnover at Indian ports is slow. Sometimes customs clearance takes days and this can prove to be a major obstacle. Poor roads, power outages, availability of land, water, labour regulations etc. are also proving to be bottlenecks. Water is required in huge quantities in the chemicals industry, for example, and in the fabrication units of microchips. Finally, while India has a large population in the working age group, much training in specific skills is needed to meet the demands of globalizing industries.

Lessons for policymakers

Large-scale investments are needed in infrastructure development since this is a critical barrier in the way of integration with GVCs. Finance has also been a persistent problem in some sectors. All firms surveyed in this research study were of the opinion that future support should target improving the business environment. Above all, a long-term and holistic approach by the government is needed to enhance integration into GVCs in contrast to the traditional piecemeal approach of functioning in the trade growth era.

Concluding remarks

The key messages of the book can be summarized into the following points:

1 It is not necessary to produce for the entire chain; there are benefits even to specialization or producing for parts of the chain.
2 International competition is fierce and participation is not automatic, as countries face many challenges in entering international production.
3 GVCs have made imports very important and low- and medium-income countries are not only importing parts but absorbing foreign technology and know-how through imports. Hence, imports of intermediates which can be used for further value addition need to be encouraged (Taglioni and Winkler 2016).

The GVC literature focuses on the potential of participation of less developed countries (LDCS) in GVCs and the benefits of engaging in GVCs. Costs (production, labour, transport, investment, and tax incentives) are the major drivers of lead firms' decisions to invest or source production in developing countries. The Indian case can be an example to many other low, middle, and large economies which face similar development problems. To move up the value chain, it is important that customization and innovation continue in a cost-effective manner. Different growth models may be required for different regions and industries to achieve these goals. India also needs to focus on sectors in which it has competencies and increase value addition in these sectors. Strong political will and favourable policies will help India move up the value chains and lead to greater integration.

References

Enos, J. L. and W.-H. Park. 1988. *The Adoption and Diffusion of Imported Technology: The Case of Korea*. London, New York and Sidney: Croom Helm.

Ernst, D. and L. Kim. 2002. 'Global Production Networks, Knowledge Diffusion, and Local Capability Formation,' *Research Policy*, 31: 1417–1429.

Navas-Alemán, L. 2011. *Industrial Value Chain Development – An Integrated Tool*. Vienna: United Nations Industrial Development Organization (UNIDO).

Pietrobelli, C. and R. Rabellotti. 2011. 'Global Value Chains meet Innovation Systems: Are there Learning Opportunities for Developing Countries?' *World Development*, 39(7): 1261–1269.

Taglioni, D. and D. Winkler. 2016. *Making Global Value Chains Work for Development*. World Bank Group.

Westphal, L. E., Kim, L. and C. J. Dahlman. 1985. 'Reflections on Acquisition of Technological Capability,' in N. Rosenberg and C. Frischtak (eds.), *International Technology Transfer: Concepts, Measures and Comparisons*. New York: Pergamon.

Index

Note: Page numbers in **bold** indicate a table and page numbers in *italic* indicate a figure on the corresponding page.